The Days Are LONG
— But the —
Years Are SHORT

Other Books by Rachel

Essay
Parenthood: Has Anyone Seen My Sanity?
The Life-Changing Madness of Tidying Up After Children
This Life With Boys
Hills I'll Probably Lie Down On
We Count it All Joy
If These Walls Could Talk

Poetry
this is how you know
Life: a definition of terms
The Book of Uncommon Hours
Textbook of an Ordinary Life
this is how you live
sincerely yours: letters in poetry

To see all the books Rachel has written, please click or visit the link below:
www.racheltoalson.com/writing

Rachel Toalson

The Days Are LONG — But the — Years Are SHORT

BATLEE PRESS

Published by
Batlee Press
Post Office Box 591596
San Antonio, TX 78259

Copyright ©2020 by Rachel Toalson
All rights reserved.
Printed in the United States of America.
Interior design by Toalson Media.
Cover design by Ben Toalson. www.toalsonmarketing.com

No part of this book may be reproduced or transmitted in any form or by any means, electronic or mechanical, including photocopying and recording, or by any information storage and retrieval system, without permission in writing from the publisher. For information regarding permission, write to Batlee Press, PO Box 591596, San Antonio, TX 78259.

The author appreciates your taking the time to read her work. Please consider leaving a review wherever you bought it and telling your friends how much you enjoyed it. Both of those help get the book into the hands of new readers, which is incredibly important for authors. Thank you for your support.
www.racheltoalson.com

Names: Toalson, Rachel, author.
Title: The days are long, but the years are short / Rachel Toalson
Description: First edition. | Batlee Press, Texas:
Batlee Press Books, 2020

10 9 8 7 6 5 4 3 2 1

First Edition—2020

*For every parent who has lived
a million years in one day
and a millisecond in a decade*
R.T.

Foreword

Blink, and they'll be grown.

It was the most confounding thing older, wiser parents told me when my first son tore into the world with a scowl and the kind of gaze that should have told me he'd be unflinching in the face of a conflict.

I didn't know what they meant; I'd spent an endless day feeding my son every 2.5 hours, another endless day changing diapers and watching him sleep and willing him to keep breathing, and a third endless day trying to figure out how to use the nose-sucker. Once he became a toddler, I spent endless days fixing three healthy meals and two snacks; picking up toys; logging requests for more milk, better food, desired toys, watch this, permission, art supplies, more stories. And the arguing alone consumed hours at a time.

In short, one day seemed to last sixty-seven hours.

And yet.

Blink, and they'll be grown.

As my sons grew, I began to understand what those older, wiser parents meant: When did his legs get so long and knobby? When did his feet turn smelly? When did he lose that precious layer of fat I used to kiss above his perfectly-shaped eyebrows?

I blinked, and he was ten, eleven, twelve.

One day could last sixty-seven hours, but one year passed in the blink of an eye.

At its heart, this book is a celebration of the madness that defines parenting—particularly parenting boys. It examines the laughable challenges facing parents at practically every turn of a kid's life; highlights rites of passage like The Funk and a parent's fall from "The Cool Club"; and laughs about the many different personalities kids assume—from listening personalities to sleeping personalities. But every essay collected within these pages contains a sometimes subtle, sometimes overt truth: one day, sooner than we can even imagine, they'll grow up.

This book is, itself, a symbol of that truth. My oldest son just turned thirteen (My other sons follow closely on his heels, shaping their own stories.). I no longer feel I can write about him as I once did; he is now in charge of his own story—humorous or not. That means this is the last humor book about parenting my sons that I will write—at least until they graduate from the volatile adolescent stage and learn, once more, how to laugh at themselves. This is the end of an era—ten years of writing funny stories about my sons.

Blink, and they'll be grown.

I hope this book will meet you wherever you are—whether in the throes of those days that seem to drag on forever or in those years where you wonder how on earth time flew so fast. I hope it will both entertain and enlighten you. I hope it will remind you—me—that nothing lasts forever; that the challenging days, weeks, months are but a single blade of grass in a large luscious green yard; that one day we'll blink and they'll be grown—so we may as well keep our eyes wide open.

Nothing slows or preserves time like a watched pot—or eyes that record everything.

January

'My New Year's Goal is Making Life Easier for My Parents,' Said No Kid Anywhere, Ever

Did you know that kids have New Year's goals? They sure do.

They're the opposite of ours.

The beginning of every year is a time in which goals, resolutions, our new ways of being—whatever you want to call it—have strong and resilient roots. Husband and I spend the last two weeks of every old year goal-setting, because we believe it's important to start the new year with a frame, even if that frame is systematically dismantled by tiny little fingers within the first few days.

Which is generally what happens to our parenting goals.

This is mostly because children are so adept at taking our goals and shoving them. I'm convinced they make goals of their own, a process that looks something like this:

We say: No more yelling.

They say: So much more yelling. SO MUCH MORE!

Husband and I welcome that first day of the new year with such high hopes. We hope that we will be able to get through an entire day without yelling. This is our hope every year—because, you know, the kids are another year older, so surely they'll be able to (a) tone down the noise and (b) stop making us so mad.

Nope. They try even harder. Not only that, but they've resolved to yell more themselves, which means when we're having chicken (always a win) for dinner, but they don't get seconds until they eat their spinach salad (never a win), they'll yell about how unfair it is that they have to eat such disgusting stuff that has so many important vitamins and minerals—why do they have to have parents who care about the health of their kids? When it's time for baths, they'll yell about how all their friends are still out playing and they just *had* to get the parents who care *way too much* about how much sleep their kid's getting. When their technology timer has clanged and they're not finished with the game, they'll yell about how we're the worst parents ever because we put a limit on how much time they spend rotting their brains in front of a screen.

What an unlucky life.

We say: This year we'll eat fewer sweets.

They say: This year, we'll sneak more sweets.

I've tried so hard to get rid of sugar in my diet. I'm not supposed to have it; it's something that could cause heart disease for me, because I have a gene anomaly (see the essay titled "How to Keep your New Year's Goal to Eat Better" if you want to know more) that prevents my digestive system from processing sugar anywhere but hips, thighs, belly (you can tell I have a hard time with this goal), and, more importantly, my (invisible) triglycerides.

Unlike me, my kids will find every opportunity they can to cram more sugar into their mouths. You'll see evidence of this at holiday gatherings, when they hover around the dessert table hoping I don't notice that a finger slid into the perfect lemon pie. You'll see it at birthday parties, when they smuggle extra brownies while leaving a trail of crumbs on the floor that lead to their hiding place (at least they can find their way back out—if they can untangle themselves from the clothes mountain in their room). You'll see it at school, where they'll swipe an extra cupcake for their friend's birthday—hey, it was free!

Oh, if we could all be so immune to sugar's plumping effects.

We say: More happy family moments.
They say: We'll see about that.

So much of my life is about getting things done. Wash the dishes, fold the clothes, cram in a few hours of work. Husband and I both work from home, and it's easy to let that work bleed into our every-day lives. So we always have this goal on our list: to soak up more happy family moments, without work-creep and rush, rush, rush.

The problem is that kids are kids. They'll take three hours to tie their shoe, because they wanted to do it themselves. They'll decide the tie they chose from the basket this morning, which they aren't supposed to have in the first place—those are reserved for special occasions, and "Pajama Party at School" is not a special occasion that warrants a tie—isn't quite the right color and will spill all the ties (which, again, they aren't supposed to have) all over the floor and think the Cleanup Fairy will take care of the mess so they don't have to lift a finger. They'll destroy the toilet and, by default, the bathroom walls, when we're already half an hour late to church.

So much for New Year's goals.

The other day, I walked into the kitchen, and one of my five-year-olds stood cramming a brownie into his mouth as fast as he could because he thought I was otherwise occupied. I almost said something, but, instead, I let him think he got away with it.

I may as well let someone in this house meet a goal this year. Because it's certainly not going to be me.

Rules for Goal-Setting With Kids: an Aside

Husband and I like to teach our kids about goals, but getting them to sit down and focus is tough. There's always a game to play, a brother to aggravate, food to eat.

So if there's always a game to play, why not turn goal-setting into a game, too? (We'll leave the aggravating brothers out of the equation, but eating food? Yeah, okay, as long as it's something with chocolate. Because you'll need it after this game.)

Here are some rules for playing the Goal Game:

1. Write down as many goals as possible—no matter how silly or unrealistic (one of my sons said this year he wants to buy all the LEGO collections that exist in the world, and I had a hard time not laughing. Laughing's against the rules. Just write it down.). The list is supposed to be comprehensive—it doesn't matter what the goals are; brainstorms are for downloading. Let them dream.

2. Don't giggle.

3. Seriously, you must not giggle.

4. After the initial brainstorm, guide your child in choosing only realistic goals for the list. You may have to explain what "realistic" means.

5. Remind them they'll have to work at these goals. Kids tend to live in a least-effort world, judging by the way my sons execute chores or fix their own lunch ("Hmm, I guess I'll just have an apple for lunch—but can you cut it up for me?") or flush the toilet (they don't).

6. Remind them again: Goals take work.

7. Be glad you now know a piece of your kid's heart.

It's a privilege to listen to the plans and hopes and dreams of our children. I hope we never forget it.

How to Keep Your New Year's Goal to Eat Better: another Aside

One of Husband's and my goals every new year is to continue the food lifestyle we've settled into. A few years ago we started eating mostly paleo, because we discovered that I have a rare gene anomaly (my doctor calls it the "superhero gene") wherein my body can process all kinds of cholesterol (Doc's words: "You could eat eggs cooked in bacon grease every meal for the rest of your life and never develop heart disease.") and be perfectly fine. In fact, my cholesterol holds steady at around 30 mg/dL or so. But if I eat carbs or sugar, I could end up with heart disease—because of my triglyceride count.

That's all a scientific way of saying carbs and sugar could literally kill me in the end (but wouldn't it be worth it? This is the existential question with which I wrestle daily.).

Fortunately, I hate bacon and grease and love all things bread and chocolate. Makes for a good and pleasurable life. And, if you can't tell, that's sarcasm rolled around in and caked with peppermint cream, which will soon be swallowed by dark chocolate (I'm making myself hungry; I need to stop.).

So, since I want to live a long life and make fun of my kids when they have kids, paleo it was.

But come January 1, when the kids have been out of school for nearly three weeks and my eyes start twitching uncontrollably, I want nothing more than a gigantic snickerdoodle cookie (it's waiting in the freezer, where I saved some from the locusts in my house. All I have to do is…No). It doesn't help that all the stocking stuffers are still around, whispering to me (*Just one bite, Rachel. Pick me, Rachel. You know how much you love me, Rachel*). When the kids are endlessly fighting for the fifteenth time in an hour, I want to open up those chocolate-covered mints and pop a few hundred calories and way too many grams of sugar.

I bet I'm not alone.

So I've come up with some suggestions for keeping your New Year's goal to eat better:

1. Get rid of your kids. (Obviously, you can't do this. I just thought I'd mention it, for brainstorm purposes.)

2. Give all the holiday treats to your kids. (Hahahahahahaha)

3. Don't buy the treats in the first place. (Too late.)

4. Put the treats in a hiding spot you'll easily forget. ((a) This could end badly and (b) who has ever heard of such a spot?)

Well, I guess since those are all terrible ideas, there's only one thing left to do:

5. Pretend sugary treats don't have calories and eat them

all yourself. Today. Right now. (You deserve it. You have all year to get back on the wagon. Best to take your time. No one wants a wooden wheel burn.)

Goals are hard with kids, which is exactly why we should enjoy this time while we can: Never again will there be another no-pressure period in our lives when we are not expected to accomplish much of anything except getting kids off to school mostly dressed.

Happy New Year to us.

Absolutes that Don't Belong in the Life of a Parent*

There is a whole world of experts out there to make the rest of us non-experts feel badly about our parenting. Some of them really know what they're talking about; they've spent time studying the brains and behavior of children and hold a Ph.D. in child development and have written volumes of books about how best to raise your children. I'll give these people permission to make me feel bad, because if they have the right advice, they don't actually make me feel bad; they call me to something higher. They admit that they, too, make mistakes, because parenting is hard.

Others, however, don't really know what they're talking about and only spout their confident absolutes because they raised one kid who was super easy.

Some of my least favorite things in the world are absolutes. How can you have absolutes with children, when they are, by their very definition, wild cards? When you have a child, you never know what you'll get. Some are so compliant you could tell them to lie down and take a nap on a bed of tacks and they would. Some are so strong-willed they'll argue with you about whether you moved their homework an inch across the counter while they weren't looking. For half an hour. Two days in a row.

I don't like absolutes, because exceptions exist. And, in the parenting world, absolutes speak of perfection I just can't reach.

Here are some of my least favorite parenting absolutes.

1. Don't ever ever ever ever ever yell at your kids.

I understand how kids can be damaged by parents yelling all the time. I don't yell all the time. I yell when it's necessary.

There's a nuance here that isn't often discussed in parenting circles, and it's this: it's all about the facial expression. Now, I'll admit, I'm not all that great at hiding my anger when my sons have just knocked off a fan blade because they were playing with a soccer ball in the house even though I've told them a billion times that what they're doing is not an indoor activity. But there are other times when I have complete and incontestable control over my facial muscles, and when I yell, I am calmly composed. I yell because they're not listening and it's effective. My sons stop and listen when Mama yells—likely because it doesn't happen often.

The point is, it *does* happen, and when it does, instead of shaming or guilting myself for this failure, I give myself an opportunity to apologize to my kids for "getting a little overworked." They get to see that I, too, get overwhelmed in the moment, that I make mistakes sometimes, that I take full responsibility for those mistakes, and that I seek to repair the relationship. They learn how to apologize, they learn they don't have to be perfect, they learn good conflict resolution skills. They learn about anger and how we all feel it at different times in our lives and for different reasons, too.

Even yelling can be turned into something good.

So I've amended this absolute to "Try not to yell at your kids. And when you do, make sure you apologize later, when the elevated emotions have calmed."

2. Always listen to your kids.

I get how this would be important in the parenting world. If you don't listen to your kids now, how can you expect them to talk to you later? This is a question I've asked myself time and time again.

The problem is that kids have so many words. SO MANY!

It's a regular occurrence in my house: I'll practice active listening for the first five minutes of conversation (it's technically a monologue), but the billions of other things I have to do start pressing on me, so I'll inch my mind away somewhere else, probably to the never-ending to-do list. I'll move. I'll try to do things *while* listening.

They'll follow me around talking about Minecraft or Pokémon or what video games their friends get to play all the time with no limits whatsoever. When the conversation (to reiterate, it's a monologue) has passed the ten-minute mark, I start to pretend I'm listening. I respond to the important parts, I give the proper vocal cues, and I daydream in my head about stories and adventures and having a minute to myself.

This absolute can be amended by changing a few words:

Listen to your kids when it matters most.

3. Never let your kid talk back.

I have several back-talkers. Sometimes that's a big deal, sometimes it isn't. When they backtalk in a disrespectful tone, with a disrespectful look, or using disrespectful words, it's a problem and needs to be addressed. But if they're trying to correct me or bring my attention to something (so long as that correction and attention-requesting is not tattling, making excuses, or pointing fingers at someone), I'm perfectly fine with the backtalk. As admitted above, I am not a perfect parent. Sometimes I hold to ideals and standards that my sons have outgrown, and they deserve to have a voice in their responsibilities and privileges and what their father and I expect of them.

What I communicate to my sons when I listen to their backtalk is that they are in control of their own selves, that they have power in a world that can often make them feel like they are powerless, and that they have the space and freedom to express their deepest thoughts and wonderings and opinions. Of course there is a right way to do it, and of course I expect them to do it the right way.

My sons' backtalk has always been valuable to our family.

The non-absolute version of this would read: Let your kid express himself in respectful backtalk.

4. Don't ever say you miss your life before kids or want a vacation from them.

There are self-appointed parenting "gurus" who will tell you this is the worst thing you can possibly think because it's disingenuous to your kids. They are blessings. They should always be regarded as such.

Voicing any version of the phrases above doesn't mean that the wonder and joy and brilliance children have brought to your life suddenly disappear. It only means that sometimes, when there are three seats to buckle in the car and you're already ten minutes late, you think it would be so nice to get in the car and leave, without seats to buckle. It only means that when dinnertime rolls around, you'd really like the convenience of ordering something (or skipping dinner altogether), but eating out for a family of eight, as opposed to a family of two, is much more expensive. It only means that when you hear footsteps at 5 a.m. on a Saturday you briefly think about how nice it would be to sleep until 7.

I appreciate and love my kids. I also appreciate and love the time I had with my husband before kids, and sometimes I'd like to have a few moments where I get to appreciate and love that time again. It doesn't mean I'd ever wish any of my children gone forever.

Every parent needs a break sometimes. Raising kids is tough. They'll climb up the walls one minute and fall asleep in the van another minute, and you have to attempt managing the transfer without waking them up so they're ready to terrorize the walls again as soon as you get home. They will one minute flush the toilet and the next forget and leave the bathroom door open so their little brother can wander in and have a ball with the un-flushed slime (hypothetically).

Amend this phrase like so: It's totally fine if you want to

say you miss your life before kids or you want a vacation from them. Because two days into a kid-free weekend, you'll be wishing them back home (sometimes it'll take three; at most five…or seven).

We can't let people make us feel guilty for these ridiculous absolutes. Sometimes I yell at my kids. So what? I get back up the next day, and I try to do better. They do, too.

It's called being a good human. And I'd rather be that than a plastic replica of perfection (have you seen what kids can do to plastic?).

The Speaking Personalities of Children

In a house like mine, there are many, many talkers. I estimate that, on any given day, before the clock strikes 7 a.m., I've already heard an average of five trillion words, which typically run in one ear and out the other.

My sons have quite distinctive personalities when it comes to talking. We have, of course, a **Motor Mouth**.

This is the kid who never stops talking. He will plant himself right next to your elbow and follow you around as you're washing the dirty dishes and putting the clean ones away. You'll have to reach over his head (if he's not taller than you yet) to get a cup out for his brother, reach around him to throw something away, and reach under him to tie the shoe of another brother so you can get on the road to school, a walk that will contain a billion more words from Motor Mouth while he finishes what he was saying—which he never actually does.

I will regularly trip over this kid as he follows me around talking about his dreams, his plans for today's stop motion movies, plus the next week's stop motion movies, and, also, the stop motion movies he'll make when he's all the way grown.

He, unlike me, never misses a beat.

We also have the **Sloth Speaker**.

This is the kid who takes incredibly long to tell a story. He has so many words and stories inside his head that he will often forget what he's saying in the middle of saying it and either start something new or just look blankly at the wall for a while until he says, "I forgot what I was saying." He will also interject "um" quite often and will unabashedly prove that he didn't really consider what he wanted to say before he opened his mouth.

A sentence like, "We did jump ropes in P.E. today" will take him at least five minutes to get out—not only because he will use all kinds of extraneous words but also because of all the excruciating pauses where he has to gather what he wants to say next. There are just too many words flitting about in this boy's brain; catching one is like an over-eager three-year-old trying to trap a hummingbird (or anything else), I imagine: next to impossible.

Then there's the **Broken Record**.

You can probably imagine that there are many interruptions in our house of eight people—six of whom have yet to successfully master the intricacies of conversation, which is simply a fancy way of saying they like to interrupt as soon as any random thought thumps them on the head. The Broken Record is the kid who will start over completely when he's interrupted—even if he was almost finished with his original story. Husband and I live in fear that someone will interrupt him when he's twelve thousand words in and he'll start over from scratch.

Next we have **Mr. Know-It-All**.

This honor belongs to one of my five-year-olds, because of course he's been around long enough to know everything about the world, and then some. He will speak matter-of-factly on every subject imaginable, even if it's to say something like this: "One of these days I'll be older than you." That's not possible, son. But I can't tell him that. He knows everything, and no one can convince him otherwise, even if they have lived longer, know more, and contain more common sense in their pinky than he does in his five-year-old body.

Then there's the delightful **Random Man**.

Random Man is the other five-year-old in my house. He offers all sorts of random information in random places. If one were to say that it's time to clean up, he would say that did you know his brother went over to Logan's house yesterday? If you tell him we're going to read a story, he will tell you that he's not wearing any underpants today. If you tell him thank you for the flower he just gave you, he will tell you that he threw up last night (it was actually three weeks ago, concerned kindergarten teacher.)

The last boy in my house is affectionately called **The Sage**.

This is the kid who often seems random but is, instead, profound. Sometimes what he says is so profound that we can't even understand him. It could be because he's only two, but I like to think it's because he has a lot of wise words to say.

Everyone gets quiet when he speaks, too—they all know he has something significantly clever to impart when he opens his mouth.

The other day I was cooking dinner, and Motor Mouth entered the kitchen to tell me about the stop motion video he'd recorded. Sloth Speaker tapped me on the shoulder, and, while Motor Mouth was still in the middle of his never-ending story (interruptions don't bother him; he's a steam roller, too), said, "I…uh…I…I uh…I was…uh…running around outside and I…uh…fell down and I uh….scraped…I uh….scraped…" He looked lost for a minute and then, finally, finished up: "I scraped my elbow." He held up a bleeding elbow.

"Oh my gosh," I said. "Let's get that taken care of."

I tripped over Motor Mouth (still talking) on my way to the bathroom, where Broken Record came in and said, "I saw…I saw the…I saw the whole…I saw the whole thing…I saw the whole thing and…I saw the whole thing and it…I saw the whole thing and it looked…I saw the whole thing and it looked like it hurt." He glared at Motor Mouth, who was responsible for the eight restarts.

Mr. Know-It-All came in and said, "He's going to bleed to death. That's too much blood." Sloth Speaker started freaking out, so I took matters into my own hands.

"You're five," I said to Mr. Know-It-All. "You don't know what you're talking about."

"I'm wearing three pairs of underwear and four socks on each foot," said Random Man.

"You're wearing twenty socks?" said Mr. Know-It-All.

"Spider!" said The Sage. He pointed. The room stilled and then exploded. We did what we always do when we see spiders—we ran away screaming.

Well, most of us ran away screaming—all except for Motor Mouth, who ran away still talking.

Things That Make You Go Hmmm, Parent Edition

Kids are confounding. One minute they're open books, relaying everything and anything—to their teachers, to me, to the world. And the next minute, they're mysteries waiting to be unlocked.

You'd think that by this point I'd have cracked the code. I'm always reading books about parenting, always checking up on the latest psychology and child development research, always trying to learn more about my duty to raise six competent human beings, whom I will one day release out into the world.

But I'm still confounded by the majority of what concerns my sons.

Take, for example, my third grader's homework. I loved math in school. I aced high school calculus and college algebra, but I can't do my third grader's math. Every day I have the pleasure of hearing him complain about how much he hates this math and how he doesn't want to do it anymore because he just doesn't understand it. And every day I have the humbling opportunity to peer over his shoulder, read some of the word problems, and feel severely incompetent. I don't like feeling incompetent, so this results in two people complaining.

After days and weeks and months, even, of listening to my son moan about his math homework, I'll find all over the house little notecards with his handwriting. On these notecards are not what you would expect to see: a note of some kind. Instead, these notecards are filled with complicated math equations. When I ask him about them, he says, "Oh, yeah, I was just doing some math."

"I thought you didn't like math," I say.

"I like *that* kind of math," he says.

Okay then.

Then there's the why of everything. One of the most frequent questions my kids ask is, "Why?"

"It's time to clean up," I'll say. Guess what's coming next. I bet you can do it. Go on. Give it a try.

"Why?" the second grader will say.

"Because this place is a mess."

He'll look around like he doesn't really know what I'm talking about. A mess? It looks perfectly fine to him.

"It's time to go to bed," I'll say after story time is finished.

"Why?" the five-year-old twins will chorus.

"Because you need your sleep to be your best self."

They'll look at each other like they're silently communicating what's going to happen in their bedroom later (I can usually always guess what this will be: They'll take all the books off their shelves, jump on and off their bed for a bit, remove clothes from their hangers and forget to put them back. They specialize in Driving Mama Crazy.).

When my sons ask me "why," I generally try to give them clear and concise answers, because (a) I know they'll keep asking if I don't and (b) they stop listening after the first five seconds anyway. Husband hasn't quite learned this technique yet, and he suffers for it every time.

Oh, who am I kidding. I suffer, too. My kids sometimes ask why so many times that my answer becomes the dreaded, "Because I said so."

My sons ask "why" out of curiosity, too—like "Why is the sky blue?" and "Why do we love cats so much?" and "Why do moms have sons?" Those kinds of questions I can't answer due to lack of knowledge, but sometimes I'll pretend they're exercises in creativity and invent an answer. The sky is blue because billions of people exhale in the world, and their collective exhales create this brilliant blue cloud that settles over the sky like a curtain. We love cats so much because in another life we lived as cats. Moms have sons because every boy needs a person in his life to tame the inner animal; it may as well be his mother.

That last one is more true than not, by the way.

What my sons wear often confounds me as well. The other day one of my five-year-olds came down to breakfast in plaid shorts, a striped button-up shirt, and a polka-dotted bowtie. He topped the look with a beanie.

"You know it's going to be cold today, right?" I said.

He shrugged. "Okay," he said, like it didn't matter one bit

that his knobby knees and spindly legs did not have proper cover.

As soon as we stepped out the door for the walk to school, he started shivering uncontrollably. When we made it to the stop sign at the end of our road (about seventy-five meters), he said he wanted to go change. I said no, it was too late now. He said I was the meanest mom ever, and then he complained the whole rest of the walk to school. Sometimes Stick to Your Guns and Let Them Suffer the Natural Consequences of Their Decisions is a very annoying parenting method.

For the school holiday program where my second grader participated in singing a handful of holiday tunes, his choir director requested that all students dress in holiday colors: red and green. My son decided to go with all green and donned a long-sleeved graphic T-shirt—backwards, so it would look like it was a solid green shirt—some green jeans that have the knees blown out because they've been through two other boys, and green shoes that were already done for the year. When we walked into the school, the first person we saw was one of my kindergarten son's teachers, who has a kid in my second-grader's class. She greeted us, and I said, by way of apology, "Yeah, he decided to wear his best clothes for the program."

What can you do? They're their own people.

What also confounds me is that when I ask who was responsible for the mess in the living room or who needs to clean up their homework before dinner or who didn't put their clothes away, they will tell me "no one." No one? Really? These toys, this homework, all the clothes belong to no one? I wish I could believe that.

One day I asked my eight-year-old why he didn't put his clothes away before he moved on to tech time, which is against the rules in our house. Work first, pleasure second.

"I did put them away," he said.

I pointed to the pile. "Then what's this?"

"Someone must have gotten them out again!" he said. I think he believed what he said, too.

I shook my head. "I guess it was The Ghost."

The Ghost is responsible for drawing all over one of my writer notebooks with a sparkly purple gel pen, taking all the ornaments off one side of the Christmas tree (no, we haven't put it away yet, don't judge), putting gigantic spit wads on the ceiling in the downstairs guest bathroom, spreading books all over the floor of our library, and leaving a poop smear on the toilet downstairs.

I'm sure you would agree that The Ghost is a very troublesome guest.

I have to shake my head at the things my sons try. Half the time they don't even know why they try them; it's just fun.

Husband has a pull-up bar in the doorway leading from our bedroom to our bathroom, and every now and then the seven- and eight-year-olds will steal in and do some pull-ups before going about their business elsewhere. One day I caught the eight-year-old hanging upside down from the pull-up bar.

"Uh, what are you doing?" I said.

"I'm doing a leg-up," he said.

I stared at him for a minute. He wasn't moving. "I don't

think it works that way."

He laughed. His face had turned red from hanging upside down for so long. "Yeah, me neither," he said. "Will you help me down? I'm stuck."

What if I hadn't come along?

He attempted an upside-down shrug. "I don't know," he said. "I guess I would've just…" He didn't have an answer.

I rolled my eyes and helped him down. I figured natural consequences would backfire on me with that one.

They'll try anything once. My sons will slide down our stairs on their bottoms and then complain about how much their back hurts the next day. They'll dare each other to make the cat so mad he'll scratch their face. They'll challenge each other to a jumping-off-the-trampoline contest to see who can fly the highest. Once they wanted to sword fight with a shovel and a rake. Fortunately, I caught them before The Death Duel could get properly started.

Another piece of the confounding equation is my sons' simultaneous love and distaste for The Great Outdoors.

I make my sons play outside every Friday afternoon, when I'm on kid-duty, so I can cook dinner in peace. I lock my twins out back (everything in the backyard is safe for the most part, even though I can never, ever predict what these two will find next) and encourage my older sons to play out front. We live on a cul-de-sac, which means they have free rein to skateboard, roller blade, and ride their bikes and scooters to their hearts' content. We have a bin of dodgeballs they can use in the side yard. We have a drainage ditch they can sled down on a slab made from an Amazon box. There's plenty to do.

Yet still they will complain about having to play outside; they want to be inside coloring or playing with LEGOs or mostly eating, because that's what they want to be doing forever and always. But then, when it's time to do their after-dinner chores, they ask to go play outside. It's already dark. Their daddy and I say no. They say they *knew* it, we *never* let them go outside. We're so mean!

"You just played outside for two hours before dinner," I'll say.

"But you never let us play outside," they'll say, like they didn't even hear me.

"I can't really argue with your logic," I'll say. "So I'll just let you think about it."

The kitchen will fade into silence while they think it over. And just when I imagine they've gotten my point, the other five-year-old will pipe up and say, "Yeah, we never get to play outside."

There's no sense in arguing with the things that make you go Hmmm. They're just yet another delight that comes standard in The Parent Life. One day maybe you'll understand. Or maybe you won't ever.

Can you live with an unsolvable mystery?

5 New Year Goals for a Successful Parenting Year

You've probably guessed by now that every new year I sit down to make parenting goals, in addition to my professional goals. Some years begin better than others—I end the old year on a laughing note and so can make humorous parenting goals that will continue to launch the laughter into the brand-new year.

This year has been a difficult year for my family, though. I've struggled through some severe depression, one of my sons is currently struggling with severe depression, and we are constantly trying to reconnect and spend time together during an especially busy season.

So this year I decided to make some more serious goals for my parenting life. Here's a look at those goals.

1. I will eat mostly healthy.

Kids sometimes make it difficult to choose healthy foods —not just because by the time the locusts have finished with our fridge there isn't much left to choose from but also because parenting is so difficult that sometimes I just want to eat all my feelings. So this year I've decided to be more intentional and make better choices on a minute-by-minute basis, one day at a time (we eat mostly healthy already, so it shouldn't be terribly hard). And the days I reach for a handful of Annie's bunny grahams or my leftover Trader Joe's peppermint patties, well, that's where the next goal comes into play.

2. I will cut myself some slack.

Though I laugh at myself in retrospect—mostly through the humor essays I write—I want to laugh at myself more in the moment. Despite how I might come across in the humor writing you've read, I very often take things too seriously. I'm hard on myself. I chastise myself for eating those Annie's bunny grahams or leftover Trader Joe's peppermint patties. I'm the first (and usually only) one to hold out the "Guilt Cap" and demand that I wear it. In the new year, I want to be nicer and more accepting of my weaknesses.

3. I will get out of the house more.

Even if it's just for a short walk in our neighborhood, I want to get out more. I walk my sons to school every day and I go to the grocery store and church once a week, but other than that, I'm a hermit, particularly when I'm going through a tough time. I withdraw, huddle inside myself, build my walls. Getting out of the house more will help me in multiple ways.

4. I will hug my kids more.

Our days are so busy that sometimes I get to the end of them and realize I haven't even hugged a couple of my sons. Some of them act like they don't want hugs anymore, but they still need them. Even if my hugs are not reciprocated, I will still give them lavishly.

5. I will let them see me cry and open a conversation about it.

This year one of my sons voiced suicidal thoughts. We've been on the lookout for depression, because it runs in both our families and was passed to both my husband and me. My sons feel when I'm sad, but they don't always see it—because I don't like to let them see it. But the more conversations we can have around this sadness—which sometimes doesn't have a specific cause and sometimes has an abundance of them—the greater understanding and acceptance they will have of their own sadness. What lives in the dark always seems scary, so we'll shine the light on it and talk.

I'll be working hard this year to make sure I take greater steps toward accomplishing these goals. And on the days I fail? Well, there's always goal number two to keep me trying again and again and again.

I've never been one to give up.

Epilogue: On Leaving Behind Sugar

Husband and I have been on a quest to clean up our diet for a very long time. We eat well, for the most part, choosing a mostly paleo lifestyle, except for that one "cheat day" a week we throw in for motivation—the one that sometimes turns into a whole cheat weekend.

This "cheat day" (that turns into a cheat weekend) is what we wanted to tackle more energetically in the new year. We made it our goal to only eat this one day a small treat at lunch and a slightly larger one at dinner, and that was it. No lazy Saturday treat, no I-didn't-pack-a-lunch-for-myself treat on Sunday on the way home from church.

This new goal would require planning, which is not our strong suit, but we were determined.

We started out the new year strong; we hadn't gone overboard on the Christmas treats, and things were looking up. The problem, though, was that Husband made brownies on New Year's Eve, to celebrate the ending of an old year and the dawning of a new one, and they were still hanging around.

Everybody knows what happens when treats hang around.

The other problem was that the kids were out of school.

Still. Like they'd been for the last ten days.

When my sons are out of school for any length of time, there is always a natural progression of "bored" that happens. First they are all excited about having their new Christmas toys, and they'll play with them for endless silent hours for the first several days. We had almost seven days of this bliss. And then the new year came, and, with it, boredom, sleep deprivation, and restlessness.

Did you know that not sleeping well has a negative impact on the healthy food choices that you're able to make? Yeah, well, I stayed up three hours past my normal bedtime on New Year's Eve, and I could certainly feel the adverse effects of that.

Those brownies Husband made started talking.

Husband had something to do on New Year's Day—he was going out to Home Depot so he could get the supplies to repair our ceiling from a water leak we'd had three months ago. The leak had been fixed the same day it soaked us and our entire kitchen with loose water, but the ceiling was another matter entirely. We were done looking at pipes and insulation and exposed innards that practically begged our children to "Come and explore." Husband decided New Year's Day would be a good day to tackle the project; we were both off work, which is important when you need one partner to watch the kids.

Good for him. He got to leave the house. He left early—probably earlier than necessary.

As soon as he left, the whole day fell right off the rails.

I had gotten up late that morning, because of the late bedtime the night before, so I wasn't able to mark my workout off my to-do list. I'd thought it would be easy enough to do this workout with all my children awake, but you probably already know, because of irony and humor, that this was very far from the actual reality. I did not plan well enough ahead. I managed my workout, only tripping over bodies twenty-three times during burpees. I skinned a few knees, did pushups with a two-year-old on my back, and huffed through twins telling me I was doing the exercises wrong.

Get out of here, thanks.

But the day actually starts earlier than that. As soon as I heard the kids moving around, I dragged myself from beneath my covers, where it was still warm and toasty, and shivered into my workout clothes for the day. The two-year-old woke up with no pants, and he couldn't tell me why. He also couldn't find those pants. I wasn't sure if I should look for them or just let it be. I thought maybe they'd show up some other time (they haven't yet). I hoped they weren't lost for a reason, like, you know, unexplained wetness (unexplained because he is a potty-trained two-year-old, and he would vehemently deny an accident. He is a big boy! Don't ever argue that point!).

I carried my newly panted son down to the kitchen, where we were greeted by the open playroom door. Playroom sounds all fancy, but our playroom is actually our garage. Someone, likely the ten-year-old who is most often the culprit, left open the door that adjoins the insulated house with the uninsulated garage. I could barely talk my teeth were chattering so hard. The twenty-three-degree weather had snuck into the house, all night, and everyone at the table sat shivering in blankets, waiting for breakfast. At least the Mystery of the Cold House was solved; my mind, before spying the open door, had jumped to the conclusion that our heater had quit. It's always worse in my mind.

Once I placed breakfast on the table—which, miraculously, no one complained about; I think they were still half-asleep...or maybe frozen—I went upstairs to make my bed. My seven-year-old, two minutes later, vaulted into the covers and un-made it.

I remade it, waved him out of the room, and walked out my bedroom door to an explosion of art pencils.

I put on *The Greatest Showman* soundtrack and took the day in both my hands. I said, "You are not going to break me. You are not."

This was only motivation for my kids to try harder.

The two-year-old dumped out all the cat treats, and I had to wrestle them away from a tame cat turned feral for salmon goodness. A few seconds later, one of my twins messed up the television I'd turned on because I needed my sons occupied for a minute (I don't like doing this, but sometimes you just need a break).

I went upstairs and glared at the laundry pile I'd earlier dumped on my bed—there was nowhere to lie down.

I tried to send my sons outside, because their noise kept swelling louder and louder, but at high noon it was only twenty-eight degrees, and I live in South Texas, which means my children don't own adequate winter clothes, and they would likely freeze to death if I insisted they play outside.

However. It would be *my* death if they remained inside—so I did my best. I bundled them up in a few shirts and zipped them into a fall-ish jacket. Their winter jackets went missing sometime around the end of November, because here in Texas, it will be cold in the morning and ninety degrees by the end of the day. My sons will shed their jackets at school like they're another skin contributing to their sweat, which, of course, they are. They then leave their jackets wherever they shed them—in the cafeteria, on the playground, in the field they lap a few times when school's out.

Five minutes later, my two-year-old came back inside and said, "My hands are broken, Mama." I knew I couldn't leave them out there. So I invited them all back in, where they fought, complained, destroyed, bounced, and otherwise orchestrated complete havoc. I caved. When Husband got home from the store, it was to the sight of me cramming leftover brownies in my mouth.

"What are you doing?" Husband said. "Today's not a cheat day."

I couldn't answer him because there were too many brownies in my mouth. I shrugged apologetically. Why were there brownies, anyway?

And then, because he's a good husband, he joined me and said, "We'll start the strict incorporation of our goals tomorrow."

That's exactly why I married him.

There's always tomorrow. Now that the brownies are all gone, I'm sure I'll have much more discipline left for resisting

Rachel Toalson

all things children and chocolate.

February

Atypical Ways Kids Show Us They Love Us

Kids are the greatest, aren't they? You tell them to handle that glass with care (they weren't supposed to have it in the first place, but they're getting older; everybody deserves a chance to prove themselves), and as soon as they nod their agreement, the glass slips out of their hands and shatters on the floor, milk splattering all over the cabinets.

They just wanted you to have something to clean up so you could feel useful. Everyone wants to feel useful.

This is only one of the atypical ways children love their parents. There are several more, including but not limited to:

1. Knees and elbows everywhere

Any time I find a minute to sit in a chair, mind my own business, maybe even crack open a book and do a little reading, it is only a small matter of time before a boy will launch himself into my lap. And by launch, I mean with missile-speed. If the book doesn't take my face off, an elbow or knee will do the trick. I've almost lost teeth in the launch process.

If I happen to stretch out on the floor for a moment of meditation (or a short ten-minute nap), boys will climb all over me, jump off me, try to turn me over like this is a game. They are the boniest creatures I've ever known. I wear more bruises on my body than I ever did when I played high school volleyball and sacrificed my hips to saving the ball.

2. Toys, shoes, clothes, EVERYTHING left EVERYWHERE

My sons have one talent that rises above all the others: making a mess. They walk out of their shoes and their clothes, and when they're doing art, they forget where pencils go and how to put away paper. They constantly leave apple cores and banana peels in places where apples and bananas aren't supposed to be consumed.

I'm sure they're just trying to show me how much they love me: the Mom Maid is still needed, after all these years.

#SoThankful.

But I swear, if I have to pick up one more smashed-to-slime banana, I'm going to leave a vomit offering on their pillows, along with a note that says, "I love you back."

3. Telling all our secrets.

My sons talk about Husband and me all the time, and because they spend the bulk of their time at school (and, consequently, miss us terribly), they air these secrets to their teachers. Their teachers now think we are parents who sing songs about bodily functions, hold regular burping contests (they're not really contests; I'm the defending champion, and the others don't even come close. It's really just a concert.), and arm-fart their prayers. They probably think we're the most immature parents ever.

Oh well. At least they haven't told about the Drunk Daddy routine. Yet. (If they *have* told you about this, kindergarten teacher, don't worry. It sounds worse than it is. Daddy is not a drunk. He pretends to run into doors and hurt himself. That's all. It's a cautionary tale for why a grown-up boy shouldn't drink, although all those giggles might completely negate the purpose.)

4. Watch this.

It never fails; I'm right in the middle of doing something important—trying to figure out whose underwear is whose, for example—and one of my sons will shout out: "Watch this, Mama!" It could be that he wants me to watch a car go down this amazing track he built (it's the car with the broken wheel, which means it will take the car forever and a day to limp down the track), or he wants me to watch a flip on the couch (he'll hurt his finger in the process and it will take fifteen minutes of Mom's Magic Kisses to take away the pain), or he wants me to see that he's mooning me (he'll only do that once).

"Watch this" is just code for "I love you so much."

5. Drawings on important papers.

Every time I have to return a paper to their school or to the doctor's office or maybe to my publisher or agent, I will find on them drawings—some tiny enough to be dismissed, some large enough to require a new copy; good thing the school always sends five duplicates of everything.

I'm sure all they're saying is, "I am here."

And I'm so glad they're here, glad for every way they show me they love me.

(Although, if you're reading this, kids, I could really do without the mess.)

How to Ban Sugar this Valentine's Day: an Aside

My sons don't need more candy for Valentine's Day. We've just recovered from all the stocking stuffer treats left over from the holidays. Add to that a January birthday party, and you get the ingredients for six really wonderfully balanced children.

So for Valentine's Day this year, I decided to do something a little different. I decided to give my sons a little coupon book of "treats."

Here are some coupons I put in this coupon book:

1. An extra hug from Mama. My sons don't hug me much anymore, because they're getting way too old to acknowledge that they may need this token of affection. They do. And so do I. So this gives them an opportunity (me an opportunity, really), to hug them again. They have to use all the coupons in the book, after all, before the expiration date. At least if they ever want another coupon book.

2. An extra five minutes with Mama on laundry day. This serves two purposes: connection time and a laundry helper. Sneaky, sneaky.

3. A chance to do the dishes and press the buttons on the dishwasher. This one might be more appropriate for the younger ones who like to press the buttons on the dishwasher. My two-year-old is especially good at this—so good, in fact, that we had to lock him out of it for the time being, or else the dishwasher will always be washing imaginary dishes, and we will be significantly disappointed when we open it to see a whole load of clean...nothing.

4. An extra five minutes of reading time. I'd much rather see them stay up late to read than sit like a zombie in front of a screen.

5. One extra movie night a week. You can accomplish a whole lot while kids sit down to watch a movie, AND you'll be the best parent ever. At least until the movie's over and you tell them it's time for bed.

Can't win them all.

Now, because of this little coupon book, I have helpers, I don't have to worry about cavities, and boys aren't bouncing off the walls because of all the extra sugar (My ten-year-old says that's not really a thing; it's never been scientifically proven, but what does he or science know about the mechanics of kids and sugar? A parent knows.).

Everybody wins this Valentine's Day.

Alternative Valentine's Day Ideas for Class Parties: Another Aside

Our family has, for a while, been taking steps to be more environmentally friendly, to cut down on costs and to live more simply and sustainably. We've already done quite a bit of work on this over the years, but there is always more that can be done.

So for Valentine's Day this year, we opted to make gifts for my sons' classmates out of supplies we already had on hand. Here are some things we considered:

1. Bookmarks

You can use old paint swatches, old books covers (because our picture books can never keep their sleeves), and that massive sheet of Star Wars stickers your first grader's teacher sent home with him last week.

2. Reusable napkins

These can be crafted from old T-shirts and sewn into squares large enough to fit on a kid's lap. If you're feeling extra crafty, you can embroider on them a design from your kids (but let's not go overboard, Miss Pinterest. That's a lot of classmates.).

3. Some seeds to plant

You can get these relatively cheap, and why not get a head start on the spring garden?

4. Recipe cards

Use recipes that are simple enough for kids to make. My kids, for now, love cooking; I may as well use that to my advantage.

5. Illustrated poetry

It's like a piece of art you can give to everyone. Print it on thick recycled paper and it makes for a fun, creative gift.

6. A small collection of inspirational cards

Everybody needs to feel encouraged from time to time. Let your kids make their own version of encouragement cards on decorative scrapbook or plain craft paper and bundle them up for their classmates.

Maybe it takes more time and effort to make Valentine goodies, but it will certainly be a Valentine's Day you won't forget (if only for the mess you're still cleaning up, four weeks later).

How to Misuse LEGOs: a Generous Guide

If you're a parent, LEGOs will likely be or eventually become an important part of your life.

Husband and I tried to avoid LEGOs for a while. I'd seen all the funny memes about stepping on LEGOs, finding them in odd places, watching them multiply with hardly a nudge. When our sons first started collecting LEGOs, Husband and I had a plan: they would remain in our playroom, where Husband had modified three long tables with edges that kept the LEGOs contained on the table and not on the floor.

Somehow the room still managed to look like someone detonated twelve bombs made of LEGOs.

My sons will play with LEGOs for hours on end. I love this during extended school breaks or short days off from school, at least until they start fighting. But I digress. How long my sons will play with their LEGOs is not the focus of this essay; rather, I want to focus on how my sons *misuse* their LEGOs.

Starting with:

Chewing them.

It never fails that halfway into a minute of releasing my sons to play in their playroom, I will hear some clicking sounds that are definitely not the sort of clicks I would be hearing if my sons were merely playing with LEGOs. These sound too…toothy. I will poke my head into the playroom and see someone with a mouth full of LEGOs.

Gross.

"Remember not to chew on the LEGOs," I'll say with so much patience I should get an award. The twelfth time I have to tell them, though, patience is not just thin, it is practically nonexistent.

I rarely understand their answer, because they have so many LEGOs stuffed in their mouths, but they will dutifully spit them out, along with a whole wad of slobber that soaks every crevice of innocent bystander pieces that were not even near their mouths. If I wanted to play with the LEGOs, I'd have to buy my own, because it is highly unlikely that a single one of my sons' pieces has not been somehow touched by saliva—and, yes, that's better than other liquids or solids that could potentially leak into the gaps, but I'd rather not, thanks.

Using them as booby traps.

I know it's cliché to say that I cannot walk into a room without stepping on LEGOs, but truly. I cannot. It doesn't matter that the LEGOs are relegated to only one room in our house; they spread. And when they spread, they assault. And when they assault, sons think that's funny and use them to assault on purpose.

Hence, booby traps.

The Days Are Long, But the Years Are Short

The other day, my two-year-old attempted to sneak into his oldest brother's room, where my oldest son keeps all his special LEGO sets that he doesn't want his brothers to touch. My two-year-old came back out of that room wailing. At first I couldn't understand why he was so upset; my oldest son wasn't in the room, and even if he had been, he would never purposefully hurt his youngest brother (the others are an entirely different story, but the baby of the family is treated by everyone as the baby of the family). My two-year-old then pointed to his foot, where two LEGO Ninjago swords stuck out, crossed like an X.

"Did you step on LEGOs?" I said, and he nodded, tears still slipping down his cute little cheeks.

"Oh, whoops," the oldest said. "I forgot to pick up my booby trap."

"Your what?" I said.

"Yeah, I was trying to keep my brothers out of my room."

He'd used a LEGO Ninjago sword, a Minecraft sword (excuse me, I thought it was Ninjago, but what do I know?), and an extra Harry Potter wand to weave a barb through the carpet fibers in such a way that it would jut out and prick whoever came close to it. Which just so happened to be his favorite brother.

After gently suggesting that booby traps were a somewhat inappropriate use of LEGOs, I had to secretly congratulate him for coming up with a creative solution to an annoying problem. In fact, I almost used the booby traps myself, the thirteenth time someone knocked on my bedroom door while

I was trying to sleep.

Refashioning them as gift wrap.

During the holiday season, my oldest son had a whole bunch of Christmas gifts under our tree that he wrapped into LEGO cages. I thought this, too, was a creative use of the LEGOs, so I couldn't get terribly mad—at least not until his brothers "opened" their gifts (which were mini figures, trapped behind those LEGO cages)—some of them clearly more efficient at this than others—and the pieces exploded everywhere. At least we didn't have to waste paper and cut down more trees. Maybe next year I'll commission my son to wrap everything in LEGOs.

Probably not.

Claiming they make good reading during Silent Reading time.

We have this fun slice of time in our house called Silent Reading time. During this period everyone—parents included—is expected to sit down and read silently for a while. These are the kinds of perks you have when your mom is a writer. Most of my sons do just fine with this time, because most of them know how to read and enjoy reading and, what can I say, we've trained them well. But every now and then the seven-year-old gets a little lazy.

One day I caught him smuggling in all the LEGO manuals.

"What are you doing with those?" I said.

"I'm going to read them," he said.

"They don't even have text in them," I said.

"Yes they do," he said, pointing to the front, on which is

printed the word "LEGO" and the name of the set. That's it.

"Not enough text," I said. He was very disappointed to learn that studying LEGO manuals was not a good enough Silent Reading activity to appease his mean author-mom.

The point of LEGOs is to encourage creativity, so I guess even when my sons misuse their LEGOs, there's a silver lining: their brains are, every time, expanding in resourcefulness, inventiveness, and innovation.

I can't really ask for more than that.

What Ice Days Accomplish in a Household: Never-Ending Fights

The other day my sons got a wonderful "ice day" off from school, because there was a winter storm that blew through South Texas, and southerners don't know how to drive in (or walk on—have you seen the videos?) ice.

I spent a year of childhood in Ohio, where it snows for almost half the year, so I felt pretty confident in my ability to walk my sons to school, which is only half a mile down the road. But I suppose not all parents have this kind of experience, and, as a result, school was closed for the day—which happened to be the day after MLK day and less than two weeks after they'd returned from their holiday break.

My sons have not yet had adequate time away from each other, which means they spent the day mostly arguing and fighting.

First it was the fidget spinner—they couldn't decide who should get to play with this one fidget spinner. They were all saying it was their turn, pointing fingers at the ones who'd already had a turn (who knows if they really had), and claiming that, anyway, the fidget spinner belonged to them. My sons all had fidget spinners once upon a time—not because they need them, necessarily, but because they were a fad. One of the grandparents provided them, and two sons promptly lost theirs, another two (see if you can guess which ones) promptly destroyed theirs, and one was stolen, according to the owner. That left only one remaining. I have no idea whose it is (but process of elimination at least narrows it down).

The two-year-old finally grabbed this fidget spinner from where it spun on the counter and took off running, with a trail of his brothers running after him, yelling, "Give it back! Give it back!"

Later that day, the fidget spinner mysteriously disappeared.

It was the same tired story with the trampoline. Sure, there's only one, but it's big enough to hold all of them. We don't have rules about the numbers of kids who can jump on it at one time (we probably should, but, well, we're tired). My sons would head outside to jump, stay there for ten minutes (if I was lucky), and one by one return back inside saying, "There's not enough room for me on the trampoline." How is there not enough room for them on the trampoline? It's a thirty-foot trampoline. I mentioned this. The first son who came back inside said, "I keep tripping over my legs."

"Well, that sounds like a personal problem," I said. I couldn't resist. Sometimes sarcasm is unavoidable. He didn't think it was funny at all, but I laughed for the both of us.

Finally, I had to gather all my sons in one place and tell

them they needed to play nicely or they wouldn't be allowed on the trampoline. They decided it was way too hard to play nicely on the trampoline, so they wandered back through the door to "play nicely" inside.

Except they elected to "play nicely" with the LEGOs.

We have a billion LEGO pieces. But apparently my sons could not decide to whom the one red piece out of six million other red pieces belonged. It came in everyone's set. They argued for fifteen minutes and then brought their disagreement into the kitchen, where I was cutting up apples for a cinnamon treat I planned to cook for their snack just to get them to shut their mouths for long enough that I could take a small "mental health" break. After their visitation to the kitchen, however, I no longer felt so generous. I ate all the cinnamon apples myself.

I told my sons there were a million other red pieces, and they said, "But not like this one. See? This one has a little scratch, and it's because…" and they each had a long and drawn-out story to tell me about how they managed to get that little scratch on this red piece that belonged to them. I picked up another red LEGO piece from the sea of others—and another and another. All of them had scratches on them.

I showed them. They sheepishly stared at the ground.

They fought about whose turn it was to pick out stories, they fought about who had the rights to play the piano (no one, until you can learn to play a different song), they fought about who didn't flush the toilet and who was the first to make it to the table. They fought about who got to read the vocabulary-word-of-the-day entry from our desk calendar, they fought about who the cat loves more, they fought about how much more, they fought about whether or not their last name would have been Patton (my maiden name) if I hadn't married their father.

Finally, I sat them all down for some good old television, for my own sanity—and they fought about what to watch. So I sent them all to bed for naps, where they fought about who would fall asleep first, why the light was still coming through their window, and what they would do when Mama said it was time to wake up.

Later that day, my ten-year-old was opening the fridge and lamenting the fact that there was no food left. I told him this was because he and his brothers had been home for 4.5 days straight, since there was a holiday and the ice day and the two-hour early release the Friday before. I said, "I was planning to go to the grocery store today, because it's my normal grocery day."

"Why didn't you?" he said.

"Because you're all home," I said.

"Oh, and you wanted to spend time with us," he said, matter-of-factly.

Yes, that's exactly why I didn't go to the grocery store today.

What My Kids Love About Me (And Yours Probably Love About You)

Any time I've asked my children why they love me, I'm always surprised by their answers. I mistakenly think they'll tie my love to the things I give them or the places I take them or the time I spend with them doing complicated things (like crafting with glitter).

But it's really much simpler than that.

1. I cook.

Because they love to eat so much, my sons feel love through food. While I don't always cook and, when I do, it's not always wonderful, they know I do the grocery shopping and the meal planning and that I gladly provide or cook the most important part: dessert.

2. I read to them.

My sons have grown up on stories, and while they may not yet recognize how important this is for them, they do know the joy of sharing novels, poetry, and true stories with their parents.

Last year I gifted my nine-year-old with a kid's literary

magazine for his birthday. He thought it was the greatest gift ever and tells me so every time a new issue arrives in the mail.

I know him—and he knows my knowing equals love.

3. I let them play outside.

I think they mean I *make* them play outside, but who's splitting hairs over unimportant things? They know they have the freedom to sword fight with sticks, build forts out of lumber, and dig holes for…well, who knows what (we gave up asking a long time ago).

4. I sign their school folders.

Most of the time—at least until the second semester of school starts and/or my pen disappears, whichever comes first.

(This year we made it to the second semester.)

5. I'm an author.

My sons are still too young to be embarrassed by my status as an author. I've visited two of their classes already this year, and they are still proud enough to come up to me and give me a hug in front of their friends and say, "This is my mom." I like to think they'll never stop loving this about me, but I know adolescence takes its toll.

My sons are remarkable kids, and I am amazed, always, by their graciousness and caring ways and their extravagant love. Even on their less-than-stellar days, when they call me the worst mom ever for telling them it's time to put their technological devices away, they can recognize, deep down, the way I love them in the limits I set.

The Car Dropoff Personalities of Children

On any given school day, Husband and I typically walk our sons to their elementary school, half a mile down the road. But this has been a cold and rainy winter, so lately we've had to pack everybody up in our van and drive them instead.

I dread these drive days. It's not simply because I really enjoy the walk and how it burns off some of that endless boy energy; it's also because I really hate anyone witnessing the state of our van's interior.

On drop-off days, I usually try to let my school-aged sons have the priority seating, meaning the seating that's easiest to climb out of. Unfortunately (well, fortunately, most hours of the day), five of them are in school now, which means we can't escape the fiasco of having some of them deep in the Way Back—their name for the third row of seats in our Honda Odyssey (her name is Lucy, by the way). This means when we're driving up to the drop-off point, I'm already coaching them to gather their stuff and spring out, because I don't want to be the one car in the line that holds up everyone else.

The Days Are Long, But the Years Are Short

We always are, though.

I already know how it will go. Of course we'll be the first car in the line of people opening their doors, and then all the cars behind me, which only have one or two students inside, will have to wait on all my sons to take their sweet time getting out of the car. I don't presume to know what the people behind us are thinking, but it's probably something like, "Are kids ever going to stop pouring out of that van?"

I've asked myself the same question.

Here's a little of what our drop-off procedure looks like:

First, **Over-Eager** will try to shove out of the car first, and he'll stare at the safety guard who didn't get the memo about how most minivans come with child protective locks, which means that kids can't open the sliding doors from the inside (I'll give him the benefit of the doubt: Maybe his mom's minivan has the automatic sliding doors, but we're a humble family with a twelve-year-old van that didn't come with all the perks). This safety guard and Over-Eager will look at each other for a minute before the safety guard will finally wrestle open the door, and then Over-Eager will dash out the door and leave his backpack, which means he'll have to come back for it. That's okay. There aren't any cars waiting, yet. I made sure to come super early.

Then we have **Trash Tracker**. This is the kid who always has pieces of paper stuck to his shoe. Our van is never clean. That should go without saying. The floorboard has a perpetual layer of papers stuck to it, and this kid will drag most of them out the door with him, and I'll pretend like they don't belong to me. Just kidding. It's too obvious to pretend. So this kid knows the drill: If paper comes out with him, he's supposed to shove it back in. He does a good job, too. I can barely see out the rearview mirror anymore with all the papers piled up behind me.

Then we have **Seat Screamer**. This is the kid who has to remain seated and buckled because he is not yet in school, and he's conveniently located in the middle of all the seats so his brothers in the back have to climb over him to get out the door. A couple will accidentally step on him and make him yell, another straddles him expertly before climbing over and patting his shoulder, and another of them will probably fart in his face, judging by the cloud I catch in the rearview mirror but, unfortunately, not quick enough to cover my nose. Now I'm almost passing out.

Then we have **Launchpad**. This is the kid who wants to race Over-Eager and claim the First One Out title, so he launches himself over everybody, not caring if a foot catches someone in the eye. He just wants to make sure that he can climb out first and get where he needs to go. I think he likes the feeling of flying when the car screeches to a stop.

What? Screeches to a stop? I don't really drive that way, especially in a school parking lot.

Then there's **Mr. Careful**. This kid will check and check and re-check to make sure he has everything. He will slowly and deliberately make sure he has his folder in his backpack (which was supposed to be done before he got in the car), his lunch box, and the shoes on his feet (which he's still wearing, but he'll just double check real quick). Once he's double checked everything, he's ready to get out of the car and face his day.

Have a good day, Mr. Careful!

Lastly, we have **Slo-Mo**. It doesn't matter where this kid sits. We've tried him in the side seats, closest to the door, and in the front seat where he can open his own door and easily climb out without waiting for his brothers, but all seats are created equal for Slo-Mo. He will still be the last one out of the car. He's so slow that the safety guards will peer in, like they're wondering why I haven't yet moved the car. I will laughingly apologize and say, "There's one more," and then hurry him along. But nothing will hurry Slo-Mo. He's like a five-foot beanpole of molasses, seeping out of the side door. He will never be the first one out, but he doesn't care. He lives in his own world, oblivious to the hurry around him.

Sometimes it's refreshing—when we're not in the school drop-off line.

The drop-off is so awkward that I've gotten to where if it's just sprinkling a little bit, we all brave the walk to school, while my sons complain the whole time that they're getting too wet and they're going to be cold all day and nobody else in the entire neighborhood is walking. But the other day it was raining too hard to tell them to suck it up and enjoy the rain, so we all packed up. Before we took off, I gave them a pep talk. I reminded them of the drill.

And then we got to the school, and Slo-Mo had his face buried in a book, Launchpad took out someone's lip, Over-

Eager rapped on the window and asked the safety guard to please open the door, even though the guard likely couldn't hear him. Finally, the door opened, and Over-Eager and Launchpad hurled themselves out to yells of "See you later!" while Mr. Careful checked for the fourth time to make sure he had his lunch box, Trash Tracker stepped out with eight Trader Joe's coloring sheets stuck to the bottom of his shoe (no wonder we never win a prize package), and Seat Screamer complained about a pinched "weg."

I thought I had everybody out and started to put the car in drive when Slo-Mo hollered from the back. I put my head down on the steering wheel and counted to ten before I looked back up to see him finally climbing out of the car.

There were twelve cars waiting behind us.

I think next time we'll just walk. A little pouring rain never hurt anybody.

March

On March Madness: Real or Myth?

It never fails: by the time we get to Spring Break, my sons are done with school.

They're done with homework, done with getting dressed, done with packing up in a timely manner. And, honestly, I'm so done with making peanut butter and jelly sandwiches they've become just jelly sandwiches.

The other morning, one of my school-aged sons came downstairs in his pajamas. I thought maybe he'd forgotten today was a school day.

"What are you doing?" I said.

"Going to school," he said.

"You forgot to change," I said.

"No?" he said, like he wasn't quite sure. He looked down at his pajamas. "This is what I'm wearing."

"You can't wear pajamas to school," I said. "Sorry."

He groaned all the way up the stairs.

The school morning routine has become complicated.

I tell the ten-year-old to get up (multiple times), and he will still act like I'm the worst mom ever (for not getting him up) when I suddenly call out that it's time to go (he didn't hear me the twelve times I said it was time to get up). He hasn't eaten breakfast, and he was supposed to take a shower this morning. I think it's all an act. He's allergic to showers; I think it's been…well, you don't want to know how long since the last shower I know about.

There's so much chaos in the kitchen they have to yell to be heard. The other morning one of my sons was trying desperately to tell me something (I don't remember what; probably a dream in vivid detail), and the cacophony around us had risen so loud that I leaned close and said, "Say it in my ear. Maybe that will help."

Not only did he say it, but he also sprayed it, and I got to both smell the delightful breath and wear the fragrant spit of a boy who hadn't yet brushed his teeth this morning.

They can never find their shoes. The shoes are right in front of their eyes. They could trip over them and still not see them.

Maybe they're just afternoon people, instead of morning people.

Several of them have forgotten what school mornings even look like (it's usually the ones who have been doing this routine for several years); they immediately head into the LEGO room, rather than sitting down at the table or packing up their folders or attempting to tie their shoes.

Most mornings, one of them is running to catch up on the walk to school, and it's not a silent catching up, it's a whining—usually a scream-whining—one. My favorite.

On a typical morning, when I get back home, I see that

someone forgot to close the back door and all our air conditioning has filtered out into the great wide world because that surely helps bring the Texas temperature down. Thanks for thinking of the rest of the world, boys!

I didn't know until I became a parent that March madness was actually a thing.

I've stopped signing folders, I get notes about overdue library books, I don't even enforce homework anymore. Guess I'm ready for summer, too.

Wait. No. I take that back. I'm not ready for summer at all.

But it's coming at me like a wrecking ball. Ready or not.

How to Get Your Kids Outside: a Partial Cure for March Madness

Playing outside does a world of good for kids. I didn't understand this when I was a kid and my mom would say, "You need to go get some sun, Rachel," and I'd argue that it was too hot or there was nothing to do out there or I was just fine inside, thank you. She insisted, so usually I'd bring a good book with me and curl up in a hammock, and that's what I called my playing-outside time. I'm not picky about my own sons' outdoor time; so long as they're outside, they can do whatever they want (well, almost).

Outdoor time gifts me with a few minutes to myself. I require my sons to play outside between the hour of 4:30 and 5:30 p.m.—and any other part of the day they wish. The required time is required so I can get dinner on the table within a reasonable amount of time in an environment that does not contain chaos and disaster at every turn.

Here are some helpful tricks to get your kids outside.

1. Give them a choice.

My kids get a choice every afternoon: You can either go

play outside or you can go to bed. Which will it be?

You know which one they'll choose.

2. Tell them an outrageous story about something outside.

This may or may not work; it depends how young or gullible your children are. I once told my twins, back when they were four, that I had seen an alien starship land in the field behind our house, and they stood on our back porch for two hours, staring at the pasture, waiting to see the green men. It was a remarkable exercise in focus, which is a feat for them.

3. Lock the door.

When all else fails, try this: tell them there's a jacket out back that you need them to get and you'll pay them a quarter for it—a dollar for the more entrepreneurial—and as soon as they're out the door, lock it. They won't be able to get back inside and you'll have your few minutes alone.

Sorry kid. Sanity preservation methods.

While kids love to complain about being required to do anything, they always have a good time outside. And what they get from playing outside—the expenditure of energy, the connection with nature, a more peaceful frame of mind—is worth the pushing.

They'll forgive us eventually.

What to Do on a Rainy Day: Sing in the Rain

It's been a rainy year. I know better than to complain, considering that most years in Texas feature more brown burned-to-a-crisp grass than the lush green kind on which you can walk comfortably with bare feet, but really. My kids are at each other's throats, they're tearing up the house, they're longing to go outside—and when they do, they come back in with gobs of mud caked to their shoes and between their toes if they couldn't find their shoes (which is highly likely). They will happily track this around the just-cleaned house. It's art, so to speak—with footprints (and they can hide nothing; they went to the pantry for an unauthorized snack? No, they say. Well, there are footprints to prove it).

With so many rainy days and so many kids cooped up inside, I start arguing with myself about whether or not it would be a good idea to enforce my daily mandatory play-outside time.

It wouldn't be that bad.
Have you seen the floor?

They'd have something to do.
They'd get all wet and muddy.
You'd have peace.

And that statement, in the end, gives me pause and necessitates one of the things I do best: an analysis of pros and cons, this one called: Pros and Cons of Kids Playing Outside In the Rain.

Pro: They get a shower.

For some of them, that's more than they got last week (what can I say? Preteens are tough). Letting them play outside means that I can skip wrestling them into baths and, instead, save my energy for wrestling them back inside. Or to bed. Multiple times.

Con: They'll come back in dripping.

Rain is cold, which means my sons will refuse to put on their swimsuits; this kind of wet is different from pool-wet. They'll need to wear layers for this, and all of those layers will get soaked. They will not think to take off those layers before coming back in—remember? It's cold!

Pro: They won't be constantly underfoot to trip me.

Particularly during the dinner hour, when tripping becomes exponentially more dangerous.

Con: But now I'll likely slip in their wet footprints.

This is what's called a no-win situation. Either way I'm going down. But baby, I'm going down swinging. Maybe. On second thought, I might need my hands to keep myself from dying. Falling's not as easy anymore.

Pro: You don't have to hear their fighting.

Research shows that kids fight every 2.5 minutes or so, and I'm pretty sure my kids are overachievers on this estimation. At least when they're outside I won't have to hear the ridiculous fights they start every other minute.

Con:

Is there a con to this point? Nope.

All things considered, playing in the rain doesn't seem all that bad. It's good for kids to be out in nature while nature is nourishing itself.

You might even decide to join them.

Games to Play When Kids are Stuck Inside the House: an Aside

If you weren't convinced by the pros and cons exercise in the last chapter, here are some games to play when kids are stuck inside.

1. Write Your Own Play

This is a fun exercise in creativity. Suggest characters or plot points, but let kids write their own. You'll be amazed by what they come up with. When they're done writing, encourage them to perform their plays.

2. Poetry Slam

Set kids up with writing notebooks and tell them to write as many poems as they can in fifteen minutes (you can give them topics and more instructions if they stare at you blankly). Give them another fifteen minutes to perfect those poems and then have them present their poems in a "slam" competition, with drama, conviction, and emotion. Encourage everyone in the room to clap vigorously and hoot wildly after every poem because why not.

3. The Quiet Game

This one's for you, Mom and Dad, and might still work with your kids if there's a prize (how much are you willing to pay for silence?).

4. The "Who Can Clean Up the Most" Game

Again, this one will work with a prize. But only once.

5. Dance Off

A dance party is always a hit in my house—at least until someone kicks someone else's eye out (it's never me; though my kids are relatively short, by adult standards, I'm still unable to lift my legs high enough to kick their faces. My middle school twirling teacher would be disappointed by my lack of flexibility these days).

When all else fails, there is Movie Marathon. There's no shame in doing what you gotta do to maintain your sanity.

The Looking Personalities of Children

Every Saturday my husband prints out for my sons a list of the library books they have checked out on their accounts so they can gather them for our weekly trip to the library. This results in weeping and gnashing of teeth as boys blame each other for their missing books—*he was the last one reading this one, where did he put it? I didn't really check this book out, it must have been one of my brothers! I can't find any library books!*

When it's time to find anything, my kids come looking for Husband and me. I'm not sure why they still come to me, since I've already proven that I'm not a great looker either (and I mean that as a verb, not an adjective), but I guess they believe I'll at least look better than they do.

And I do—I don't even have to try that hard, actually.

My sons have some very distinctive looking personalities that emerge as they're wandering around the house searching for something.

Probably the most vocal of these lookers is **Mr. Memory**

Delay. This is the kid who will look and look and look, and only after he's spent hours looking for something (sometimes it only takes half an hour, but that's if we're really lucky), will he suddenly remember where he put the something for which he's looking. And then, of course, when he goes to look in that fortuitously-remembered spot, there it will be. If only this could be Mr. Memory without the Delay.

I have spent so much time looking for Mr. Memory Delay's things. Just the other morning he lost his wallet, which has his school ID card in it, which allows him to ride the bus home and purchase something from the lunchroom, which he's not permitted to do unless he leaves his lunch at home (guess how often he can't find where he put his lunch). We both spent half an hour looking—well, calling what he did "looking" would be a stretch for him; he wandered around the house musing about how he put it on his desk and his brothers probably moved it and now he's never going to be able to find his ID card because his brothers are pests—before he remembered that he did *not* put the wallet on his desk, he put it in a drawer.

There it was, snug inside the drawer. Thanks for the massive waste of time, love.

Next in line is **Mr. Perfect**. This is the kid who rarely loses anything because he's so responsible that he knows where everything goes and he makes the effort to get it there.

The eight of us in my family share a smallish house, which means it's necessary for everything to have a place, to avoid the oppressive weight of clutter (I find it, literally, oppressive. If there is clutter in my home, I can scarcely breathe). And this kid, miracle of all miracles, typically puts things back in the place where they belong. I'm always impressed when Mr. Perfect stands ready at the door for school, without a single "Remember to get your folder" and an answering, "I don't know where it is." If he happens to lose something, he doesn't even bother Husband and me about it; he looks in the place where he knows it belongs, and, if it's not there, a place that makes sense to him, and just like that he's found it all on his own.

Good job, Mr. Perfect. Maybe eventually you'll rub off a little on your brothers.

There is a downside to Mr. Perfect, however. If he can't find something, that means it's really gone, and he will grieve for days.

Next we have **Mr. Doomsday**. This is the kid who says he's looked and looked everywhere, and it's nowhere and he's probably never going to find it and will you please help him even though he's never going to find it but you may as well try and he surely won't be able to find it without the help of a parent and he wants to give up and he'll never ever ever have his jacket ever again, because it's gone forever.

Mr. Doomsday can often be seen roaming around the house, scanning the walls and doorways (as if he'll find anything but scratches and hieroglyphics there). After a few minutes of this, accompanied by some moaning, he will plop down on the couch, a boneless blob—right on top of the jacket for which he's looking. He won't believe us when we tell him, but yep. There it is.

Mr. Wanderer wanders around staring at things but not really looking at anything specific. He tells us he remembers putting his shoes where they were supposed to go, and he has no idea why they're not in the right place right now. If you tell him he should probably look, he'll say that's what he's doing and continue wandering around staring at the piano, the toy cabinet, the puzzle spread out on the coffee table, the brownies I accidentally left out on the counter, which he'll nonchalantly "taste" as he walks by.

What whips Mr. Wanderer into action is when I tell him that if I go outside and look by the trampoline and I find his shoes, he's going to pay me some money. After the first time I found them in plain sight and he had to pay me a "looking fee," he mostly learned his lesson. He'll scramble out the door before I can even finish my sentence, and it's nothing short of a miracle when he finds his shoes exactly where I thought they'd be: by the trampoline.

Mr. Wanderer will wander back in and say that someone else must have taken his shoes and put them by the trampoline, because it certainly wasn't him.

Yeah, okay.

Next we have **Mr. Distractible**. I'm sure most parents can identify with being the parent of this kid, but mine is a notch above the rest (raising a gifted kid with ADHD and processing disorders is fun). He will start to look for something, but in his looking, he will see something else that looks so interesting he can't help but touch it. It's probably his brother's nerf gun that was a Christmas present. He'll look around to see if anyone's watching (he should know, by now, that someone is *always* watching—me), and then he'll pick it up. When I call his name, he'll practically jump out of his skin.

"What are you supposed to be doing?" I'll say.

"Looking for my book," Mr. Distractible will say. And off he'll go to look again, until he's distracted by the next shiny (or dull; it really doesn't matter) thing, which will be in approximately three seconds.

Lastly there is **Mr. Immovable**. This is the kid who doesn't really care that he's lost things because (a) his parents usually look for it anyway (I mean, he's only two) and (b) he's not really attached to anything. Ironically, he's the best finder we have in the house.

One day Mr. Memory Delay couldn't find his favorite LEGO mini figure, and he looked everywhere and was almost ready to give it up for Lost Forever and Ever when I asked Mr. Immovable, who earlier that morning had found my phone after I'd looked everywhere for it, if he'd seen the mini figures. He walked right over to the laundry basket and pulled them out. Mr. Memory Delay was impressed, but I knew the reason Mr. Immovable found those mini figures was because Mr. Immovable stole them from Mr. Memory Delay while the latter wasn't looking, and, after playing with them for a good long while, he set them on the clean clothes and called it a day.

Still, Mr. Immovable has found my water bottle, my writing notebook, the book I was reading, a magazine I needed, a brownie I set down (I shared the spoils with him),

Rachel Toalson

and countless other valuable things.
    Now if only he could find my keys…

Kids and Conversation: a Harrowing Examination

The other day Husband and I were walking across the parking lot at our church, and one of my five-year-olds raced ahead. I could see him from where I walked. I watched him politely hold the door for an older man, who stopped to chat with him, likely to thank him for this small kindness.

Any time someone talks to my five-year-old twins, the first thing they do is tell their audience that they are five years old, because they're very proud of this. The next bit of information is always a wild card; my twins are usually thrilled that someone is talking to them in the first place. They're used to being overshadowed by older brothers.

This particular morning my son decided to follow up his age announcement with some rather personal information.

"My mom is fifty-six," he said.

Besides the fact that he was WAY off on his estimate, Husband and I have also been working with him and his twin on what is good information for people to know and what is unnecessary information. His mother's age is most definitely unnecessary information for people outside the family to know.

I didn't worry much about it, though. I don't look even close to fifty-six, so I was able to laugh—at least until I noticed the new gray hair in the bathroom mirror on my way in to the sanctuary.

This experience got me thinking (as many experiences with my children do; thanks, kids, for the critical thinking challenges) about how kids offer so many bits of random information to strangers without really considering the implications of their word vomit. A more age-conscious woman (and that's saying a lot; I'm very age-conscious) might have been offended to hear a kid call her fifty-six when she's still in her thirties and feeling vibrantly alive most days, with the exception of cold days that make her hips ache, warm days that make her feel bloated, and all the days in between that make her feel like she's been run over by a truck—or a parcel of rowdy boys.

Sometimes these random bits of information can get somewhat embarrassing for a parent. When my second son was in first grade, he wrote a whole essay about the pet he wanted: a frog, because it would catch all the flies in the house (and there were so many that year. It took months of creative solutions and endless complaining to get rid of them all.). That's information you don't really want circulating the halls at your kids' school—that you live in a house with hundreds of flies you can't seem to get rid of (lest you think we're breeding them within the walls of our house, how absolutely disgusting,

I'll assure you that these flies seem so invasive because of a constantly revolving back door, bananas left half-eaten and unattended on the table, and kids who can't be bothered to close the front door when racing out to play with their neighborhood friends). But such is life with children.

There are, of course, some important requirements for the details that kids offer freely to other people—preferably strangers who don't know the least bit about your family.

1. The information must contain highly personal details.

For my sons, this often translates to kids commenting on what their mom's underwear looks like (they saw it this morning when they followed me into the bathroom, much as I tried to hide it), how much their dad weighs and how much weight he wants to lose (they love listening in on conversations that don't belong to them), how they've been wearing the same pair of underwear for three days, what their poop looked like this morning, how long it's been since anyone in their house cleaned. The more personal these details are, the better.

Once my third son was talking to a friend's parent, and he said, "Our house is always messy because my mom doesn't like to clean." I would not have been all that offended by this except for the fact that we work so hard to hide it from the outside world. People show up at our house and they just think our house is magically tidy all the time. If unexpected visitors show up at our door, we have a drill. The kids know what to do: close their mouths, hide, and pretend no one's home.

Well, the secret's out now.

Kids have no idea what it means to keep secrets from the public. Their life is an open book, and, honestly, sometimes that's refreshing. Just not when the details involve me and my facades.

2. The information must be random.

The next requirement for the bits of information my kids offer complete strangers is that it must be random. My oldest son will likely offer some random fact about Minecraft—and he's gotten better with this tactic; now he'll actually take a subject of conversation and artfully bring it back to Minecraft. For example, if I'm talking to another mom, laughing about how difficult it is to leave the house with children in tow (and in shoes), he will interject to say, oh, yeah, it's really hard to leave your Minecraft construction, too, because you only have a certain amount of time to finish what you've planned to do. It's a clever trick, but it doesn't erase the fact that this unsolicited information is completely random and unconnected to the conversation at hand.

My second son is a skilled conversationalist, even at eight, so he doesn't usually offer random information. My third son will say something about how he was the P.E. student of the week, because we're all searching for significance.

My twins are the most random of all, if you haven't already gathered that from the story I already shared. They will periodically announce to all the parents at my sons' school one of the following:

They took a poop this morning and it was really long and really green

The Days Are Long, But the Years Are Short

They threw up this morning (it was actually a morning last month)

They watched a movie at their Nonny's house (no one knows their Nonny)

They colored a picture yesterday

The more someone says, "Yeah?" or "That's really great," the more they will feel encouraged and empowered to find more random things to say. I usually gently extract them from the conversation after less than a minute, because I know that the more mortifying personal details will start trickling in if I don't.

3. The information must be as embarrassing as possible.

You might think that all personal details are embarrassing, and you'd probably be right. And some of the random bits of information my twins offer to passersby are certainly embarrassing. But here I'm talking about a level up from embarrassing: I'm talking about details like how long it's been since their daddy mowed the backyard (they learned to count by marking the days) and how every time they go out there to the wilderness (what we now call the backyard), they get sticker burrs in their pants. They'll talk about how their mom yelled at them before they got in the car (but they'll leave out the part about how they tripped her as she was walking out the door because they were already supposed to be in their seats; she yelled in surprise, in distress, and, finally, in terror). They'll tell everyone that their car looks like a trash dump on the inside and follow that up with the fact that their mom told them their family doesn't have any money but leave out the part where that was in response to the question could I buy a new car to replace the trashy old one.

I'm sure that eventually my sons will grow out of this tell-the-world-everything-there-is-to-tell phase, but I suspect it won't be before they release out into the nether many, many more personal, random, embarrassing details.

Oh, well. It's kind of exhausting living behind a facade anyway. So thanks, kids, for sharing all my best and most embarrassing secrets.

How to Leave the House With Kids: a 5-Step, Foolproof Plan

Every parent knows that leaving the house is one of the most difficult things to do—at least when you have your kids in tow.

This is mainly due to the disasters that follow children everywhere. There are the shoes for which you have to search (because no matter how many shoe repositories you've set up in your house, your kids will hardly ever use them for shoes—but maybe for Smuggle Candy they're not supposed to have), milk you have to clean up (because of course a kid will help himself to a generous glass of this cool and refreshing beverage and spill it as soon as you're about to walk out the door), and the things they need to gather in their backpacks that almost certainly will not be found in the rush of a moment.

Here's a foolproof method for leaving the house when you're a parent.

Step 1: Make the announcement.

(At least five minutes pre-departure time; if kids are exceptionally bad at leaving, make this ten)

You'll have to repeat this announcement at least five times (for the mathematically challenged, that would stretch into an announcement every sixty seconds until the time for departure arrives) in order to make sure it's heard (and someone will likely still pretend he didn't hear it). It's not even necessarily that they aren't listening. Well, yeah, it probably is. They have better things to do than listen to a parent proclaim that the family van will pull out of the driveway in five minutes. They don't want to go anyway, because it's never fun when they're required to get in the car (except the times you actually surprise them with a trip to the frozen yogurt place and regret it all the way home). They especially don't want to go anywhere that requires buckling their seat belts (which is every place, kids. EVERY PLACE. Don't argue.).

Because kids likely won't listen the first four times you make this announcement, it's imperative that on the final one-more-minute warning, you raise your voice to stage-level proportions and repeat yourself in rapid succession (much like they do when they think you haven't heard them). They'll likely turn on you and say they heard you the first time, which may or may not be true. And you'll say, "Well, that's how I feel when you tell me the same thing a billion times."

It's a good object lesson.

Step 2: Start a countdown.

(30 seconds pre-departure time)

If your kids are anything like mine, they need a countdown for everything. We use countdowns for getting to the dinner table on time, for getting out of the bath, for putting that book he stole from his brother back in Brother's hands. Departure is simply one of the many occasions for which we use a countdown.

It usually sounds something like this: "You have ten seconds to get in the car. If you are not in the car in ten seconds, I am subtracting from your technology time a minute for every minute you're late." For the younger ones it sounds more like, "You have ten seconds to get in the car. You can either walk to the car or I can carry you to the car. If you are not in the car in the next ten seconds, I will assume that you want me to carry you."

Don't ask me how often this works; that's not what this essay is about.

Almost every time Husband or I count down from ten to one (we even give them an extra second, with a "zero" added to our countdown), our kids are still not ready. They express outraged surprise that we've already reached zero and that now they must deal with the consequences of their choice to play for an extra ten seconds rather than using that valuable time to walk themselves to the car. We're the worst parents ever when we carry them to their seat, when we don't let them grab something "real quick," and when we enforce the consequences of which they were already made aware.

Oh, well. Life's hard, kids.

Step 3: Announce that it's time to go and wait to hear someone say they don't have their shoes.

(0 minutes pre-departure time)

At least you haven't pulled out of the driveway yet.

"Why don't you have your shoes?" you'll say.

"I couldn't find them," he'll say.

You'll sigh. Looking for shoes has got to be one of the top time wasters of every parent. How many millions of seconds have I wasted on searching for lost shoes? I don't want to know.

"Where did you look?" you'll ask.

He'll say he's looked everywhere, he thinks they disappeared, one of his brothers lost them, maybe there was a burglar and they just took his shoes (as if this would really happen; I know for a fact that every pair of shoes in my house smells). You'll walk inside the house, ready to prove him wrong.

Step 4: Locate all the left shoes in the house.

(1 to 17 minutes post-departure time)

I don't know if this is a universal phenomenon or if it just seems like one in my house because there are so many kids and so many shoes, but any time one of my sons can't find The Other Shoe, he is missing only one shoe in particular: the right one. We have so many half-pairs of shoes with only a left shoe in attendance and a right shoe missing in action that I'm wondering if there really *is* a burglar with a missing left leg who enters my house only to steal all the right shoes in size 1.5.

It's a sad world when a kid has to wear two left shoes, but, after searching for what feels like hours, that's exactly what must happen in order to leave in the next century.

Step 5: Rush out the door.

(17+ minutes post-departure time)

Depending on the weather, the shoes you're wearing, how

tall the lip of your front door's threshold, and your age, you should take care with this rushing out the door. If you're my mom, you'll likely fall regardless of how slick the ground or the bottom of your shoes or the thickness of your threshold, but everyone else has a hope of getting to the car in one piece. Don't ruin the day with a trip before the trip.

Step 7: Still be late.

(20 minutes post-departure)

As a parent, it doesn't matter how early you try to get out the door; even if you start leaving an hour before departure time—you'll still be late. You'll hardly ever be on time anywhere anymore, so today's a fine day to debut into that brand new always-a-little-bit-late life.

If you haven't already made that debut—many times over.

April

The Joke's On You: An April Fools' Tale

April Fools' Day is always a fun and exciting time in our home. I live with a bunch of pranksters, which means they keep me on my toes all day. No one is safe this day—not even Mama.

Every year, I painstakingly contemplate what sorts of tricks I'd like to play on my kids. Here are some I considered this year:

1. Steal their underwear.

I imagine this prank would go something like this:

Me: Are you missing anything today?

Him: No.

Me: Nothing?

Him: No.

Me: How long has it been since you changed your underwear?

Him: I don't know.

I doubt he (and by he, I mean any one of my sons, take your pick) would even notice, without my explaining to him what I'd done, so I skipped this one. Maybe I'll try it in a couple of years, when he actually cares about how he smells.

2. Hide their shoes in random places.

The problem with this little idea is that my kids don't really need any help with losing their shoes. They leave them in odd places and accomplish this not-so-creative-after-all trick on their own—every morning, without fail.

3. Stuff all their socks inside one lucky sock.

One of the five-year-olds does this on a regular basis, so I don't think they would really appreciate my work on this one. Why waste all that time?

When I asked them what they use this monster sock for, they said "Hitting each other." Of course. They call it a sock bomb.

4. Pretend the hot water got turned off for the one who actually cares about taking a shower.

I feel like that would discourage him from taking a shower, though, and we definitely don't need that. Boys aren't exactly the most hygienic people around.

5. Turn all their clothes inside out.

Oh, wait. This happens every laundry day, because that's how they put it in the dirty clothes hamper, and I don't have time to turn it all the right way. A few of them take it a step farther: They wear their clothes inside out. Accidentally or on purpose? They'll never tell.

Well, at least next time they put it in the laundry it will no longer be inside out.

6. Replace their morning milk with buttermilk.

My father did this to me when I was six. How many people can remember memories from when they were six?

Exactly. It was traumatic. I took this one off the table.

7. Tell them they don't have school today.

This would have been really fun, except that April Fools' Day fell on a Sunday this year. Also, I imagine that when the day falls on a school day and if I actually executed this prank, there would be some messy cleanup when my sons discovered it was a joke. And by messy cleanup, I mean lots and lots and lots of whining.

8. Tell them it's "dress like a Dr. Seuss character" at church today.

This one I actually managed (only a couple of them bought it, but it was still a victory).

I'm glad we can have a house that embraces pranks.

But now that I can't find my left running shoe and there's a stick-bouquet hiding under my covers and someone switched out my favorite soap with hand sanitizer, I've realized that I'm really good at dishing it out—but not so great at taking it.

Mom was right all along. Imagine that.

When the Rain Won't Go Away: How to Entertain Kids Indoors

This spring has been a rainy, rainy season (you can probably tell by how many essays address what to do with kids when they're stuck inside the house; when I'm in danger of losing my mind, humor is what pulls me through, so…sorry, not sorry)—so rainy even *I'm* getting cabin fever, and I'm a hermit. You know it's bad when Mama starts saying, "We need to get out of this house."

Because the rain seems to never, ever stop, we've gotten really good at playing inside. Here's a list of things you can do inside your house to keep kids entertained:

Idea #1: LEGO station

This station will work nicely until one of them decides he owns the table, he owns all the LEGO pieces, and/or he owns all the ideas (it's probably "and").

That tattling and fighting will drive you to:

Idea #2: Art time

This art time will entertain them well until someone goes renegade with a permanent marker that wasn't supposed to be mixed in with all the other markers, and now you have a spider on your dining room table that you'll always think, for the briefest moment, is real.

Well, it's good for your heart, you tell yourself. Like interval training.

Idea #3: Reading time

The kids will likely fight over who gets to sit on your back, who gets to pick stories, who gets to exist. So then it's about time for:

Idea #4: Nap time

They'll fight you on it, but if you're really lucky, you might get two or three minutes of rest out of it, while older kids try to figure out how to sneak something past your ninja senses (Yes, I can see you. Even when I'm sleeping.).

Idea #5: Board games

They will terrorize your board game closet so it's hardly recognizable, and by the time they're done with the games, your house will be unrecognizable, too. In fact, you might not be able to find your children underneath all that Monopoly money, those Uno cards, and the Spot It deck. No one wants to clean it up, because no one—absolutely no one in this house—made the atrocious mess. That's when you know it's time for a bribe: those who clean up get to watch a movie.

Idea #6: Movie afternoon

Sometimes there is no sweeter sound than the silence that a movie affords you (if your kids aren't like my oldest son, who likes to narrate scenes just to aggravate.). It's okay to give in. You'll try harder tomorrow. In fact, you'll have a do-over every day this week, because the rain is here to stay.

Oh, look! The rain has stopped for a minute. Send them outside until the next storm comes rolling through so they can come back inside looking like a mud monster.

Hey, at least you got a five-minute break.

The Smell of Feet: a Terrifying Tale

One night Husband, my sons, and I were all gathered in our home library, each of us stretched out with a book in our hands, when a smell assaulted my nostrils.

I don't mean this was just a regular kind of strong smell. I mean it reached up into my nasal passage, all the way to my brain, and wrenched a hole in my head. Or that's what it felt like, anyway.

Smells are not an unusual thing in my house. In my ten years as a mother of sons, I have grown accustomed to the myriad smells—both good and bad, but leaning more heavily toward bad—that accompany boys. We have not even hit the puberty years, and I know it only gets worse from here. God help us. I might have to walk around my house with a clothespin clenching closed my nostrils.

The problem is that I have a very sensitive nose. When I was pregnant, it became superhuman in strength. Before we opened the front door, I could tell that someone hadn't washed the ranch dressing off his plate. Five miles away I could tell that someone hadn't flushed their toilet. Husband couldn't take off his shoes for nine whole months.

This superhuman ability faded only slightly after I had my sweet little baby in my arms. It was blissful in the first few months; when people talk about that new baby smell, I could really *smell* it.

However. This gift is not a gift now. And the smell that night in our home library was truly offensive. I'm not sure if I've ever smelled anything so offensive (but ask me again in three years, and I'm sure the story will have changed).

I surreptitiously glanced around. None of my sons had their shoes on; the stench could be coming from any one of them. But then I locked eyes with my oldest son, who had just removed his socks. That's when I realized, with sickening and startling clarity, from where the smell hailed.

"What?" he said, when he noticed me looking at him.

"You should go wash your feet," I said.

"Why?" he said. He looked confused, like he was completely immune to the smell, which, of course, he was. Actually, everyone in the room except for Husband (who has been somewhat domesticated, living in such close proximity to a woman for the last fifteen years) was oblivious to the smell. They all looked at me. I knew why; I'm always telling them to be quiet during Silent Reading, and here I was breaking the rules, talking. But this was important. My stomach was not going to make it through the fifteen minutes of reading time.

So I said, "Your feet smell."

That's when my son threw his nasty, wet, stiffened (yes, I am horrified to report, they can be wet *and* stiff) socks at my face.

The Days Are Long, But the Years Are Short

The sound I released was one of the most primal sounds you might ever hear in your life. Every single person (except for me) dissolved into laughter right there in our home library, during the middle of what was supposed to be Silent Reading. "You sounded like an animal!" my second son said.

I'd jumped up from where I was sitting so fast that my book flew twenty feet across the room. One nasty sock landed on top of it, and I knew I was going to have to burn that book —and I love books.

My oldest son, the sock-thrower, loosed an evil, villainous cackle. I've never heard him laugh that hard. He could not stop laughing.

Silent Reading time was over by that point. My sons were all too riled up. Chortling one minute, then wrinkling their nose the next as the atrocious smell disbursed all around the room through socks flying and displacing odor molecules so efficiently no nose was left untouched.

When this son was younger, his teachers would reward good behavior with a shoes-off day in class. I noticed they stopped doing that in fifth grade—for good reason, judging by our Disgusting Sock Smell Experience. The smells on the bottom of my sons' feet have gotten so bad I've had to stop demanding that they take off their shoes when they burst through the front door, because whatever they're tracking on the shoe soles is nothing compared to what's on their feet.

Later that night, in our room, Husband disappeared to work on a documentary he's been filming and producing, and I lay down to read something in a book, because this was normally the time when my sons were occupied with books of their own and I finally get a couple of minutes to read whatever I want. I kept smelling that same gross-feet smell. I washed my own feet in the bathtub, since I'd worn my TOMS all day without any socks. I thought maybe it was me. But the smell did not go away. I kept glancing at Husband, wondering if it was him. Then I wondered if maybe my nose was just irreparably damaged from earlier.

A knock sounded on the door.

My oldest son poked his head inside. "I have a confession to make," he said.

Husband and I both waited, surprised by his candor.

"My dirty socks are behind your desk, Daddy," our son said, giggling through the whole sentence.

"Oh my gosh," Husband said. "I kept smelling something and wondering if it was me."

Our son burst out laughing.

"That's going to get in our books and into the fibers of everything in this room," Husband said.

"I've been reusing my socks because I didn't feel like doing laundry this week," our son said, another unsolicited confession.

"Gross," I said.

"They're kind of crusty now," he added. "I take them out of my drawer, and they're still in the shape of my feet."

"That is so disgusting," I said. "Socks are not made to be reused."

"Go wash your feet—and your socks," Husband said.

Our oldest walked out the bedroom door, with his smelly, reused, crunchy socks, laughing.

Husband looked at me. "You know it's just going to get worse," he said.

"I know," I said.

"Times six."

"Don't remind me." I was still plugging my nose, because the smell of boys is a lingering, pervasive one.

"We'll have to get them their own house," Husband said.

"A detached mother-in-law suite. A kids suite."

Husband shook his head, his eyes wide. "It's going to be bad."

"When they grow up and leave, the suite will probably have to be burned down."

"We may even have to burn this house down."

Not really. But maybe. Those smells don't come out easily, and my nose hairs are starting to shrivel up and die.

I started a diffuser, to rid the air of the lingering stench. I chose an essential oil at random; I wasn't picky. I just wanted that smell gone.

Turns out I picked an aphrodisiac. It didn't work because of stinky feet.

The Listening Personalities of Children

My family works exhaustively on listening in our house—because instructions are important (and can often even save lives in the homes of impulsive children like mine), and, also, we show our respect and love for one another in the way we listen—or don't.

Because we work so hard on this, because Husband and I remind our kids, incessantly, how important it is that they listen, because I am always on the lookout for good listeners (notice of the good listeners in my house multiplies the good listeners, I've discovered), I've also observed some very different listening personalities in my sons.

My favorite of them is **Mr. Half-Heard**.

This is the kid who only listens to half of what you say and so becomes the rumor-spreader in the family. He will listen to you say, "You're going to Nonny and Poppy's house," and he will not hear the last part of the announcement, which included, "next weekend." He'll tell all of his brothers that they are going to Nonny and Poppy's house *today*, and everyone will

The Days Are Long, But the Years Are Short

get excited that they get to miss three days of school, and when you tell them they have the dates wrong (because of course they don't ask you for confirmation, they just run with Mr. Half-Heard's information) they respond with moans and a chorus of "You lied to us!"

Whenever I point out to my sons that they are, once again, relying on the faulty information of Mr. Half-Heard, they look at me blankly.

"Hasn't this happened before?" I tell them. I even give them a hint. "Like, yesterday, when someone thought there was going to be a birthday party last night?"

They shake their heads, utterly bewildered.

Mr. Half-Heard spreads his rumors most consistently any time Husband or I mention the pool, the store, or pizza for dinner.

What Did You Say is my second favorite kid.

No matter what, he needs to hear you say it twice. You could be two feet from his face, saying something in a normal-volume voice when the whole house is absolutely silent, and he will respond with, "What?" Sometimes I think it's just a bad habit, although sometimes the noise level in our house is such that I'm not surprised no one heard what I said. At least he's actually interested in knowing what he may have missed. That's more than I can say for five others boys, who blissfully don't hear and never ask "What?"

The problem, though, is that one of my pet peeves is repeating myself, so What Did You Say and I are often locked in a battle of wills—he wants to know what I've said, I don't want to repeat it (usually because it doesn't really matter). The best is when What Did You Say inserts himself into a conversation not meant for him, and every other minute, he says, "What?"

Second Timer is high up on my list of "Listeners I Love," too. This is the kid who, even if you call his name while he's staring right in your eyes, will not hear his name—or anything, for that matter—until the second time you say it. Two times is actually a generous estimate; sometimes I've called his name five times or more—while he's looking at me—before he snaps out of his own world and says, "Yes?" At least he's polite about it.

Husband, for a while, even counted the number of times he had to say our son's name. He would say the name, then say, "That's one." Name—"That's two." He was trying to get our son to respond before the third time we said his name. He's gotten better, but still not good enough to graduate out of the nickname Second Timer.

The other night Second Timer sat reading a book, and I wandered around the living room, trying to find my own book when I tripped over his shoes. It took me seven calls of his name to tell him he needed to pick up his shoes from the middle of the floor. And after I delivered the words, he tilted his head and said, "What?"

Mr. I-Know-What-You'll-Say-Already is another favorite. He, like Mr. Half-Heard, will stop listening halfway through a conversation—but it's not because he gets distracted, it's because he thinks he knows what you're going to say already.

Ever watched that scene in *Frozen* where Anna and Hans sing a song in which they finish each other's sentences with random things? One line from the song goes like this:

[Hans:] I mean it's crazy

We finish each other's

[Anna:] Sandwiches!

Living with Mr. I-Know-What-You'll-Say-Already is like singing that song over and over and over again and when you're tired of it, you have to sing it again.

Here's a recent conversation:

Me: Its time to get some shoes on, because we're going to the—

Him: Library. I know.

Me: No. What I was going to say is we're going to the museum and you should—

Him: I know. Get my shoes on.

Me: No, you should pack up your notebook if you want to take notes. I know you like to do that. And make sure—

Him: I know. Make sure I get a pencil.

Me: I was going to say make sure you go to the—

Him: Exhibit with the dinosaurs, I know.

Me: Bathroom before we leave.

Mr. Looks Like He's Listening is a master of deception. This kid will look so convincingly like he's listening that I will go on and on and on, with elaborate instructions along with detailed discussions about what we're going to do and what time we're leaving and what *he* needs to do to get ready for all of that, and he will blink, nod, offer me proper vocal cues to reinforce the idea that he's listening, and by the time it's all finished, he hasn't heard a word. He gets the instructions mostly right, because he's really good at following his older brothers. One of these days, Mr. Looks Like He's Listening will probably be listening.

But how will we ever know?

Lastly, there is **Eavesdropper**. I get this kid. He is me, when I was a kid.

This son is really, really good at listening in on conversations that are not meant for his ears. These aren't terrible conversations, more like discussions about our sons' grades or plans for the weekend or a trip we might want to take later this year. Eavesdropper is stealthy; often we don't even know he's there until he says, "We're going to Florida this year?" Other times he'll announce himself with a "You know I can hear you." Most of the time it doesn't really matter if he overhears, but when we're behind a closed door, Husband and I have been known to check periodically to make sure Eavesdropper isn't anywhere around. Any time a curse word slips, you can bet Eavesdropper heard.

The ironic thing about Eavesdropper is that he can hear all of these not-meant-for-his-ears things so well, but when we say something actually meant for his ears, he hears nothing.

Last night Husband and I met in the kitchen to finish up dinner preparations while our sons (we thought) played outside on the trampoline. Unbeknownst to us, both Eavesdropper and Mr. Half-Heard were still in the house, listening in on the conversation about the Family Fun Day we wanted to have not this weekend but the following weekend. Mr. Half-Heard ran out to tell his brothers we were having a Family Fun Day tonight, Eavesdropper spilled all the details about where this Family Fun Day would happen (it was supposed to be a surprise—I guess we should know better than to discuss things until the entire house is asleep), What Did You Say responded with his characteristic, "What?" and Mr. Half-Heard and Eavesdropper repeated their information dutifully. Second Timer, in typical delayed fashion, said, "I don't know, I think Mama and Daddy should take us to—"

"The children's museum, I know!" Mr. I-Know-What-You'll-Say-Already interrupted.

Second Timer tried again. "I was going to say—"

"To the pool, I know!" Mr. I-Know-What-You'll-Say-Already chimed in.

By this time What Did You Say caught up with the conversation and said, "Let's go get ready!" Mr. Looks Like He's Listening followed his brothers like he knew exactly what they'd all said.

After a minute, our sons came pounding back down the stairs, full of questions they should have asked in the first place: where were we really going and how long were we staying out and the most important one of all: Why were we having a Family Fun Day on a school night?

Husband and I looked at each other. Husband said, "Have we ever had a Family Fun Day on a school night?"

"No," Second Timer said.

"Do you really think we're having one now?"

Our sons looked at each other, the realization spreading across their faces. But instead of expressing their frustration at the bearers of nothing more than rumors—Mr. Half-Heard and Eavesdropper—they instead turned to Husband and me, pointed a finger, and said, in a synchronized chorus of boy-child voices: "You lied to us!"

How Parenting Helps Us Understand Our Own Parents

It took me a while to get here, but I've officially reached the point where I can fully understand my mother and all the knocks she took raising my brother and sister and me.

There are things my sons do that drive me absolutely crazy and things I do that likely drive them crazy. I remember as a kid saying things to my mom that made her mad and my mom saying things to me that made me mad. It all comes back around, eventually.

I have turned into my mother now. And I want to say, once and for all: I'm sorry, Mom.

I'm sorry for saying, "He's looking at me."

I remember fondly the times that we were driving along in the tiny Ford Escort hatchback, my brother and sister and me crammed in the backseat where we always sat—at least until we were old enough to sit in the front seat and would then argue about whose turn it was to ride shotgun. We always seemed too close to each other. Back seats are not big, roomy places, especially on long trips. My sister was the youngest, so we usually made her sit in the middle. My brother and I got the favored window seats, where at least we could watch the passing landscape and pretend we were almost there.

Periodically along the trip, that closeness would annoy us. Significantly. One or the other of us would say, "He's touching me" or "She's invading my space." Mom would patiently tell us to try to keep our hands to ourselves, our elbows to ourselves, our legs to ourselves, then our sleeves and pants to ourselves. Our complaining would then devolve into, "He's looking at me" and "She's trying to stare out my window."

My kids do this now. I know how exasperating it is.

Once my mom was so fed up with this particular complaint that when she rolled to a stop at a red light, she looked at the person in the car next to her and said, "She's looking at me! Stop looking at me! Look, she's looking at me!" It served to break the tension. We all laughed. And five minutes later, we were back at it again.

Poor Mom.

I'm sorry for saying, "That's not fair."

I can't even begin to estimate how many times my brother or sister or I said that something wasn't fair. Kids are so consumed with wanting everything to be perfectly fair, and by fair they mean all completely equal. If someone gets a piece of cheesecake, they will measure every dimension of it to make sure that it is exactly the same size as their brother's. The other day I gave my sons some popcorn, and they all wanted to make sure they got the same number of pieces. I'm pretty sure a few of them were eating as they were counting because a discrepancy of five hundred kernels was a little too obvious for the care I took filling up their cups.

You take what you get, and you don't throw a fit.

I'm sorry for saying, "I'm bored."

I like to think that when I was a kid I was never bored, because I was a voracious reader. But I suspect this isn't true, because I have a couple of avid readers, too, and they still, from time to time, will say they're bored. My mom usually just put up with it, but I've heard of other parents who told their kids that if they're bored, they can certainly find something for them to do. Like extra chores. Or cleaning tasks. Or some additional homework or a book report or menial math task.

My mom worked for a time as a teacher's aide, and then as a school librarian, so she had entire summers off with us. How fortunate, right? Unless you're hearing a billion times a day, "I'm bored." Based on my kids, that might be an underestimate.

I'm sorry for saying, "You're such a mean mom."

Kids like to call their parents mean when they don't get everything their hearts desire. Any time I tell my sons that they can't have an extra hour of tech time, they call me the Meanest Mom Ever (it vacillates between that and Worst Mom Ever). And when I make them do chores, they say I'm the meanest mom ever and they don't have any friends who are required to do chores, and why should they have to do the jobs that moms and dads are supposed to do in families?

I just about split my gut laughing.

And now I'm sorry for calling *my* mom so mean because she wouldn't let me sit and read all the time instead of helping out with the dishes. I'm sorry for calling her a mean mom when she took away my beloved recorder because my brother and I were recording our little sister crying like a wambulance (that is not a typo. That is a Rachel-and-Jarrod-invented-it word). I'm sorry for calling her a mean mom when she didn't order my world like I thought it should have been ordered.

There are many intricately complicated things about parenting that you don't even understand until you become a parent yourself. Your perspective changes about the mean things your parents did, and, thankfully, with that perspective comes a deeper understanding of what they did, the mistakes they made, and the ways we endure as both child and parent.

Which means one day my sons will understand, too.

I just may be waiting a long, long time.

The Parent Trap: the Myriad Ways Kids Trip You Up

My kids are masters at laying out traps and snagging me in them. They have the uncanny ability to weave a story around me, wrap me up around their finger while I'm not even aware of it, and use my sudden captivity to do all sorts of things. They tangle my words, they make me forget what I'm saying, they try their best to have the advantage in any battle.

Sometimes I feel like I'm living in The Parent Trap.

Last week, my two-year-old was looking like the cutest kid in the whole world, and I was sipping a chocolate peanut butter smoothie, and he ambled up to me and said, "May I please have a taste of your smoothie, Mama?" He asked so politely that I couldn't deny him the pleasure of one taste. So I let him have a taste.

That was the beginning of the end. Every few minutes, he walked back over to me and said, "May I please have another taste, Mama?" And when I finally caught on and started saying, "No, this smoothie is mine, baby," he said, "Just one tiny taste," held up his fingers to show me just how tiny, and…

well, what could I do? We pretty much shared the smoothie. Actually, no. We didn't share it; he finished it in less than a minute and suffered a brain freeze for his indulgent pleasure. I had to console him in his pain while also consoling myself about the fact that I'd just given up my delicious breakfast—albeit to someone cute, but still.

A few days ago, my oldest son, who is currently grounded from technology time after Husband and I discovered that he'd stayed up all night watching Minecraft videos on YouTube (a thing I'll never understand: why kids will watch a video about a video game and not just play it themselves), told me that he was supposed to get his tech time back today.

"I don't think so," I said. I looked at the calendar. I couldn't actually remember if his daddy and I ever talked about when he might get tech time back, but it didn't seem like a long enough deprivation period had passed yet; it had only been a week. I vaguely recalled that we'd settled on two weeks, or maybe that was my own opinion, which is almost always tempered by Husband's less-extreme opinion.

"But you said!" my son said, and then he launched into a cry-fit about how we always say these things and then we forget that we've said them and he's the one who has to suffer the terrible, horrible, no-good, very bad consequences for that and he wishes he could be in another family.

I couldn't really feel all that sorry for him, as terrible as that sounds, because he's the one who stayed up all night watching YouTube videos in the first place. But his tearful diatribe, which he continued all the way up his stairs and into his room, did make me question whether or not I had actually forgotten what was originally agreed upon, which made me waste ten minutes going upstairs to ask Husband, who was on the toilet, for clarification. It was confirmed: Our son did not yet have the privilege of tech time back.

I delivered the news with impassivity, and the house shook with the volcanic eruption of my son's disbelief. I fled downstairs before the lava could burn me.

A recurring theme in The Parent Trap is the "that's not mine" conundrum. My sons are really good at saying that they didn't play with whatever's strewn all over the floor, cluttering up the house. When I trip over a jacket left beside the couch, they cast a cursory glance at it, claim it's not theirs (most of their jackets look the same; I have no idea how they can tell it's not theirs from one hundred feet away), and go about their merry way. I collect the jacket into a "lost and found," which means they won't be able to wear it the next time a cold front blows in; that's what they get for claiming the jacket belonged to the ghost that must be living in our house, leaving his clothes all over the floor.

One of my sons likes to ask, "May I read for a little bit longer?" when it's time for bed. Tell me who among you would make your child go to bed when he's just asked for a little bit more time to read. I'm an author, after all. I believe in the power of reading and its potential for changing a kid's life. I don't like telling him he can't stay up to read for a few more minutes.

Such a terrible trap.

Last Sunday, one of my five-year-olds asked his daddy if he could go outside and play. We had just finished leading worship for church, and he was getting antsy inside. The problem is that this kid is a wanderer, and the church sits off a semi-busy street. I had already answered the question in the negative. Husband was just coming out of the bathroom, and my son saw his opportunity to ask the question of another parent (the nicer, more permissive one) and likely get an affirmative response. Unfortunately for him, I happened to pass through the hallway at the exact time he asked his daddy the question, one of the rare instances I'm in the right place at the right time.

Husband spotted me and didn't answer the question quite like my son thought he would. "Ask Mama," Husband said.

My son looked at the floor. "I already did," he said. "She told me no."

This launched Husband into a lecture about how our son can't ask one parent and hear an answer he doesn't like and then go ask the other parent, hoping he'll get a different answer. I remember doing the same to my parents, when both were home. Yet another trap.

My oldest son has a habit of saying, "I just need to do this real quick." The problem with this trap is that "real quick" is a variable term in a kid's mind. They lose track of time (a trait they got from their father), and then half an hour later they're still trying to finish the piece of art that has now exploded into something way more complicated and they just need a little bit more time to finish it. "Real quick" has become an expletive in my sons' vocabulary, at least to my mind.

A few days ago one of my sons noticed that one of his friends left a jacket at our house. He said, "I'll just run to his house real quick and take it back to him." He failed to mention that his friend's house was two miles away.

Probably the biggest Parent Trap for which I most consistently fall is the "I'll do that for you." No matter how many times this blows up in my face, I am always flattered by the kindness my sons exhibit when they offer to do something for me—when they see that I've lost my phone and need help finding it, when they see that the dishes have piled too high and I'm really tired, when they realize I'm making cookies. They will want to stir the cookie batter for me, and I'll let them do it and then next thing I know it's all over the counter and, also, hanging from their chin because they snuck a quick bite to see how it tasted. Now not only will cleanup take longer, but I'll have two fewer cookies baking (it was a big bite he took).

One of my sons offered to put all the socks away one day after I'd finished the laundry, and I gladly assented. He left a trail of socks all the way up the stairs and didn't even notice. Two of my sons really like re-shelving books, without realizing they're shoving them into other books and ruining the spines in the process.

I should be glad they want to help, right? Well, I am. But sometimes I'll just go ahead and do it myself, thanks.

Kids are pretty crafty. They're wildly smart. They know how to play a parent to their best advantage.

Fortunately, they don't always realize they have a smart

mom. I know what they're up to. I just gave the little one a taste of my smoothie, told the oldest one he could do something real quick, and said two other sons could read for a little bit longer before starting on their dreaded homework.

I'm sure they're not trying to trap me this time.

May

What I Really Want for Mother's Day

"What do you want for Mother's Day?" Husband asked me the other day. Mother's Day is two days away. Husband is notorious for his last-minute planning. It is one of the most frequent and most entertaining conflicts in our marriage.

I figured it was too late for anything large and impressive, but, fortunately, I am easy to please. The things I want for Mother's Day are relatively simple things. They might even be called provincial, though I like to think of myself as a sophisticated, cultured person.

I want to walk into the kitchen and see only six dirty cups instead of thirty-two. I don't know who is responsible for so many dirty cups, but I'm getting tired of reminding my kids they don't need a new cup every time they desire a drink. They have name-labeled cups, even. They're only supposed to drink out of their own cup.

One morning, as I was grumbling about this very problem, I watched Husband pour himself a glass of water, set it down, and five minutes later pour himself another glass of water. Thirteen minutes later, he'd lost both of the glasses and poured himself yet another.

Happy Mother's Day indeed.

I'd also like to read for an arguably short period of time without an interruption. Even if I'm reading aloud to my children and they are fully engaged in the story I'm reading, it is inevitable that someone will interrupt me by saying, "Did you hear that fart?" Or "Do you smell that?" (Yes, I can always smell everything, likely before you do), or "Hey, I was sitting here first!" Sometimes they'll interrupt to predict what they think might happen in the story. I don't mind those so much, because at least they're paying attention. But quiet would be preferable.

I'd also like to use the bathroom without someone commenting on how pretty (or not pretty) my underwear is. There is a thing called privacy, and I would like to covet it. I already avoid any of the bathrooms frequented by my sons (because boys), which means the only bathroom available to me in my home is tucked away upstairs in my room. And, yeah, maybe I dally a little. Maybe it's necessary for someone to come looking for me when they can't find their socks or their brother stole their favorite Pokémon card or they have a wiggly tooth they want to see if I can pull out. I just want a few minutes to myself. Ten, at the most.

Once my sons come looking for me, for one reason or another, the encounter usually ends in one of two ways:

"Oh, wow, your underwear is pretty."

"Mama, you need some new underwear."

Thank you for noticing, son. If I wasn't constantly buying you shoes I'd splurge on some new undergarments.

I would like to take a shower without drip-drying because the last person who took a bath in my garden tub stole my towel. I'm not a big fan of drip drying, although Husband would disagree, based on the number of times he's nearly broken his neck entering the bathroom after one of my showers. He thinks I don't dry off at all. He might be right.

I would like to set the table and not have to pull forks from the dirt in the backyard just to have enough to eat like decent human beings (at least the human beings after the fourth century). I would like my forks to remain in the silverware drawer, instead of being hoarded by sneaky boys so they can continue digging their tunnel to Spain or wherever it is they're headed this week. All the soil in my backyard is full of rocks that could subjectively be called boulders. They're not getting farther than the tree's roots, but that won't stop them from trying. And the number of forks I own without bent prongs grows smaller by the day.

I would like to walk into a bathroom and not see all the cabinets open, especially the one that stores the Band-Aids. My kids think they need Band-Aids for everything. Kids don't need Band-Aids for everything. I know it's hard to believe that you're not going to bleed to death from that thorn-prick you got picking blackberries, but you're going to be just fine. And just because you got a rug-burn on your knee doesn't mean you need a bandage. And trust me, no dressing is thick enough to stanch that snot dripping from your nose. Don't use a Band-

Aid.

I would like to drink a cup of green tea with peppermint while it's still hot. Every single morning I get ready to drink my tea, and someone initiates a crisis that must be attended—they can't find their shoes, they can't tie their shoes, someone misplaced their backpack, they forgot they had homework last night and now they have to do it real quick before school, they feel sick, someone stole all their underwear (No one stole it. They missed laundry day; if they don't have their clothes in the hamper, it doesn't get washed, hence no underwear. Not my problem. Turn the ones you're wearing inside out and wear them another day.).

I would like to eat my leftovers from Husband's and my order-in date night without a scavenger hovering, asking if he can have a bite, just one small bite, please, Mama, let him have a bite? I've already fed him lunch. Plus a snack, when he said he was still hungry. I would now like to eat my own lunch in peace, without hearing every other second, "That looks really good" or "I wish I could eat something like that." Have you ever read *The Pigeon Finds a Hot Dog*, by Mo Willems? I feel like the pigeon every time I sit down with my yummy day-old food.

I would like to walk into a room that doesn't look like a crime scene happened while I was out. There are clothes stretched out on the floor in strange positions, there are toys scattered and papers everywhere and pens uncapped and upended, and there are shoes that look like someone ran right out of them. I would like to be able to walk across my living room without my feet tangling in someone's sweat pants (emphasis on the sweat), sit on my couch without a LEGO Ninjago sword puncturing my backside, and open my front door without brushing aside shoes. In short, I would like my sons to clean up after themselves once in a while.

I would like to walk around a corner in my house without a child jumping out from an impossible hiding place (which is why my guard was down) to scare me because they think it's hilariously funny. They're everywhere, and they do it all the time. Someone's gonna get hurt. I've already told the cautionary tale of Husband's one and only time to frighten me. I punched him. In self-defense. They care not. Like most kids, they think they're immune to the natural consequences of scaring me. But one of these days…

My wish list for Mother's Day is no more attainable than it is refined, but, like I said, I'm not particularly hard to please. Do these things for a day, and I might be able to endure another year of the opposite.

Key word being: maybe.

The Creative Gifts Kids Give on Mother's Day

Mother's Day is one of the woefully few days when everyone makes a concerted effort to think about Mom—the kids are still in school and make her all sorts of gifts during class, Sunday school teachers help kids trace their hands and use each finger to tell Mom why she's so special, the stores put their best flowers and chocolates on display.

In short, moms get a lot of gifts for Mother's Day. Some are more keepable than others.

Here are some of the wildcard gifts I've gotten on Mother's Day:

1. Info sheets

These are, of course, hit or miss, depending on the kid. One kid will say my age is sixteen, one will say I'm five, and another will say I'm one hundred twenty. It's the same with the details—you can tell which kids are paying attention and which kids are completely stuck in the World of Me, Me, Me. The kid who wrote that my favorite thing to do in the whole world is wash the dishes must not be listening to all the complaints I air every night at 6:30 p.m. Either that or I must look really happy doing those dishes (I can't fathom how this could be).

2. Pieces of kid-made art

These are also hit or miss. One year one son came home with a delightful flower pot that, unfortunately, faded when I set it on the window sill but which was still lovely, years later (I still have it). Another son once came home with a clay cupcake he'd painted to look incredibly appealing (except that the icing was green—artistic liberties). It sits on my desk so that every time I take a break from writing and look at it I can crave cupcakes heaped with buttercream icing. Darn it, now I'm going to have to go make some. Right now.

Another son recently came home with a portrait of me—which was actually quite frightening. That went in a drawer.

3. Old used things

One of my sons once gave me a toothbrush that had already been used. I could tell because hanging out between the bristles was a collection of dried toothpaste, along with a few bits of hair and maybe a tiny bug.

They've also given me stuffed animals they took back at bedtime, half-eaten cookies, and old toys they found buried out in the yard (they generally hand them over without even washing them—how considerate!).

Well, it's the thought that counts.

4. Wildflowers

These are some of my favorite gifts, because my sons collect wildflowers without anyone suggesting it or overseeing it. They simply gather the flowers, stick them in a cup, and thrust them in my face. Even if I get splashed with wildflower water, nothing quite compares to the offering of wildflowers. Except maybe

5. Time to myself

Of course what every mom *really* wants for Mother's Day is time to herself. This can't happen without the support of a partner or friend. A few years ago, Husband left me a note on Mother's Day. It said, "Hey, I thought you might like a Sunday off leading worship, and since it's Mother's Day I figured today would be best."

Sweet, right? The note also said, "I left the kids at home so you could spend some quality time with them."

He never did it again after I re-gifted that one for Father's Day.

I have a whole bin of all the wonderful terrible gifts my kids have given me on Mother's Day—because no matter how awful they are, it's still nice to know your kids appreciate you.

And I can always sneak that well-loved bunny back in bed with him once he falls asleep and take, instead, the memory of his angelic face.

How to Snag a Few Minutes Alone: an Aside

One of a mom's greatest desires is to have a few minutes to herself. And it's not often that she gets it, if you're like most parents, with one or both partners working and kids who demand a whole lot in the down-time hours. My kids are everywhere—there's always someone who needs me. "I want to have you, Mama," the little one says. And I want to have him, too.

Still, I'd like a few moments by myself.

If you're feeling short on alone-moments, here are some ways to get a few minutes to yourself:

1. Tell your ten-year-old son you're on your period. He took the puberty class at school. He'll high-tail it out of the bathroom, where he followed you still talking, faster than you can say, "'Bye, love."

2. Drop a load. If you hide away in the bathroom like I'm known to do, drop a load and make it really smelly (you can use some of the cat's litter if you need to—just don't put it in the toilet; your pipes won't like that). When they walk in,

they'll walk right out—unless your house, like mine, is filled with boys who no longer have any sense of smell because of all the noxious gas clinging to the walls.

3. Tell them they'll get a treat if they leave you alone. This is otherwise known as a bribe, and there is no telling whether or not it will work. It might make everything worse, so use with care.

4. Run away. If you're lucky, you might be faster and get a few minutes of peace before they catch up, whining, "Why are you walking so fast?" (Hypothetically.) You'll refrain, with a massive dose of self-control, from retorting, "I was running, not walking."

5. Pretend you're a robot. This will so annoy them that they'll leave you alone for at least the next two minutes.

6. Tell them you have something important to say. They will immediately lose interest and wander away.

7. Tell them their birth story, with all the gory details, and every time they approach you, pick it back up where you left off.

I sure do love my kids, but, like every parent, there are times I'd like just a minute or two to myself. So, as one is tapping me on the shoulder while I'm trying to write this, I prepare to respond.

This time I think I'll be a robot.

Kids are Some of the Best Eavesdroppers Around

My sons have a severe problem with eavesdropping.

I try not to get annoyed about it, because when I was a kid, I did the same thing. My mom used to get so mad at me for listening when I wasn't supposed to be listening (and likely not listening when I was supposed to be) and overhearing all sorts of things I wasn't supposed to overhear. I specifically remember hanging out in doorways, just to hear what the adults were talking about.

What can I say? I was a nosy kid (that's probably why my first career was journalist).

Nosiness does not skip a generation.

The most frequent place my sons eavesdrop is in the car, since car manufacturers have yet to produce the police-car divider that I believe most parents want between the front and back seats—so their kids can fight without a parent hearing, so their kids can ask their billion "Are we almost there?" questions without a parent hearing, so their kids can say all sorts of things without a parent hearing. And vice versa.

Husband and I drive a Honda Odyssey. This lovely vehicle has three rows of seats, eight seats total, and, for us, every single seat is filled. The kids in the middle seat are the ones most privy to any important conversation Husband and I might be having. But the van is not the only place that eavesdropping occurs. Sometimes it takes us by surprise, when we're flippantly commenting on something inside one of the rooms in our home.

One day Husband and I were in the kitchen, discussing, jokingly, The Funk (a pervasive smell that resembles something between sweaty armpits, dirty socks, and un-flushed toilets. Don't worry. I've written an essay on it later in this book. You'll get all the horrendous details.) and how it's begun to overtake our house in significant proportions, and I said, "Yeah, it makes me want to get my own house out in the backyard where I can hide away for some peace and quiet and lovely smells."

My oldest son was sitting in the living room. He crept into the kitchen and looked at me. He said, "Wait, are you moving to a new house?" He wasn't concerned about divorce or anything; he was just curious about this concept of a mom moving to a different home.

Imagine the rumors he could start with that question.

We carefully displaced the misread sarcasm and told him he probably shouldn't listen in on conversations that aren't his to hear.

"Okay," he said, exactly the same way I would have said it when I was a kid. He's almost eleven. It's expected.

The Days Are Long, But the Years Are Short

This morning our sons all gathered at the kitchen table, and Husband and I stood at the counters, where we usually eat on Sundays because it's a crazy day of herding little incompetent sleepyheads out the door, and I said something about going to the library. I was staying home from church to get a few things done, and Husband was taking everyone else to church. One of my twins said, "We're going to the library? But I want to go to church!"

He clearly hadn't heard the words, "Later today when we go to the library," only "go to the library" and made his own assumptions (which are, ninety-nine percent of the time, incorrect; you'd think with a track record like that he would have learned his lesson). He was distraught that we were about to go to the library, and they hadn't even had time to gather their books! What a terrible day!

Husband and I rolled our eyes and didn't bother to listen to his complaints about how he dressed for church and he really thought we were going to church and Miss Cassie said next time they went to church they would get to play with LEGOs and he really wants to play with LEGOs. I kissed Husband goodbye and said, "Have fun with that one."

I'm sure he calmed down as soon as he recognized the way to church. Actually, *that's* probably not even assured; this is the kid who will argue with Google maps that we're going the wrong way.

During their eavesdropping, my sons have heard things like we're moving to New York (instead of we're visiting New York), Mama and Daddy are leaving (instead of Mama and

Daddy are going to a conference), we're having a Family Fun Day today (nope, it will be in two weeks), they have a day off from school, we're going to have a birthday party this weekend (it's actually a whole month away, but we like to plan ahead), someone is in trouble, someone is getting something they aren't, someone has a doctor's appointment who really doesn't.

It's slightly maddening trying to straighten out all the misinformation that flies through our house, especially when the one who overheard incorrectly first spreads a rumor and only once the rumor takes root thinks maybe it would be a good idea to have a parent confirm or refute.

When I was a kid, my mom didn't talk to me about a lot of things because she thought it better to protect me from the hardships that hammered us. And it's true that things were hard. But oftentimes, I imagined much worse than was really happening. I can't say for sure it would have been better to talk and lay it all out in the open, but I can say that sometimes I wonder if the silence was one piece of the fuel for my lifetime battle with anxiety.

Husband and I have tried as much as we can to include our kids in important conversations, because we like them to know what's going on, and we want them to see that we trust their input on the decisions we make. And we know, from personal experience, that the truth can be better than a child's imagination—particularly when that imagination is large and robust.

That said, there are still conversations we'd like to have in privacy. When a kid is standing outside our bedroom with ear

The Days Are Long, But the Years Are Short

pressed to the door, in hopes of overhearing the conversation taking place inside, that's when you know you're not safe anywhere. If we want to discuss sensitive information about a particular kid, we'd like to do that in the space of No Child Listening. In that case, the safest place is often a walk around our neighborhood. We learn to work with what we have. At least we're getting exercise.

One day last week, we were all in our van (in case I haven't mentioned it, this van is as old as my oldest son, named Lucy, and affectionately called Old Girl). Our oldest son sat in the seat closest to mine. Two of his brothers played Rock, Paper, Scissors in the seats beside him. Husband said something about needing a new van, because Lucy was getting so old and she wasn't quite as reliable for long trips anymore, and the oldest piped up with his jump-to-conclusions observation: "We're getting a new van?"

All my sons cheered.

"No, no, no," Husband said. "That's not what we said."

Everyone groaned.

I had no idea they were so keen on ousting Lucy and replacing her with a sleeker, newer model.

When everyone had resumed their conversations, Husband and I looked at each other and laughed. Our oldest son leaned forward so his head hovered in the space between our seats. He said, "You can tell me if we are. I won't tell my brothers."

Yeah, right.

"We're not," Husband said. "But you'll be the first of your

brothers to know if we do."

Three weeks later, Husband came home with a new van, and not a single child acted surprised. It was somewhat disappointing.

Well, I guess you can't really have surprises in a house with such master eavesdroppers.

The Challenge of Minimalism When You Live With Kids

Husband and I have been trying, since the beginning of the year, to not only make our house and habits more environmentally friendly but also embrace the concept of minimalism.

Owning fewer things is a much simpler, more environmentally friendly way to live, because the fewer things we own, the fewer precious resources it takes to make them. We want our sons to know and understand that every possession they bring into their lives has an impact on others and the state of the earth.

This particular part of environmentalism—the minimalism part—is an ideal that has had our hearts for quite some time; I am the kind of person who feels anxious when surrounded by too much stuff. And kids come with so much stuff.

But now that my sons are out of their infant and toddler stages, which are some of the most crowded (as far as things, time, and, well, everything else), Husband and I thought this would be a good season to focus on minimizing even more.

My original plan was to finish minimizing the house within the year, but since we're still only on the first room, I think that goal might be a little idealistic.

The problem is kids.

They want to be a part of this process—and they should be; this is their home, too. But they are also really terrible at getting rid of things.

I recently spent an entire day going through every bookshelf in our house—and there are many; we have a designated home library, a library in Husband's and my office area, and at least two bookshelves in each kid's room. It's no wonder this process took all day. I was proud of my efforts when, at the end of the day, I'd cleared off the equivalent of four entire shelves and stacked books with broken bindings and missing pages in one pile and books we'd outgrown or never really enjoyed reading in another.

I was all ready to congratulate myself for minimizing one of the most difficult things for me to minimize—books—when my oldest son wandered into the room.

"Oh, wow!" he said. "I love this book!" He picked up a book from the discard pile that was flapping from the first few pages because it long ago lost its cover. He started to leave.

"Uh . . . What are you doing?" I said, perhaps a little too aggressively.

"Taking this to my shelf," he said.

"No, you're not," I said. I proceeded to explain to him what the piles were and why they were necessary—which was a huge mistake. He dropped down to his knees and started rifling through the discard pile and the donation pile, rendering them no longer piles at all, as kids do so well. I went to fetch Husband for help.

Husband was much more reasonable than I was; he let our son choose three books from whatever pile he wanted, so long as there was room on his personal bookshelves and the books didn't end up on the floor.

It's been story after story of this same kind of thing. Upon clearing out our art cabinet, one of my sons opted to keep every one of his already-used journals—even the ones he'd scribbled in as a toddler. I couldn't even talk about touching the toys without every one of my sons protesting the donation of anything with which they no longer play. The other day I caught another son rifling through the recycling, saving papers for himself that I'd already sorted and tossed.

I understand how difficult it is for kids to get rid of anything. They don't have the experience we have to say that ridding ourselves of one thing makes way for something better —or simply opens up space to breathe. But they will. They'll notice the difference, and while they may not learn from the first thousand experiences of this kind, eventually they *will* learn. And they'll remember it when they grow up and have homes and families of their own.

So I guess I'll keep chipping away at the reduction, letting them exercise their negotiation skills, and enjoying the wide open space of owning fewer things—however fleeting it is.

Environmental Jobs that will Capture Kids' Hearts: an Aside

When a family makes a concerted effort to focus on more environmentally sustainable activities and earth care, it requires the entire family to accomplish this goal. Some kids are less enthused about the details—"Why can't we buy this candy anymore?"—but with specific jobs aimed at targeting carbon footprint reduction, they can all get involved.

Here are some fun and friendly jobs to propose:

1. The Light Leprechaun

This is the kid who will move silently behind his siblings to turn off the lights once they leave rooms. Speaking from experience, he'll never complain of boredom, with all that work to do.

Warning: He will sometimes abuse this privilege by turning off a light while his brother is still in the room. Most likely the bathroom.

2. Water Warrior

For some reason, there's a certain five-year-old in my house who has a habit of walking out of the bathroom without turning off the faucet. I know I should be glad he washed his hands after going potty, but really? Please turn off the water.

The Water Warrior's job is to periodically check bathrooms to make sure faucets aren't dripping (or worse), and toilets aren't running.

Warning: Our Water Warrior delights in announcing that a toilet is overflowing (his word for "stopped up") and describing, in intricate detail, just what caused the clog.

3. Door Defender

This kid's job is making sure all doors that lead outside are closed and secured.

Warning: A rule will likely be needed—no closing the door when a sibling is walking through it.

4. Compost Conqueror

This kid's in charge of taking food scraps (no meat or dairy) out to the compost pile and turning the pile every few days. He will likely find great pleasure in watching food rot and turn into fertilizer.

Warning: Another rule may be needed—Do not taste the compost. Hypothetic—never mind.

5. Recycling Renegade

This kid makes sure all recycling is cleaned out and in its proper place (which is, to clarify, the recycling bin outside).

Warning: I advise against assigning this job to the kid whose philosophy in life is "everything can be reused," or nothing will make it into the recycling; it will, instead, be repurposed throughout your house, causing an anxiety-meltdown level of clutter.

6. Cheering Champion

Reserved for the youngest of the bunch. Everyone needs to be cheered in his efforts to reduce his carbon footprint.

Way to go, team!

The Subjectively Fun Games Boys Play

During extended holidays and lazy days, my sons are really great at making up games they can play together to pass the time. Some of these games—typically those played outside on the trampoline, include somewhere in the title the word "fight," which means they're not as big a break as you would think, because I can almost guarantee someone will soon come back inside the house crying because the game got a little out of hand. It's so predictable.

In spite of this little hiccup in the playing world of boys, I am always impressed by the creativity of my sons. I don't know why I'm surprised; I should know by now that when they are faced with a wide empty space on the schedule, they can do nothing else but create. And games are some of the funnest things to create.

Here are some of the recent games my sons have imagined and with which they have experimented (some were more successful than others):

Who Can Stand the Longest

My sons usually play this game on the trampoline, but that is no hard-and-fast rule; it can be played anywhere. As far as I can tell in my limited observation, the rules are something like this: someone takes a ball and lobs it at someone else's legs, and whoever is left standing at the end of the game wins. Some of the players can take more hits than others, and typically this will result in a revolving door of boys coming in to tattle on their brother for throwing a ball at their legs, to which I generally reply, "Were you playing Who Can Stand the Longest?" When they sheepishly admit that yes, yes they were, there is really nothing more to say.

There are variations to this game of course; it can also be played in the yard (preferably in the rockiest spot) and with a foam sword (or plastic one if you're the angry brother who lost all preceding six games). Sometimes, when my sons are really testing my patience, I want to join the game myself, as the sword wielder or ball thrower.

The Fight Game

This game has the longest shelf life in our home; my sons play it practically every day. I'm not completely certain what the rules to this one are, either, just that they only play it on the trampoline and it appears that the object of the game is to jump and try to hit each other in mid-air so the assaulted one doesn't land on his feet but on a head or an arm or, even better, the backside. You'll notice that this one is very similar to Who Can Stand the Longest, except without a ball or foam sword; they use their hands and legs and feet instead.

This game has resulted in a bruised knee, a couple of black

eyes, and some loose teeth. Husband and I try to discourage the play of such a brutal game, but every time my sons head out to the trampoline, I can hear their whispers (because kids are the loudest whisperers on the planet): "Do you want to play The Fight Game? Just don't tell Mama."

Yeah, right. Like I'm not gonna know when someone comes in with a bloody nose.

Get There First

My sons will play this game any time they're eating, leaving a room, trying to pick up a library book, heading upstairs, and going to the bathroom. They play it for everything, actually—everything, that is, except getting in the car.

They will race each other for dinnertime seconds, even though we only dish out seconds when everyone has finished their firsts (we thought this rule might result in less stuff-it-in-your-face-as-fast-as-you-can-and-make-sure-you-don't-chew eating behavior, but what it really amounts to is more boys complaining about how hungry they are while they wait for the "slow eaters" to "FINALLY!" finish.). They will race each other up the stairs for some imaginary prize, or maybe just bragging rights. They will shove each other out of the bathroom doorway, because one has to go worse than the other (or so they say).

If you ever accidentally wander into the path of a boy playing Get There First, you'll discover how much like a wrecking ball they can be. Just ask the yellowing bruise on my shoulder.

Whack a Brother

This game is exactly what it sounds like: They will use foam swords as makeshift hammers and hit each other (it doesn't matter where) until someone begs mercy. They'll run around the backyard shrieking like banshees while one chases the other with a foam noodle that we turned into light sabers (you always think it's a good idea at the time). They hide around corners with foam pirate swords. They whip through the cul-de-sac with Thor's foamy hammer.

I'm just glad they're not using real hammers.

Follow the Reader

If there's anything my sons fight about most, it's books. Okay, they fight about LEGOs more, but when we've just taken a trip to the library, my sons will fight over the books checked out, as though they don't each have their own library books they just spent the last half-hour choosing. Someone else's book is always better—that's why the library is such a magical place. I'd just like to have some peace and quiet, maybe a little reading time, after a library trip, not this constant fighting over who had the book first and whose it is and why the original reader doesn't need it right now.

Here's a typical scenario: Son 1 will follow Son 2 around the house, because Son 2 has a book that looks exceedingly interesting, and Son 1 wants it. Son 1 will politely use his words and ask if he might read the book, and if Son 2 says no or, more likely, doesn't respond because he is deep in the throes of narrative, Son 1 will steal the book right out of Son 2's hands.

I'm sure you can imagine what happens next. We have unauthorized play of Whack a Brother.

Stealth

My sons use this game to steal things—particularly food. They don't really steal anything else. My older sons have grown out of this, for the most part—probably because it's unnecessary for them to steal food; they get what they want. But my twins would eat all day if I let them, and they like to play this game every Monday, Tuesday, and Thursday afternoon—times that, ironically, correspond to when Husband is on kid-duty. He doesn't pay as close attention, and they know it. They're not actually very good at Stealth, but when I take over on Wednesdays and Fridays, they operate under the erroneous assumption that they *are* really good at it (because they got away with it on Husband's shift). They forget that Mama has eyes everywhere. And I mean everywhere.

Why Can't I

This game is every parent's dream. Here's how you play it: A parent refuses a kid some kind of request, say, "I want to go to the pool by myself," and upon parental refusal the kid will say "Why can't I" over and over and over again until the incessant asking breaks the parent down so efficiently they start rocking themselves in a corner, crying, because they can't take another minute of this question. Hypothetically.

Your kids don't do this? Oh, well, neither do mine.

While these games are creative and subjectively fun, I try to encourage my sons not to wear them out—that is, don't play them so often you get tired of them. Once every blue moon is fine, but every day?

It's more for me than for them, but they don't have to know that.

The Enormous Cost of Raising Children

Children are delightful, aren't they?

When my sons aren't leaving dirty socks and underwear all over the floor of their rooms, forgetting to hang up towels so cats think they're a nice little place to urinate (the Cat Whisperer didn't do his job of cleaning out the litter box this week), or slipping out of the kitchen like something's on fire because now that their bellies are full they don't really feel like doing after-dinner chores, they're truly enjoyable people.

Sometimes I catch myself staring—when one of them is putting together a puzzle with that crooked-mouthed concentration or when someone else is helping a brother hunt for his shoes (the never-ending quest) or when another is trying to draw his name with the new letters he learned today, and his eyes won't leave the page no matter how many silly things I do to catch his attention. Half an hour can pass while I watch these little people grow up. I enjoy it—but my work sometimes suffers.

This is, of course, one of the hidden costs of children. I've written similar essays elsewhere, but for this one I'd like to focus on something that is not quite so common to the raising-children experience.

My sons have avoided childcare because Husband and I arrange our days (and we're incredibly lucky to operate this way) so that one or the other of us is in charge of childcare. This is fantastic in terms of family togetherness, but not so much when it comes to the costs of always being home, which can be felt (and seen) in many ways.

1. The electricity bill

My sons mistakenly believe there is a fairy who flits around behind them and turns off their lights. And they do a really good job of keeping her employed. It doesn't matter that a chalkboard tally is adding up what they'll owe us for "energy costs" at the end of the month; they simply don't pay attention to the fact that they are leaving the room (which can also be witnessed in the number of times I have to say "Shut the door!"). They are oblivious to the world around them, unless it's dark and they need a light. Of course that light should stay on; why should they have to deal with darkness when next they come into this room three hours later?

The only time they really make an effort to turn off a light is when a brother is peeing in the bathroom and they suddenly remember they left the light blazing.

Ha. So funny, kid.

So far we haven't had to pay out an allowance to any of them, because they're all paying for our electricity bill. Natural consequence (that has no learning curve, apparently, but still.

Principles.).

Recently a bulb in their bathroom burned out, and I almost didn't replace it, because I thought about how often I pass by that room and find the light still on and no one inside. And then I thought it was probably better to replace the bulb, because boys are bad enough at aiming without the added challenge of darkness.

Some days when I emerge from my room to begin the breakfast preparations half an hour before my sons are set to rise, I find every lamp in their rooms on. I have no idea how they sleep with so much light; it can't possibly be restful sleep.

Someone likes flipping on all the outside lights so once the sun comes up I don't even notice. Who knows how much energy we're wasting with lights we don't need. Sorry, world. I'm really trying.

2. Plungers

This should not have a place on a hidden cost list, but my sons are really, really bad about flushing the toilet.

Husband remarked to me the other day that just after he purchased a plunger for every toilet (because no one could remember where they'd last seen the one we originally had, so frequent were the toilet stoppages), he noticed a marked decrease in the number of times he stumbled upon a clogged toilet. I said it's probably because there's a marked decrease in the number of times the toilets have been flushed lately. No one notices a clogged toilet if the toilet is never flushed in the first place.

I'm sure we'll need one any minute now.

3. Food, food, food, food, food

Of course kids need food, but I tell you what, I should have a revolving door installed on our fridge for the number of times it gets opened in a given day. One of our refrigerators (yes, we have two—might even need three in a few years; a mom can only get to a grocery store so many times in a week) quit working not too long ago, and I think it's because my sons opened it too many times. The fridge lost the ability to suction its doors closed.

My sons are constantly rummaging for a snack, even though we have specific snack times in our house. They get two snacks a day, anytime between 3 and 4 p.m. We set these rules because if we didn't, our sons would eat all day, and our grocery budget would be more out of control than it already is.

Fortunately, it doesn't really matter what's left in the fridge by the end of the week. If there's a container of wilting spinach, they will cram it into their starving mouths. If all that remains in the crisper drawers are a few flimsy carrots, they'll fight over who gets to eat them. If there is nothing but shriveling, freezer-burned strawberries, sans packaging, scavenged from the darkest corner of the freezer, that will suffice.

And, if all else fails, there's always the insects outside, which my five-year-olds seem to love.

4. What happened to your shoes?

Husband and I operate on a pretty tight budget. We both run our own businesses, and they're creative businesses, which is to say sometimes money is good, sometimes it's really bad. Regardless, we keep a shoe budget in circulation. This is because at least twice a year, my sons will need their shoes replaced. It doesn't matter how expensive the shoes are in the first place, they will wear out within four to six months, sometimes sooner.

My sons use their shoes for a variety of things—brakes for the downhill slide on the scooter, weapons with which to "shoe fight" on the trampoline, noise makers for the asphalt outside (preferably the tips of the toes). Two days after I handed over the brand new tennis shoes I bought my five-year-olds, one of their shoes already had all the color scraped off the sides. He complained about it. I asked him how it had happened. He showed me how he was running on the way home from school —one foot dragging behind him, then the other foot dragging. It's no wonder his shoes lost all their color. I explained that he would have to keep these colorless shoes for six more months, until it was time to buy new shoes. He tried to steal his twin brother's, but I'd already twin-proofed that—initials, in permanent marker, all over the insides.

By the time shoe-buying rolls back around, my sons' soles will be flapping along the sidewalk with us as we walk to school. No matter. They say it makes them run faster.

5. Destruction as far as the eye can see

The paint on our walls is peeling off. The bookshelves are scuffed and marked. The carpet is worn and decorated with marker.

I once left my twins downstairs alone when they were around two; I was dumping out laundry on my bed. I heard a crash and leapt down the stairs, almost breaking my foot in the process. They had overturned a sofa table with a stack of books on it. It was a heavy table, too. They took off running as soon as it happened so they could stammer out that it wasn't them. There was proof, though: their shoes, flattened under the table. I have no idea how they wriggled out of that one.

These same twins regularly sit on baskets that are not sturdy enough to hold their forty-pound frames, dig holes in our backyard with the same spoons they use for Monday morning yogurt, and cut out horses from the back covers of Magic Treehouse books. They're set to start receiving Christmas and birthday gifts again in 2025, once they've paid off all the damage they've caused around here.

6. Lost library books

Before I had kids I never lost a library book. Books are precious things to me; that's probably not surprising, given what I do for a living. But now we lose so many library books we've had to start a "library" line in our monthly budget. And because I'm a parent who believes strongly in the importance of reading, I don't forbid my sons from going to the library; I just make them pay their fines.

The most annoying part of it is that we usually find the library book, eventually. When we find it on a day that falls outside my library's thirty-day return window, the receipt for our payment is always where it should be: in Husband's wallet. When the finding happens within the thirty-day return window, which would allow us to get our money back, the receipt can never be found.

I just consider this my generous contribution to my local

library. They rarely get enough money as it is. I can pay them twenty-five dollars every month or two.

7. The egregious waste

My sons use all the soap to blow bubbles. They do food experiments, even though they should know what a precious resource food is in our house. They will use so many pieces of computer paper to draw their own stories (which I totally wouldn't mind if they didn't abandon them halfway finished) or make a bevy of origami swans that the next time I need to print out a manuscript, no paper's left.

The other day my two-year-old disappeared down the stairs. I thought maybe he was just getting a book to read, since the rest of us were in our home library reading books. But then he didn't come up after a while, and Husband bounded downstairs to check on him. He came back up with the two-year-old, who had painted himself bright white.

Needless to say, that resulted in ruined paint, a ruined shirt, some ruined slacks, and a spot of ruined carpet.

Children are delightful, aren't they?

June

A Sincere Thank-You Note to Involved Dads

Recently Husband and I went to visit my mom, and for practically the whole time we stayed he and my sons played baseball outside. The boys had fun until the other team scored a run or they thought they should have another chance at batting but the game was actually over.

Truthfully, most of the games ended in tears (but they didn't start that way).

After one such game, when I could hardly keep my eyes from rolling out of my head because of the broken hearts (they were exceedingly loud communicating this broken-heartedness) of the losing team, Husband plopped down in the seat next to me and said, "I love playing with them."

"Even when they whine and complain after the game's over?" I said.

"Yeah," he said.

And I was struck, right there on my mom's front porch, which faces the open yard and, across the street, a cornfield, by how much children gain from the involved presence of their dads (not for the first time, and most likely not for the last, either).

Dads offer something incredibly important to their children, and here are some of those things:

1. A confirmation of their identity

This is the most important thing Husband does for my sons. It's the most important thing, in my opinion, that any dad can do for their kids. A dad can reinforce to their children the truth that they are important, they are beloved, and they are worthy of the love they are lavished.

I think here of my own background, where a dad did not stick around. What it spoke to me, the hole I carried around—and still carry around on my worst days—is that I was not worthy of his love.

Dads, with their continued involved presence, affirm who children are; they speak into their lives in an authoritative way, one that stands strong against the arrows those children will take when they are someday grown. Dads tell their children, through their involved and interested presence, that those children are worth being loved. And this means the world to a kid.

2. A role model

Dads model for boys who to be. Boys will try to walk like their dads and talk like their dads and sometimes even think like their dads. But dads also provide an essential model for their daughters. They show girls how to be loved. They show their daughters that they are not loved for their beauty but for who they are—and in a world like ours, this is an essential message to pass on.

Dads show boys how to treat girls, and they (the good ones) show girls how they should expect to be treated by boys.

3. A voice of wisdom

Moms are wise and capable. Dads offer another dynamic of wisdom, a reinforcement, an underlining of that wisdom. A mom can exemplify to her children how to treat others, how to be kind and loving, how to live with courage and strength. But when that message is reinforced by dads, it grows spectacular wings.

I'm exceedingly grateful to the man in my life and all the hands-on fathers like him. Thank you for what you do.

What Dad Really Wants for Father's Day

It's the day before Father's Day, and I'm just now thinking about what to get my husband to celebrate his presence in my sons' lives.(I do realize that last month I wrote an essay that began with Husband's procrastination regarding Mother's Day. My life is one big exercise in irony.)

It's not that I didn't see this coming. It's just that there's so much to keep up with. And it's summertime. My kids are driving me bonkers.

Well, if Husband says anything, I can simply remind him of that one Mother's Day I was pregnant and he didn't even give me a card (because "You're not technically a mother yet, are you?" Say what? Maybe you're not a father yet, but I most certainly am a mother. Who do you think is making me crave and eat hamburgers all the time?! I don't even like hamburgers! My back aches so badly I'll never forget what it feels like to walk with a somersaulting bowling ball strapped to my frontside. Let's see…why can't I sleep—because there's an elbow in my spleen. Not technically a mother yet. Ha.).

Here are some Father's Day Gift Ideas for Husband (and other dads) I've assembled in no particular order.

1. Time to play.

Husband, every now and then, likes to take out the Nintendo Switch (which will likely be an outdated system by the time this essay goes to press) and imagine he's thirteen again and spend all day playing a video game. Maybe for Father's Day, I'll gift him with the time to play.

There are other ways to play. Send Dad outside to play baseball with the kids, schedule him a night out with friends, let him spend all day writing songs. Play is important for dads and for all of us.

So encourage him play.

2. An "All About Dad" book.

This is a great keepsake for dads. Fill it with questions the kids have answered about their dad. Dad will now forever remember that his kid thought he was three years old and weighed five hundred twelve pounds.

Always a winner.

3. Some new socks.

If your kids' daddy is anything like mine, socks get crusty and gross by about the third week of wear. Get some new ones so they don't slice his toe next time he tries to put them on—or, worse, take off your toes when he's getting in bed.

4. Some no-ride-up underwear.

Every man needs a pair of underwear or boxer briefs that don't ride up. A man who's comfortable is a man who's less grumpy.

5. A free pass to sleep late.

Husband is always in need of more sleep (or so he says). He faithfully searches for small windows of time when he can sneak in a quick (or not so quick) nap. Maybe I'll give him a whole day.

If all else fails, just cook an elaborate meal; my Memaw always told me the way to a man's heart is through his stomach. As the mom of six boys, I can tell you: it's true.

The Sports Personalities of Children

Not too long ago, Husband and I took our sons to visit my mom's house, which has a big open field for a yard because it sits out in the middle of nowhere. It's a place where kids can be kids and shout and scream and whine all they wish. On this particular visit, Husband went outside with our sons and played some baseball.

They don't often get to do this together, because they don't have the space in our suburban cul-de-sac (at least not without the danger of breaking a window for which I don't want to pay) and Husband doesn't always have the time. But this weekend trip afforded both space and time.

My sons unfortunately don't know much about baseball. They haven't engaged in club sports (we're not quite ready for the madness that introduces to a life, and they haven't really expressed much interest in it), and Husband and I are not sports people who watch games on television. When something like the Super Bowl rolls around, we typically (a) have no idea which teams are playing and (b) avoid all parties

—not because we boycott football or something, just because it's not exactly a high priority or interest, and when you're the parents of six kids, prioritizing matters.

Husband did an efficient job of teaching our sons how to play baseball, and once they caught and understood the basic concepts, their sports personalities, to which I had never previously been exposed in any formal capacity, began to emerge.

There was, of course, **Rule Keeper**. He's needed for so many things, isn't he? To keep score, to make sure someone doesn't mistake a foul ball for an actual live ball, to determine how many outs have been logged. So Rule Keeper wouldn't be such a bad addition to any team except that our Rule Keeper kept making up his own rules. For example, he would move the bases without anyone noticing, and when someone ran for their life toward a base, the poor runner discovered that base was no longer where it was supposed to be. Rule Keeper took giant advantage of this little oversight; he would retrieve the ball and race toward the confused runner, who would make a valiant effort to avoid the ball in the glove by sprinting in circles, shrieking, "Where's the base?"

Rule Keeper is good at keeping rules—but only the rules that benefit him.

Then I noticed **The Perfectionist**. This was the kid who stood at the mound as a self-proclaimed pitcher, and every time he would pitch a ball instead of a strike (and he pitched a great many strikes, because he's graceful and catches on quick), he would cover his face and call himself the most terrible baseball player in the history of the game. The Perfectionist can be a little dramatic sometimes. After covering his face and calling himself the most terrible baseball player in the history of the game, he would pitch three strikes. And then he would pitch a ball and cover his face and do the whole dance again. And then he would pitch five strikes.

I guess his rose-colored glasses were a little cracked today. Maybe the competition was a little too fierce.

Next I observed **The Opportunist**. This kid was so fast, like a flash, that no one could keep track of him. They couldn't see where he was at any given time during the game, because he was always stealing bases—every time someone turned around or bent over or blinked. He'd steal a base and everyone on the other team would get mad and say he was cheating, and Rule Keeper would announce that there was no stealing bases in this game and Husband and I would have to mitigate a loud and passionate argument about how many bases you could steal in a game before you were disqualified (all of them is the answer. You can steal all of the bases and never get disqualified; our sons didn't like this answer). And every time we had to stop the game to have a discussion about the fairness of stealing, The Opportunist would creep toward home. Eventually he'd make it, and his brothers would look at each other, wondering what just happened.

I'm pretty sure The Opportunist scored all nine of the runs his team had by the end of the game.

Then I noticed (though I could have done without noticing) **The Whiner**. This was the kid who wanted to pitch, but he was not elected the pitcher at the beginning of the game, mostly because he is five and every time he threw a ball you weren't really sure if it was going to hit you in the face or go far into left field behind him. His brothers, being kind, gave him the opportunity to pitch a few balls, and he lobbed three—one hit a tree, one hit Husband's shin, and the last sailed off into the horse pen fifty feet behind him—before they told him maybe he should just stick with batting. Thus began the whining, which endured the entire game. The Whiner whined about how many runs the other team was getting, how he struck out and it was unfair, how he didn't get to pitch, how he missed the ball when someone hit it directly to him because he thinks there was something wrong with his glove, how he made a run and no one even tried to tag him out.

There's really no pleasing The Whiner.

I noticed, too, his twin brother, **Clueless**. This kid clearly didn't know the locations of any bases (and this was even before Rule Keeper moved them), although it was pointed out at the beginning of the game. When he finally got a hit off The Perfectionist, he stood at home plate and looked around, like he wasn't sure what he was supposed to do—but he knew there was *something*. And when someone told him to put down the bat and run he only heard the last part and took off running for his life, all the way to first, or very near it, passed it (without stepping on it) and headed straight for second, which was a brick in the middle of a swing set. He crashed into the swing set, toppled, and started bear crawling to third base, even though he didn't know where it was and he hadn't touched the other two bases. Somewhere along the way he lost the bat. We're still looking for it.

Clueless provided the comic relief for the game.

And then there was **The Roamer**. He was the cutest one of all, because he wasn't on anybody's team and he wasn't technically playing, he was just enjoying being out in a great big field with his big brothers. He happily watched them at bat and would take off after the ball when it was hit, and then he would take off running in the opposite direction when he retrieved the ball his brothers were too lazy to retrieve, while they yelled at him to bring it to them, fast. He was hilariously entertaining, like any little brother should be.

Husband and my sons took a little break after the seventh inning, when they'd tied up the game. They needed some hydration and a snack. After fifteen or so minutes, they ambled back out to finish the remaining two innings. I sat out on my mom's front porch, with my mom and stepdad, to watch.

I'm glad I was there to see what happened next.

Rule Keeper threw the ball right at Husband, saying that if the ball hit him he was out (he'd probably confused the rules for dodgeball with the rules for baseball; easy mistake), The Perfectionist yelled at himself for not getting the ball into the hands of another teammate besides Rule Keeper, The Opportunist stole another five bases (and he only had two left), The Whiner complained that he made it home without anybody throwing the ball at *him*—why'd they throw it at Daddy instead of *him*? Clueless stared blankly at everyone and seemed to wonder what on earth was going on, and The

Roamer clapped his hands at the performance that erupted around the final game-winning runs:

Tears.

The game ended in tears for practically everyone, except for the Silent Observer, who wrote it all down in a notebook.

The Hidden Perfection of Reading Time with Children

As soon as I became a parent, I sectioned off a wedge of time in our evening routine called Reading Time. This, of course, wasn't the only Reading Time my children would have, but it was an extended Reading Time that would also allow me to read. I imagined it would be a magical time of peace and quiet and calm. I thought my children would cooperate perfectly with little or no intervention. I dreamed of actually reading a book.

Turns out there's no such thing as peace and quiet and calm in a house full of males.

However. I have never been one to give up.

So this summer, since my sons are home from school all day every day, I instituted an hour-long Silent Reading Time that is mandatory before they earn their tech time for the day. During this time, my sons are supposed to take out their books, put their feet up, and read. It's simple, really.

Nothing's simple with children. You should know that by now.

Silence is practically impossible for my sons (unless they're doing something they aren't supposed to be doing). This time almost always includes a child complaining about someone looking at their book while they're reading; they don't like people peering over their shoulder (I understand this; I don't, either, though my sons apparently believe they're the only ones with this pet peeve, judging by how often they do it to me.). They tattle about a brother who accidentally nudged their elbow, and now they've lost their place. They announce to the world that they finished their book and they need a new one.

I know how valuable it is for kids to see their parents reading; we can talk to them all day about the importance of reading, but if they never see us read, do they believe us? Likely not. So Silent Reading Time is a significant opportunity to not just read ourselves but also show our sons we walk what we talk. We keep trying.

There is also another significant time in our routine: Read-Aloud time. I've been asked the question often: Are kids ever too old to hear stories read aloud?

No, no, no, no, no. I will do this forever.

I will confess, however, that our Read-Aloud Time looks very different, too, than I imagined it once upon a time. On any typical night, it looks like this:

One kid jumps on the chaise lounge while the youngest tries to walk across it, on his way to a table, where he'll stand to look down on all his minions who are supposed to be providing a good example of what it looks like to listen to

The Days Are Long, But the Years Are Short

Mama read a story. One of the five-year-olds uses a scarf as a jump rope while he looks at Pokémon cards over the shoulder of his brother, who is about to open his mouth and lodge a complaint for this very offense.

Another five-year-old talks to himself about planes and trees and the ladybug he has in his pocket, which he'll dig out as soon as I'm caught up in a really intense part of this book and drop into my lap. I've had years of practice bolting from the insects my sons drop in my lap, so this is just yet another practice session. I'm very good at it. I don't even miss a line on the page.

Another kid whispers really loudly to his daddy (if you don't already know this, kids find it impossible to whisper; it's more like a shout in a breathy voice.) about the page he read in his book before I started reading aloud. He'll use twelve hundred more words than what is printed on the page to do it.

One of my sons sits completely still, listening.

Another kid sneaks off to the bathroom to do God knows what with a plunger and toothpaste, which are the first two items he grabs on his way inside, effectively smearing toothpaste and, well, you don't want to know, on the book still in his hands. It's a library book. We'll clean and sanitize it before we return it.

Another kid tries to see how high he can jump before he cracks his head on the ceiling fan, which is turned on high.

Wait. That's too many kids? Well, I lost count.

It's like a six-ring circus around here.

But I've noticed something hopeful over the years. Even

when my sons don't appear to be listening during my read-aloud time, because one of them is whispering to another; and one of them is looking out the window daydreaming about the story he'd like to write with a bird and a song that needs to be found; and one of them is standing on his head without any underwear; and one of them is turning around in circles, trying to hit whomever he can with his flailing hands; and one of them is stomping on a table because he's proud he got there; and another one is pulling book after book after book off the bookshelves so he can look through all the pictures and maybe tear a few pages, unnoticed, while he's at it—they're still listening. Their noise and activity don't mean they don't hear.

I know this, because they have to write in journals about what they've read for the day, and they always nail it. I don't know how they do it. If I were standing on my head while listening to a book, I'd be too distracted thinking about how long it will take for all the blood to rush to my head and knock me unconscious. Not that I'd be able to do a headstand in the first place. I'm too lumpy to do that anymore. And my arms are too fragile. And my neck is already stiff enough. (Aging is fun.)

Sometimes kids have to move when they're listening. Sometimes they have to stand on their heads or turn flips or jump off a couch into the great abyss of a cavern that exists only in their imagination.

So maybe Read-Aloud time doesn't look the way I expected. But at least they get a few words out of it now and then. And a few words eventually make a whole story.

What the Word "Maybe" Means

One day last week my second son asked Husband and me if we were going to go to the pool at any point that day. It's summertime here in Texas, which means, often, three-digit-degree days, so it's a time when my sons might logically assume that we would, in fact, schedule a visit to the pool. The problem is really that we've been going to the pool so much that Husband and I both are a little tired of it.

Husband said, "Maybe."

My second son said, "Great. I know that means no."

"Why?" I said.

"Because any time we ask you if we're doing something and you say maybe, we don't do it," he said.

"We answered maybe yesterday and we went to the pool," I reminded him.

My son looked at me, and his eyes were so mournful that it was impossible not to say we would go right now, this minute. Of course I resisted because I'm strong. But it was very, very difficult.

My kids hate the word maybe. They hate it because they know that it usually means their daddy and I haven't really thought about whatever they're asking and if we think about it, we're probably going to say no. If I run the statistics briefly in my head, the answer typically boils down to no—but, then, I was never great at statistics; maybe I'm just projecting what my sons have said ("Maybe *always* means no") onto the situation. Sometimes maybe means yes. I think. I remember it meaning yes once upon a time. Have we corrupted the word maybe?

What complicates the question-and-answer process in my home is the fact that I have several strong-willed, sticky-brained kids, which means that when I say we're going to do something and we don't do it, I have not just one meltdown on my hands but several. They sound like a wailing choir. And I know this, because it's happened more times than I'd care to admit. When he was younger, my oldest son had a very difficult time putting things away when it was time for a transition (he still does; he's on the autism spectrum, and this is one of the classic characteristics of the autistic brain). Husband and I would tell him, "You'll be able to color as soon as you get up from your nap," and when he woke up from his nap, the first thing he would say to us was, "I get to color now?" Like he had been dreaming about coloring the entire time he slept.

A strong will is good to have. But it's also incredibly difficult for parents to manage. Because things change, sometimes unpredictably. Husband and I can have the best of intentions and then a whole day will fall apart and we're not entirely sure we can put it back together—ever. These times call for improvisation. Strong wills don't like improvisation. I know, because I also have a strong will.

This is where the word maybe comes in handy. Husband and I don't have to technically commit to anything. It's a gray area—note definitively yes, not definitively no (and I get why kids would hate this word. I hate vague answers, too.). Will I get tech time when we finish this Family Fun Day? Maybe (but probably not). Can we please go to the store this afternoon so I can look at the LEGO sets? Maybe. (That is a hard-and-fast pass, my dear. Remember what happened last time?) Are we gonna have brownies for a treat since you're making so many? Maybe (if I don't eat them all first).

Husband and I try really hard to follow through on any commitments we make, specifically because of the diverse and sometimes difficult personalities of our children. So we use the word maybe more than we probably should.

Here are a few of the maybes we've used in the last couple of weeks:

"Are we going on a trip this summer?"
"Maybe."

I'm not a last-minute person. In fact, I'm the opposite of a last-minute person. If I could schedule all the things I need to do in a year back on January first and know with complete certainty that absolutely nothing would disrupt those plans, I would be a very happy woman. But when it comes to planning anything with my family, I tend toward the last-minute-person personality. It's strange. I can't seem to get on the ball with planning things like birthday parties, special get-togethers, trips to see the people we love. So while I'd like to tell my sons we're going to take at least a trip to see their grandparents this summer, I know my sons will hold me to it if it doesn't actually pan out, and then they'll be so disappointed it's all they'll talk about for the next three years.

"Remember that time you said we were going to take a family trip and you lied?"

No thanks.

"Can we go out to eat?"

"Maybe."

Our sons are somewhat deprived in the eating-in-restaurants department. Husband and I hardly ever take them all out to eat, mostly for economical reasons. A dinner at a sit-down restaurant (not the fancy ones, the burger joint ones) will cost us seventy-five dollars or more, and that's before all our sons hit puberty. That's more than our current budget allows. It may be more than our budget ever allows, because our unlucky sons happen to be the kids of an author and a documentary filmmaker. Cash doesn't exactly flow.

"Can I have quiet time instead of a nap?"

"Maybe."

This is never "maybe" for the ones who truly need a nap (which is defined by age, by volume of whining, and by how much a kid happens to be annoying a parent that morning). Our older sons rarely ask this question anymore; they always get quiet time, because they're (mostly) responsible and can take care of themselves for a couple of hours a day. But our twins are getting older, and Husband and I are trying to give them more opportunities to prove that they can follow instructions—which includes remaining quiet for three hours during the youngest's nap time—so this is a maybe that depends on them. They don't quite get the concept yet. They may never.

"Will you fix this?"

"Maybe."

Actually, this answer is never "maybe," but it should be. Instead, I back myself into a corner with a yes. My sons typically ask this question when a beloved stuffy has picked up a hole or a pair of their favorite pants is ripped. I used to sew them all manner of things—bowties, ties, blankets, pillows, library bags. They know when it comes to thread and a needle I'm at least competent.

It's just that I don't have much time to do it anymore.

My third son, when he was five, had a stuffed crocodile he really, really loved. His hugs soon wore a hole in its tail. He asked me to fix it. Two years later, it's still sitting on my sewing table, along with an overflow of books I put on hold at the library, some old bills in need of filing, and a box of treats I keep for myself. The poor kid has forgotten about it by now—at least until he walks into my closet and sees its green tail, still waiting for someone to sew it.

"Will we ever be done cleaning?"

"Maybe."

In order for parents to sign off on their tech time, my sons have to make sure the house is tidy. They complain about this, but it's only logical; they are the ones who make the mess, so they should be the ones who have to clean it up. They disagree.

They say they always have to clean it up, why can't Mama and Daddy do it?

"Did we make the mess?" I'll say.

They'll stare at me blankly, like they don't understand. The person who makes the mess has to clean it up?

Inevitably, during this cleaning session, one of my sons will ask the above question. Husband or I will then lecture them about how clean-up time wouldn't take so long if everybody picked up after themselves. We've gotten really good at this lecture, considering we've practiced it at least 2,578 times. And how woeful it is that I just went downstairs to see what my sons were doing (it was suspiciously quiet), and they'd taken everything out of the art cabinet and, before putting it away, moved on to the LEGOs, which they'd spread out all over the kitchen table.

Come tech time, their granny in California will be able to hear their groans.

"Do you like this song?"

"Maybe."

This may seem like a strange response to such a question, but my sons are always telling Husband and me about songs they like, which they've heard somewhere with a friend or something, and then they show it to us, and it's Minecraft music, which is defined as taking popular songs and putting Minecraft lyrics to them. So, no, I don't really care for it, thanks. But you can't tell a kid that. So maybe suffices.

"What's for dinner?"

"Maybe—I mean…"

Yeah. Dinner. Every night. It's exhausting. I'm currently training one of my sons (middle school is the inauguration period) to cook one night a week. He gets a budget and furnishes me with a grocery list and then he cooks it all.

I'll let you know how it goes when he actually completes the challenge. So far he's provided us with pizza pouch dough (it wasn't as bad as it sounds), a hastily-tossed salad of romaine lettuce leaves left whole, and cereal. Today he told me he wants to order pizza for his cook night.

"With your own money?" I said.

"Maybe," he said.

I know what *that* means.

How to Take Things Apart: a Step-by-Step Process

There are very few things in my house that my children will not at least attempt to dismantle.

There is something about seeing an object completely intact that makes a certain population of kids—not all of them, mind you, just the overzealous ones; I have four of those in my home—want to take it apart and see what's inside. See this handy contraption that cuts up our vegetables into pasta-like strings? I will take it apart. See this brand-new rotisserie oven that is roasting our chicken to perfection? I will take it apart. What about this interesting shoe that has to be put on so I can leave for school in another five minutes? I WILL TAKE IT APART.

It doesn't happen all at once; the take-apart process has several steps—most of which go unseen even by the most trained eye: the mother's.

Step 1: Notice something interesting

Interesting is widely variable in a little boy's life. Sometimes they find interesting the container that holds their crayons, sometimes the complicated device that is cooking their meal. Sometimes interesting is simply their brother's face (which they will also attempt to take apart). This means that everything is on trial in your house: Is it interesting enough to take apart? Bookshelves, bathtub fixtures, and especially soap dispensers will all become victims of a boy's untamable curiosity.

Step 2: Smuggle it

I'm convinced that some boys are born part-ninja. They are *really* good at stealing something when I'm not looking. Or maybe I'm just not observant enough (naturally, I don't think that's what it is). I have one kid who thrives on his parents being distracted in any way they possibly can be. He spent his first year of school in a classroom with twenty other kindergarteners, and in the span of five weeks, he came home twice with a gaping hole in his shirt (because, apparently, his shirt was really interesting and so were those scissors). The first hole erupted in the middle of his belly, and the second one was not so much a hole as it was strings. He came home with a shirt that looked like he'd stretched a flag football belt into a top.

This kid will smuggle anything and everything, and sometimes I won't notice until it's too late. It was, of course, an accidental dismantling.

Step 3: Take it apart

It doesn't take a boy long to dismantle anything. This is because they're made to do it. I think it's some quirky part of their brain that they can switch on and off; I remember my brother doing the same thing to my tape recorder when I was a kid. That happened only once. What happened more than once was the destruction of my Barbie mansion, which he said was destroyed by his He-Man superheroes and a really terrible tornado. His nephews have all followed in his footsteps and have, to date, dismantled bikes, CD players, cell phones, earbuds, a laser sword (don't worry, it wasn't real), the hinges on a cabinet, door stoppers, and all sorts of things I'd rather you not know (including a toilet that had not been flushed in days).

Step 4: Lose a piece

It's not hard to lose anything in my house. It doesn't help that my sons are terrible at looking. So when they've dismantled something and they want to put it back together to (they hope) avoid getting in trouble, only to discover, halfway through the fixing, that a necessary piece is now missing, what do you think they do? That's right. They put it together anyway. I'd like to tell them that the vegetable pasta maker doesn't really work without the crank. A CD player doesn't work without the lid. A cell phone doesn't work without a screen.

They always think we won't notice, but how could we not? The toilet doesn't have its flusher.

Step 5: Feign innocence

Pretend nothing happened, you didn't see a thing, you weren't even near the item in question. My sons are great at abandoning a dismantled project right in the middle of reconstruction, especially when they realize there's a piece missing and they can't find it, which renders reconstruction impossible. They will forget about it, and the next time their mother is on dinner duty and wants to make zucchini pasta primavera or they try to play something in their CD player or they pick up the family phone because it's their designated technology time, they will vehemently deny they had anything to do with the dismantling. It was that pesky ghost that lives with us.

Husband and I have had to replace so many things around our house because of what my sons take apart. I know it's just a natural expression of curiosity, but that doesn't make it any less annoying.

The other day I walked into my five-year-old twins' room and saw thousands of tiny little pink pieces on the floor.

"What in the world?" I said. Only one was in the room. I had a sneaking suspicion that he was also the one responsible. "What did you do?"

At first he shrugged, but then I flung my best Mom Look at him, and he said, "I took apart an eraser."

"Why would you do that?" I said.

He shrugged. "I don't know."

And it's true. He doesn't. He saw something, he found it interesting, he dismantled it.

One of these days, maybe one of them will take things apart and put them together for a living. I'll bill them for all the things they never repaired after curiosity had its way.

I've got a running tally going already.

The Never-Ending Nuances of Rule-Making for Kids

In a house with so many children, I have the distinct privilege of encountering all sorts of lovely behavior that needs addressing and/or correcting. I try to do this in an always-gentle and compassionate way (though I am far from perfect and many times fail at this parenting goal of mine). Any time I address behavior, however—specifically something that might bring danger or unwanted consequences to my sons but that seems especially fun or enjoyable—the one thing I can always count on is what they say next.

"Why?"

As if "Don't sword-fight with a knife" needs an explanation of why.

I'm glad they ask why. Husband and I have cultivated this Questioning Practice in our household, because we believe questions are how we learn and determine our own opinions and beliefs. We want, more than anything, to raise children who know how to think for themselves and how to respectfully challenge authority in ways that will make a positive difference.

The problem is that there are many, many opportunities to exercise this Questioning Practice, because there are many, many instances where parents must intervene before children accidentally harm themselves.

Here's a look at the typical day.

No, you may not walk in your roller blades when you need to go upstairs.

Q: "Why?"

A: Because you could die.

The threat of dying, it must be said, is not a significant deterrent for boys. There is some of the "that won't happen to me" at play here, but there is also a considerable lack of foresight when it comes to imagining what might happen if one walks up stairs in roller blades and slips. They imagine (I've asked them) they will simply roll down the stairs on their feet, one jarring step at a time. They do not imagine or even consider that the stairs might beat them up on the way down and possibly break every bone in their body.

On a recent day, when they again asked why they could not achieve this bucket list feat, I tried to remind them that I once walked down the stairs in my running shoes, missed a step three stairs from the bottom, and cracked my foot. They said, "Yeah, but you always trip on things." Which was not the point.

No, you may not break the plastic shirt hangers you have in your closet so you can make a device that's surprisingly efficient at picking the lock on the fence.

Q: "Why?"

A: Because it keeps you safe and the backyard secure.

There is a reason our backyard is locked. For one, Husband and I don't want the neighbor kids coming over while we're gone, jumping on our trampoline, breaking one of their bones, and suing us even though it was unauthorized play. For another, we don't want our five-year-old twins or our two-year-old to escape into the front yard and get flattened by the tires of a car taking a turnaround in our cul-de-sac. Locks mean safety.

Also, a lock pick that works on the back fence would likely work for our bedroom, and kids do not want to see what's inside when the door is locked. I mean, usually we're sleeping, but better safe than sorry.

No, you may not wear five shirts at the same time in the middle of summer.

Q: "Why?"

A: Do you want to do laundry?

For some reason, my sons like to play dress-up. There's nothing wrong with this, and we have an entire basket of old Halloween costumes we keep for this specific purpose. The real problem comes when they decide they want to use their closet, which is full of regular clothes, to dress up.

The six-year-old came down the stairs the other morning looking like a football player.

"What are you wearing?" I said.

"Six shirts," he said.

"You only need one," I said.

"We're playing the Bashing Game on the trampoline," he

said. "I need some padding."

I looked at him for a minute, shook my head, and said, "Well, you'll have to figure out something else, then. I'm sure you don't want to do all that laundry come laundry day."

A few minutes later, he walked out with pool noodles Duct taped to his body. He was the only one who wasn't hurt during the Bashing Game.

No, you may not take the screw out of the kitchen table leg and use it for your own invention.

Q: "Why?"

A: Because your mother will be wiping off the table after lunch, and she will lean a bit too heavily on the table, and it will cave under her weight, and she'll bust her face and lip in the fall, and, also, she will not be able to move tomorrow.

True story.

You might wonder how a kid would be able to unscrew an entire leg from the table without my noticing. Well, it's a madhouse in my home. Someone is always demanding attention, and the ones you have to worry about are the ones who don't demand that attention. They see the opportunity, they take a little time, they have a pocket full of screws that they will stash under their bed and pull out during nap time so they can scrape lines and rivers onto their walls.

I kid you not: Sometimes I wish for the monotony of a dull moment, because they don't exist here.

No, you may not de-fluff your stuffed animals.

Q: "Why?"

A: Because I don't want to walk around on a bunch of

animal carpets.

My twins, for a while, went through a de-fluffing stage. I say they *went through*. They've never actually come out of it. Every now and again Husband or I will graciously allow them to take one of their remaining stuffed animals into their room for the evening, and the next morning there will be an animal carcass (you know, the stuffed animal kind) lying on their floor, and they will swear they had nothing to do with it. Must be the same ghost that keeps leaving out the crayons and art supplies even though no one used them.

Recently, my mom decided she felt sorry for my twins because they don't get to sleep with any stuffed animals. She bought them both stuffed cats for their birthday. Two days later we texted her a picture: one had a limp tail, the other was tied to the lift cords on their window blinds in a knot we had to cut. The cat still has its too-tight collar, courtesy of the lift cord, but that's okay; his head has been de-fluffed.

No, you may not eat three pounds of frozen strawberries in one sitting.

Q: "Why?"

A: Remember the Cherries?

"Remember the Cherries" has become a mantra in our home now. My second son once ate a whole pound of cherries, possibly more, in one sitting, and the next day he threw up the entire day. That remarkable consumption might have been unrelated to the vomiting, but in our infinite wisdom, Husband and I linked them. Now "Remember the Cherries" means something in our house. My sons, when invited to remember the cherries, get wide-eyed and nod. Yes. Yes, they do.

They put most, if not all, of the strawberries back and wait for us to advise them on portion size.

Works every time.

No, you may not rot your brain on video games every hour of every day.

Q: "Why?"

A: Because I care too much about you to let you ruin that extraordinary brain of yours.

It sounds like so much fun: spend every waking moment holding a device, playing on a device, being entertained by a device. But I like my children to get creative about what to do with boredom. My oldest son came to me the other day and read the prologue of a series of books he wants to write. Okay. Yes. Please.

Boredom is just a door into the creative mind.

Sometimes my sons can get persistent when it comes to technology time. I usually give them the standard response: they can cultivate creativity when they're not distracted by a device all the time. But sometimes the argument devolves and I find myself caught in the following exchange:

"Why?"

"Because I said so."

"Why, though?"

"Because technology eats your brain."

"Why can't I?"

"Because.I.Said.So."

I never thought I'd use those words my mom said to me when I was a kid, but it turns out having inquisitive children is sometimes annoying. Sorry, Mom.

One might logically think that offering reasons for certain rules within the household would cultivate children who are more aware of the nuances that exist for said rules. But, no, I just caught my oldest son with the skateboard at the top of the stairs, which he intended to ride all the way down, because I told him he couldn't walk *up* the stairs in *roller blades*.

They both have wheels, but that nuance is apparently lost on the young and fearless.

Guess I'll have to add another rule to the list. I have a feeling this will be a never-ending story.

July

The Broken Processes of Summer

By the time summer break rolls around, we are ready for school to be out—at least on the first day of summer. After that, well…things get a little old.

You know what? I'll even give it a month.

June passes in a flurry of activity and so many I'm-so-glad-I-get-to-spend-time-with-you hours, but by the end of that month, the family togetherness starts wearing on us all.

Pretty soon we're all fighting about everything—what toys to play with, who that pen belongs to (usually me), how many snacks they're allowed within a three-hour window (no, you're not going to starve if you don't eat every hour).

This is usually the time when Husband and I begin to realize that most of our processes have broken down.

The Breakfast Process: I usually get up later during the summer. Actually, I get up at the same time (4:15 in the morning), but I make my kids sleep an hour later, which really only means I emerge from my room to put breakfast on the table an hour later. But what this usually amounts to, if kids don't burst into my room and scare the heart out of me, is I emerge from my room to loud complaints about how they're all starving and why isn't breakfast ready yet, they're usually eating by now?

I'll go with what's easy: toast.

Too bad we can't have toast every day. Breakfast is a problem every morning; my creativity can no longer keep up. I think it's time to start teaching them to cook.

The Cleanup Process: Kids aren't great at cleaning up in the first place, but when school's in session they're occupied all day, somewhere else—which means the grand total of mess they can make is much smaller than it is during the summer.

Right now there is a wide open space for mess-making and no initiative to do anything about it. Husband and I start out so well, with a whole list of things our kids have to do before they earn screen time: play outside, write in journals, read, tidy the house. So the tidying gets done every day. And the mess is mostly handled.

Once July hits us, though, we're reassessing why it's so important that our kids only get an hour of screen time every day. Can't they just watch all day? What would it hurt?

The Clothes-Wearing Process: By July it's so hot my kids are either spending all their time in their swim trucks or their skivvies—and, honestly, I'm wishing I could do the same.

The Keep-Your-Patience Process: I keep my patience really well with my children—when they're away from me for seven hours a day. But all this family togetherness has been sitting on my nerves and suffocating my patience.

I can't be held responsible for how it all blows apart. And —judging by my twitching eye—that'll happen soon.

I love our time off. I love the stretching out of summer days, the opening and closing (mostly opening) of the back door as boys rush out to play, the trips we take around our city with no deadlines looming over us.

But I sure am getting ready for school to start.

Parenting is a pile of paradoxes, isn't it?

How to Make Summer Interesting (Or At Least Endurable): an Aside

If your kids are anything like mine, they stepped all over your last nerve for Summer Break Patience at sunrise on July 1.

It's not that Husband and I don't like having them home, like I said before. It's just that…there are so many of them.

I know. It's our own fault. I'm not complaining; in fact, I'm problem solving.

Here are some ways Husband and I have found to harness the elementals and make summer break work for us (at least for another month). Maybe they'll also work for you.

Water

If you don't have a neighborhood pool or access to one that is close, set up some sprinklers and let your kids run around in their swimsuits. This was one of my favorite things to do during the summer as a kid. Spread out a slippery tarp; just make sure there are no rocks (you don't want to know why. No, really.).

When all else fails, pretend the bath tub is their pool.

Wind

Let your kids run outside and feel the wind in their hair. Or use the wind to fly kites or paper airplanes that have to be picked up after they're flown.

If there is no wind, tell your kids to pretend *they* are the wind. Works every time. For at least thirty seconds.

Fire

It's too hot here in South Texas to harness the power of fire, but every now and then we'll use an outdoor fire pit (and stay well away from it) to roast some marshmallows or tell stories.

Just don't make those stories too scary or you'll end up with a night walker in your bed.

Earth

Spend as much time as you can outdoors, during the hours when it's not too hot (what would those hours be here in South Texas?). Take nature walks, play kickball, do some grounding walks (walking around on grass with your shoes off and your eyes closed), or lie down in the grass and imagine shapes in the clouds.

As difficult as summertime gets, I always try to remember: there will be a last summer. And I want to make sure each one between now and then counts.

Here's to summer and family togetherness.

The Traveling Personalities of Children

Every time Husband and I take the kids on a car trip, I always wonder what exactly we were thinking—kids cooped up in a car can drive you crazier (in less time) than a cat that jumps out and claws your feet every time you pass the bed (and that's saying a whole lot, in my opinion.).

We recently road-tripped (yes, that is now a verb) to see my mother, and the entire way my sons were being their typical drive-us-insane-in-the-car selves. They are very good at branding. Maybe I should take some lessons from *them*.

Time Keeper kept detailed track, as he always does, of how much later we were than what we'd originally planned. Math comes easily to this kid, so it's simple and enjoyable for him to figure out how much distance we have left to reach our destination and how long it will take us to get from where we are on the roadways to that destination. He's like a Google map —except one that does not tell you where to go but, instead, tells you how far you're off in the time realm. He likes to provide his useful updates about every five minutes. They sound something like this:

"Two hours and forty-five more minutes. We'll be there one hour and twenty-three minutes later than we said we would."

That's great. Thanks, kid.

An update like that one is about the time someone will yell that they really need to pee, a stop that will add another half hour to that running-behind time.

"Well," I'll tell Time Keeper, "now we have to stop for someone to go to the bathroom."

"Didn't he already go before we left the house?" Time Keeper will say. He's a boy after my own heart; he doesn't like stops, either, and would prefer to drive the entire way with no bathroom break—which is entirely possible, by the way. My mother only lives about three hours from us.

"Well, yes, but it's your father," I'll say.

Everyone knows that when Daddy has coffee—which he needs to stay awake at the wheel—he has to make frequent stops. This could be alleviated if I took the wheel every now and again, but I'm not a fan of driving. So I ride. And read. And work on the computer. And generally try to ignore the arguing in the backseat.

Time Keeper will usually sigh and say something like, "Well, if we stop for ten minutes that means we'll be there in two hours and fifty-five minutes." And then, during the stop, he'll keep a constant watch on the clock to ensure that Daddy does not take longer than ten minutes. He'll rejoice (loudly, I must say), if it's even fewer than ten minutes.

Delighted to Be Alive will, throughout this road trip, look out the window every other second and say, "Look at the clouds! They're so pretty. And they're moving so fast. " He keeps us remembering the reason we're traveling—to be together and to enjoy every other second.

The problem is that he has an opposite, and it's **Worst Case Scenario**. Worst Case Scenario will see the clouds outside the window and say, "It's probably going to be a tornado. Mama, is it going to be a tornado?"

"No, baby, those aren't tornado clouds." I don't tell him that I don't actually know what tornado clouds look like, because I'm not an expert, although I did obsessively watch the clouds outside my childhood home every time it stormed to make sure no tails started dangling from the clouds. I was unreasonably afraid of them—as in, I would hide in a bathtub if it rained and the wind picked up even a little bit, sure that a tornado was on its way to carry us all away to who knows where—maybe Oz, but probably not.

Matter of Fact will pipe up from the back and say, "Tornadoes don't hit out here," even though he's only five and doesn't have a clue where tornadoes do and do not hit. But he likes to be sure of everything he says. His twin brother, **The Victim**, will usually argue with him and get a big smack to the side of his jaw, and he'll wail in the loudest voice imaginable some garbled version of his brother hit him and it really hurts. Once the whole story unfolds, we discover that he also hit his brother—likely first—but The Victim never tells the whole story, only the one that resulted in *his* unfortunate smack. And then Husband and I get to play the game called "Who Did What and Why." Or, more often than not, the game of "Just Ignore Them."

Thankfully, we also have **Sleeps Anywhere**, who will get a little extended shut-eye—for the entire three hours we're traveling, even though Mayhem with Monkeys has broken loose in the interior and it's a miracle he can sleep through five minutes of it. I appreciate this kid so much, because he doesn't add words or fights or tattles or farts (that last one might be incorrect) to what's already circulating in our cabin. Sometimes Sleeps Anywhere will jolt awake, after a well-timed shriek, and all he will do is start singing to the radio.

It's not unusual that I will peer into the third row of our minivan early in the trip to see my twins with their bare feet on the windows. They will usually dispose of their shoes as soon as they climb in the car, which means the air we're breathing is delightfully clean, especially if they were wearing yesterday's socks (which happens much more often than I would like to know). Someone's second-row knees are usually pressed into my back, even though they have plenty of room. It's like riding on a school bus again.

But it's the middle of the trip when everything *really* falls apart.

Nerves are tired, rear ends are tired, parents are tired. Everything's tired in the middle of the trip.

My sons will get so bored they'll start playing in the back row. Delighted to Be Alive will dance in his seat for the sheer and utter joy of it and, in perfectly executing his stellar dance moves (which mostly consist of elbows and hands in varying positions), will probably accidentally hit The Victim, which will set off a cascade of crying, complaining, pointing fingers, retaliation, and general tattling.

They will shake the car to make it seem like it's running out of gas. During one trip, Husband and I tried for several seconds to figure out why Lucy, our Honda Odyssey who is ten years old, was shaking so badly while we drove up a hill, and we turned around to see everyone in the back executing a well coordinated shake, snickering into their hands. We were so happy about the cooperation we almost didn't tell them to stop. Would it ever happen again? Who knows?

They will slap each other in jest, which is as fun as it sounds, because someone will always get hurt and then, instead of hysterical laughter, the car fills right up to the brim with hysterical crying.

And they're so loud that sometimes Husband has to tell them (my voice is not nearly loud enough to rise above the cacophony) they need to calm down and be quieter if they want to reach the destination safely. And today. And with their mother and father subjectively sane. And what he says is true —if you've ever tried to think about how to use a blinker with screeching voices surrounding you, you know how impossible it is.

We can't forget the tattling on each other. I know I've mentioned it a few times, but I just love tattling, don't you? My sons will tattle about anything when they're in the car. It sounds like this:

The Days Are Long, But the Years Are Short

He's looking at me.
He won't stop touching me.
He took something of mine.
He's thinking about taking something of mine.
He's trying to look out my window.

It's ridiculous and maddening and sometimes I wonder why we don't just tape their mouths shut before we leave the driveway. Just kidding. That would be inhumane. But also kind of wonderful.

And, lastly, there's the trash.

The Victim and Matter of Fact like to rip up the papers they've hidden in compartments in the Way Back (my sons' term for the third row of seats in our van). Usually they are papers from church. This is especially annoying because they do not clean it up when we reach our final destination.

If we happen to stop and get them a snack because we're more than an hour past the time we said we'd arrive and everyone's hungry, The Victim and Matter of Fact will finish their snack and throw down the trash because they don't want to hold it anymore.

The state of the car when we stop anywhere is usually a cross between Appalling and Humiliating. We really do clean it out. Frequently. It's just that kids destroy it quicker than we can find the energy to care.

As we neared the end of this particular road trip, Matter of Fact said, "There's the lake!" It wasn't really the landmark he was looking for—the lake right before the road where we turn to get to my mother's house. It was some other lake. But we let them think it was the right one. It quieted them for at least the next ten minutes, until they discovered for themselves that it must have been the wrong one, because the rest of the trip was taking entirely too long.

"We're almost there," Husband said into their chorus of complaints. "Just not quite."

"Two hours and twenty-seven minutes late," said Time Keeper.

"I can't wait to see Bailey!" said Delighted to Be Alive.

"She's probably already asleep," said Worst Case Scenario. "And we missed dinner."

"It's already time for breakfast," said Matter of Fact. (No. It's not even close.)

"My legs are broken from my brother kicking me, so you'll have to help me out of the car, Daddy," said The Victim. He was still talking about the injury his brother gave him at the beginning of the trip (which was a retaliation injury, remember).

Sleeps Anywhere didn't say anything, because he was still asleep.

And, miraculously, we pulled up to my mother's house still alive.

What to Do With Kids When You Need a Little Self-Care

There are seasons of my life when I live in a perpetual state of burnout. Summertime is one of them.

It's not just because all my sons are home. It's also because it is incredibly difficult to get anything done during the summer—and, yes, that's because all my sons are home. I always begin my summers with grand plans: I'm going to finish that minimalism project for the house, I'm going to catch up on phone calls and household items that have occupied space on my to-do list for far too long, I'm going to remember to water the plants.

Even that last one is difficult to achieve with kids at home, when they're every other minute asking what's for lunch (it's still a good three hours away), how many snacks they can have (as if they don't remember), where all the cups are (check beside the sink—last I counted, there were thirty-three).

What every parent needs to combat burnout is a regular practice of self-care. Some minutes to yourself. Some time to think without interruption.

How's it possible? Well, here are some things kids can do while you're in your self-care bliss:

1. Play outside

There is no shame in locking the back door for ten minutes or so. I won't tell you how long I've locked the door before when I needed a break from all the questions my sons were asking. They're not going to die out there. Remember what we used to do when we were kids? (On second thought, maybe you should go ahead and forget what we used to do—at least I don't live near a train track, so my kids can't do what I did...)

2. Nap/quiet time

If you think nap time fades away when kids reach a certain age, have I got some good news for you: It doesn't. It just becomes a different time: Quiet time. This is a time in our house when anyone who wants to nap can nap if they so desire (usually it's one or both parents), and everyone else in the house is quiet. It might take a few days or weeks of practice to establish that quiet time, and you might have to define the word "quiet" multiple times, but after a while, they'll catch on —especially if you tie "quiet" to how much screen time they'll earn.

3. Watch a movie

When all else fails—turn on a movie. There are times when nothing else works. (Here's a bonus hack: If your kids don't get much screen time, this will actually work wonders; they're mesmerized by a screen. You can get so much more time to yourself when they're glued to the screen because they never get to watch it.)

And remember (I know I've said it before, but it's worth saying again): There will be a last summer. Make this one count.

The Astounding Number of Decisions Parents Make Daily

I recently read a story about a man who wears the exact same thing every day. He has multiple gray shirts in the exact cut and style, so when he goes into his closet, he doesn't have to think at all about what he will choose to wear. He just pulls on a pair of jeans and a shirt.

I wear pretty much the same thing every day, too—a ponytail (usually unwashed), workout pants, a sports bra and a T-shirt to which I likely donate two pounds of sweat, between walking my sons to their elementary school down the road, huffing through my interval training workout, and running a few miles.

The reason this man in the story wears the same thing without fail, he said, is because it minimizes the number of decisions he needs to make in a day. He's a business owner, and, as far as I know, doesn't have children.

I'm a business owner, too, and also the mother of six young children, which means the number of decisions I have to make in a single day runs in the thousands.

Here are just a few of them.

1. What's to eat.

I face this decision at least four times a day—breakfast, lunch, dinner, and snack. While I often make a meal plan for breakfasts and dinners and my kids have the same thing every day for lunch—peanut butter and jelly sandwich, some kind of vegetable, some kind of fruit, a homemade snack mix of nuts and dried fruit—I'm still left with the wildcard of hungry boys. There's no telling if we'll have much of anything left at the end of a day. Our refrigerator can be most closely compared to a revolving door. We're often out of everything the day before grocery day, which means my kids will likely be having for dinner that evening a piece of bread, some popcorn, and the frozen eggplant they claim they won't touch (but hunger is a strong motivator).

The hardest decision I face, however, is what Husband and I will eat. We try to avoid carbs as much as we can. Because of our schedules, we trade off on whose responsibility it is to fix breakfast and lunch for the other. When it's Husband's turn to prepare meals, he will ask me what I'd like. My standard response is: I do not have the capacity to decide what I would like to eat. Choose for me.

Because this is the point of trading off.

2. When will I [fill in the blank]?

Every parent knows the slippery nature of time. Kids are like black holes when it comes to fitting in everything we'd like to accomplish in a day. There's never enough time. When will I take a shower? When will I clean up? When will I make that call that needs to be made? When will I have some time alone?

Husband and I use Sunday mornings, on our drive to church, to address some of these decisions in a scheduling meeting. But there are many more "When will I [blank]s" than even that can solve. Things will fall through the cracks. It just comes with the territory.

3. Where to put [fill in the blank].

This blank could go on forever and ever and ever. A few of my favorites: the mountain of papers that come home from school, the toys my sons refuse to clean up, this random thing someone brought in the house, the digital devices so my kids won't find them.

Parenting can sometimes be likened to putting together a massive, never-ending puzzle.

5. Should I engage this battle?

There are many, many battles that happen every day in my house, so this question is one I often ask myself. Is this battle worth it? Will it accomplish anything? What is the cost analysis? (These are also questions you can ask when considering whether or not to enter a battle on Facebook.)

When my sons are throwing out the words, "I hate you," I engage. When they're digging a hole in the backyard with a fork they smuggled from the silverware drawer (yes, they still do this. I don't think they'll ever be too old to dig with forks.), I probably won't engage, because I know that soon enough I'll have to engage in the intervention of a pushing-down fight about who the hole actually belongs to and who is given authority to dig in it and who gets to keep the snails they uncovered down deep.

I'll have to engage in an argument about why they shouldn't be playing Power Rangers on the trampoline (one came in with a missing tooth, another with a bruised shoulder, and still another with a broken toe, so he says), so I ignore the battle about whether or not he *really* wants to wear a jacket in one thousand-degree weather.

This is not even half the decisions I have to make in a day. There are so many. And this is why, if you see me out and about, I'm likely wearing the same thing I wore yesterday and the day before that and the day before that, too. It's because I know that my decision-making capabilities will be used up on other, more important things, and that means the less important things—like what to wear—are automated. I don't even notice picking out clothes anymore; I'm on autopilot. And it's wonderful.

Except that one day, when I had a meeting and came downstairs in jeans and an off-the-shoulder top, my sons dropped their jaws and said, "Who are you? Where's Mama?"

Which makes me think I should maybe wear regular clothes more than once a blue moon.

Sometimes I Want to Change My Name

When I was a little girl, I distinctly remember my mother occasionally saying, "I sure wish I could change my name." Sometimes she said this under her breath (I was always listening, in case I missed something wonderful someone said about me). Sometimes she uttered it in our hearing, fed up with arguing or complaining or any of the other billions of things my brother and sister and I did to annoy her.

I remember this so clearly because it was a confusing thing for me; why would anyone want to change their name?

Now that I'm a mom, I completely understand and feel I must profusely apologize to my mother (I seem to do that often now, too). We are in the throes of summer at my house, and if there's anything my sons repeat more than "I'm hungry," it's my name, Mama. This simple word has a variety of tones and urgencies when my sons use it: annoyed, whiny, desperate, sad, happy, all the above at the same time.

I'm starting to get tired of my name.

They use my name to tattle on each other.

The Days Are Long, But the Years Are Short

Let me just tell you something you may or may not already know about me: I really hate tattling. I don't use the word "hate" for many things, because it's not one of my favorite words, but I will use it for tattling. I *hate* tattling.

When a son comes to me specifically to get his brother in trouble or so that he can be absolved of responsibility in some circuitous way, I feel the annoyance rise to the surface of my skin, a heat blanket in the middle of summer—which is never a good idea here in South Texas. I don't know what to say or do in response, because the steam barrels toward my mouth faster than I can close it, and I *really* don't want to say something I'll regret later.

We used to live next door to a little girl who would ring our doorbell specifically to tattle on my sons. She knew our family well enough to know when my sons weren't supposed to be doing something—like putting rocks in their mouths or tearing leaves off the trees or digging holes in the front yard (we stopped caring about the backyard). Even if she had been participating in the forbidden act right along with them, every few minutes, once she grew bored of its prohibited thrill, she would ring our doorbell to tell me exactly what they were doing, how they were doing it, and why I should care.

Sometimes a mom just wants to pretend she doesn't see, and tattling prevents this.

Husband and I have talked endlessly to our sons about when to tattle and when to let it go. Tattling, in our house, should happen if someone is about to harm themselves or someone else—or if they already have. Tattling should happen if there is some danger we need to know about. Tattling should happen if someone is destroying something important. This, in our opinion, is not tattling at all; it's informing.

Of course our sons get lost a little in the nuances. Often, they will race inside the house to be the first to tattle about a brother who smacked their shoulder, conveniently leaving out the fact that they first karate-kicked their brother in the stomach and stole his very breath (according to the extremely specific clarifier).

Tattling, in these cases, presses on my nerves so hard I want to lock the back door and pretend I don't hear their cries for help. But that would be terrible mothering, so instead I take notes and write humor essays about tattling.

They use my name to tell me something that will take them a thousand years to finish.

My eight-year-old will come to me in the early morning hours, when I'm trying to get breakfast on the table while listening to an audiobook, and tell me in graphic detail the dream he had last night. It will take him fifteen minutes to download the entire plot. The ten-year-old will ask me if I've seen a particular movie and if I answer in the negative, he will proceed to give me the longest possible summary of a movie plot you've ever heard in your life. I could have watched the entire movie, and he'd still be summing it up. The seven-year-old will provide a digest of everything his best friend said during a recent conversation, in such great detail it takes half an hour to remember and replay (the silences alone, during which he's trying to remember, are excruciating).

Words are my favorite thing ever.

They use my name to interrupt me in the middle of a conversation.

I had originally planned to use this summer to catch up on all the doctor's appointments and dental appointments we needed to schedule so my sons didn't have to miss school unnecessarily (and, also, I didn't have to miss work). I probably don't need to tell you that insurance is ridiculous in the first place and in the second place, every time I get on the phone, this exchange happens:

Son: Mama! Mama! Maaaaamaaaa!

Me: Hold on a second. [Cover phone and shoot a Look (you know the kind) at the interrupting boy] I'm on the phone. What do you need?

Son: Z's trying to see what will happen if he throws a marble into the fan.

Me: [long, long sigh]

It's impossible to have a conversation during the summertime. My kids have been taught the proper way to interrupt, but do they use it? No. Well, that's not true. They use it about .99 percent of the time.

They use my name to determine where I am in the house.

Sometimes, I have to admit, I'm hiding out in the laundry room because I've had just about enough, and the last thing I want to hear is someone calling my name to see where I am. So I usually don't answer; I can tell by the lack of urgency in their voice that this is not an emergency. I'll wait to see how long it takes them to find me, and then, when they confront me with the inevitable accusation, "I thought you had left us!" I mumble something about needing to do laundry and pull from the dryer last week's forgotten load, which I definitely do not want to fold right now.

They use my name to complain of their infinite boredom.

My sons are always complaining about being bored, despite the fact that we live in a house with more than a thousand books waiting to be read. Despite the fact that we live in a house with journals and sharpened pencils and gel pens and coloring books and drawing pads and charcoal pencils and things most kids would love to have. Despite the fact that we live in a house with a trampoline and a cul-de-sac and bikes and roller blades and wall balls and all manner of entertaining outdoor supplies.

They never like my host of responses to this confession of theirs, which generally include the words, "I really wish I could be bored. I'll trade you places."

They use my name to ask if they can watch something or if reading time is over yet or if it's tech time now. They still have six hours to go, and the whole house needs to be tidied before they're given permission to play, so…

They use my name to tattle.

Wait. Did I already say that? I forgot, because it happens so often.

"Mama, he took my crayon!"

"Mama, he threw my shoe over the back fence!"

"Mama, he's looking at me!"

Excuse me while I go pillow fight with my bed.

The Days Are Long, But the Years Are Short

I've been pondering this problem for a couple of days now, and I think I've come up with a solution. I'm going to change my name to "Dear Lord" so that every time my kids call my name to whine or complain or tattle, they'll be praying. Because that's exactly what I'm doing—praying that I make it through the rest of this summer with a shred of my sanity intact.

August

What to Do When Family Togetherness Reaches its Saturation Point

By the time August rolls around my sons have had more than enough of each other.

This summer we've gone swimming together, read together, written together, played basketball together, built LEGOs together, watched movies together, baked cakes together, laughed together, traveled together, done pretty much everything together.

So what do you do when kids have had too much togetherness and all they seem to do anymore is argue, whine, and tattle?

Here are some suggestions for separating kids while they're still together at home:

1. Stations.

Set up a reading station, an outdoor play station, a LEGO station, a coloring and drawing station, a writing station, and any other kind of station you can dream up—even a craft station if you're feeling brave. Set a timer for half an hour and let your kids rotate through the stations—with only one kid at each station at a time. Chances are, by the end of the day, they'll be ready for each other's company again—especially when it comes to outdoor play. Who wants to play a game of gaga ball on the trampoline all by his lonesome?

2. Group activities.

Get them out of the house. Go to the park, the museum, the local pool. If funds are low, get them outside and do a group interval training workout—the exercise will release some of the tension, and you'll burn a few calories, too.

3. Call in the grandparents.

There's no shame in asking for a little extra help. Some of my favorite childhood memories are of the summer weeks and weekends I spent with my grandmother, eating way too much candy, running wild through the streets of the neighborhood, staying up later than my mom ever let me stay up. Sure, it'll be fun detoxing them once they're back home (and by fun I mean the complete opposite of fun), but they'll be together in a different environment, which is often enough to get the brotherly (or sisterly) love working again, and, maybe even more importantly, you'll get a break from constantly arguing kids.

Admittedly, August is the most challenging month for goodwill and family relations. But with a little creativity and some pleas for help, you can reclaim those final summer weeks as Renewal Time, rather than Mama's Having a Breakdown Time.

The Money Personalities of Children

Husband and I are entrepreneurs who have run our own businesses since our first son was born ten years ago. Those businesses have metamorphosed over the years, but the fact remains that we are incredibly fortunate to set our own working hours, work entirely from home (if we so desire; Husband likes to get out to coffee shops, I like to play hermit), and spend as much time with our children as we want. It's true that sometimes we have to forgo things like chaperoning every field trip or volunteering for every class party or attending every single event schools host for kids nowadays, but our sons understand the demands on our time. I like to think they are secure enough in our love not to equate it with how often we can attend events that won't really matter in the grand scheme of things. We make memories at home and out in our city.

Because of our business-ownership dynamic, Husband and I often engage our children in money conversations. We talk to them about budgets, about business expenses, about how to be good stewards of what we have and earn.

I'm not sure the lessons are sticking yet.

My sons have very distinctive money personalities, and

some of them make me cringe a little—or a lot.

Take, for example, **The Spender**.

When this child has any amount of money stashed in his pocket, it will burn a hole right through that pocket. On his birthday last year, several friends gave The Spender gift cards, and during his sleepover party, I overheard him asking Husband if they could "just run to the store real quick." The store is not a quick trip; it requires a parent, a car, and a superhighway that is not a superhighway at all but is a glorified feeder road with too many lights between home and store. You think it's hard taking your kids to the store? Try taking other people's kids.

I'd much rather not.

My brother was The Spender when we were kids, so this money personality is not all that foreign to me. My son will spend his money on extra food, extra toys with which he won't play, and, if something he really wants to buy is too expensive, he will settle for something else less expensive—just so he can spend that money.

Though I would like to pretend this money personality does not exist, one of my sons is the very definition of **The Credit Man**. This kid always wants us to buy something and doesn't understand the concept of money, no matter how many times we've reviewed it with him. He can often be heard arguing with us about how we have a card in our wallet and all we have to do is use *that* to buy them some pizza for dinner tonight. We can use the card to purchase hundreds of dollars worth of gift shop merchandise at the local Witte Museum—

isn't that what it's for? We can use the card to give him everything he wants—forget the budget.

Husband and I have facilitated lesson after lesson with this kid about how money doesn't grow on trees and there is a limit to our spending and we can't always buy everything and blah blah blah but he's only five, so maybe there is still hope.

Otherwise, I'll make sure he doesn't put my name on any co-signing deals.

Thankfully, to balance out these two personalities, we also have **Mr. Content**—though, to be honest, sometimes Mr. Content can be *too* content. I'm not saying it's not great to be content, but contentment can be taken to an extreme, like anything else. This kid doesn't really care about being wealthy or poor; he's rather clueless when it comes to monetary value and the things money can buy—such as food and shelter and clothing. While a life free of caring about money and how much one has would, of course, be somewhat liberating, it doesn't bode well for the future, when he will be out of our home and on his own. This child is tempted to do whatever he wants and to ask for no money in return. No matter how many times I offer to pay him for his artwork (which is really amazing; I think he could do it professionally), he is oblivious to the importance of this negotiation. It's not that he doesn't value his artwork; he simply doesn't care about money.

Contrast him with **The Hoarder**.

This kid searches for money everywhere. He will turn our couches upside down to find an extra penny, which I hate to tell him is not worth very much anymore, because the cost of living has skyrocketed. He still collects them in a little container that he shakes all over the house, and if anyone inside these walls accidentally drops a coin—even if it's a silent drop on the carpet—this boy is faster than a vulture on roadkill. He will locate that metal carrion and add it to his collection, asking all the while what it will buy him (still not much, I'm afraid, sweet boy).

The Hoarder regularly pats our pockets to see if we have extra change, checks the washer to collect any coins that might have slipped out of laundry, and combs the car for downtown-parking quarters. He will claim them all as his own. This, as you might imagine, has sparked many a fight with The Spender, who is about the only one who comes home with change but unfortunately can't ever keep hold of it, since his pockets have gaping holes in them.

We also have **The Opportunist.** This is the kid who's always asking what he can do to earn a little extra money. Can he mow the lawn (No, you're five.)? Can he sweep the floor (last time he did it, he broke a light because he forgot he was supposed to be sweeping and turned the broom into a sword and had a self-directed sword fight with a chandelier.)? Can he clean our room (this kid has a history of coloring walls black with permanent markers, which reside in my bedroom from now until eternity.)?

I admire his entrepreneurship, but maybe we'll wait a few years to take him up on his offers.

The youngest son is much too young for a money personality, so I'm leaving him out of this assessment. But I'm hoping he'll be like me: **The Saver**. Because we need one voice of reason in the middle of all these irrational ones.

Though my sons apparently require much more guidance about money and saving and credit and budgets, I am still often delightfully impressed with their entrepreneurial spirits. They set up art stands and sell their original art; they work hard at extra chores to earn the most money possible; they produce homemade newspapers and comic books and sell them on the corner.

This summer they want to start a lawn business. The Spender has already mobilized his brothers to do all the work, while he'll control the budget.

I'm thinking this venture will demand more important conversations in our future, starting with How to Get Rid of a Boss Who Refuses to Work and Collects All the Money. But we'll take those as they come. What matters is: They're learning it's possible to build their own business and be their own bosses.

And maybe that's worth all the altercations required with The Spender and The Credit Man.

Maybe.

7 Reasons I'm Looking Forward to School Starting

Summertime is a wonderful time of connection and laughter and play. I enjoy it for almost all of the first month. By the second month, everyone is a little tired of each other, so fights show up more frequently and food gets consumed in greater quantities (I'm not sure how anyone else in the world deals with drama, but food is a comfort) and words appear in abundant supply—even when they're not really wanted.

By the third month, I can hardly keep my head on straight.

This year my sons' school started much later than it normally does, which was a gift to them and also one to me. At least when they were all in bed, sleeping, and I could venture out into their rooms and gaze at their angelic faces and remind myself they are sweet, kind, delightful kids.

When school starts this year, I'll have all but one son in elementary school. This means I'm already entertaining fantasies about a quiet house, monumental tasks accomplished in a day, and a mostly tidy space—because my youngest son is the easiest kid I've ever known in my life. I really lucked out with this one.

That's not the only reason I'm looking forward to school starting. I have, of course, a list.

1. No more fights.

I know that I will still have interactions with my sons in the morning, as they ready themselves for school. But those fights will be nothing compared to their summer fights. My sons fight so much. They fight about whose turn it is to wear the blue shirt, which amazingly fits them all (it doesn't; some just have a little trouble parting with old clothes and don't want younger brothers wearing what they remember wearing), they fight about whether or not this is *really* a blue shirt or if it's actually cerulean, they fight about who gets to pick the movie for movie night next week. They fight about which day of the week it is (and usually I can't resolve this one, because I don't even know). They fight about anything and everything, and I am so tired of mediating.

I do it, still. You don't want to know what happens when boys don't have a mediator.

2. I'll be able to have a snack myself.

If there's anything I've come to expect from summer, it's the phrase, "I'm hungry." I hear it so often that sometimes I hear it when my sons haven't even spoken. They look at me for a minute and I hear, "I'm hungry." They wander into the house and I hear, "I'm hungry." They're playing with the LEGOs in the playroom and I hear, "I'm hungry." No one's said a word. It's just the ghost of hunger, circling like a buzzard.

My sons, during the summer, eat like locusts. I'm ready to

have enough food left in the fridge to snack myself.

Once I asked my second son how he and his brothers possibly survive without twelve snacks a day when they're in school. He looked at me with a confused expression on his face and said, "I don't know. But can I have a snack now?"

Shouldn't even have said the word.

3. The back door will stay closed.

When my sons walk outside into the great outdoors, there's one thing I can always count on: The door will be left wide open for all the world (and all the flies) to enter. An air conditioner has no power over a Texas summer when a door is left open for five minutes because I was putting laundry in the dryer and didn't promptly yell, "Shut the door!"

Sometimes, because I live in a house of boys (which is synonymous with a house of smells), the flies that meander in during these wide-open-door minutes will decide to stay a while. There's plenty of food and drink and fly-heavenly lures here, not the least of which is the trash that Trash Man forgot to empty (accidentally or purposefully? He's not telling, although the LEGOs with which he chose to play instead are). Maybe they'll even reproduce and give me quite a fright when I tiptoe down the stairs to fix breakfast the next morning.

The most chanted order during the summer is, "Please close the door. Please."

4. No more paper airplanes

Two of my sons really, really enjoy making paper airplanes. They will make them out of old report cards, out of art that didn't make the Keep it Forever cut, out of bills that need to be paid. I can't believe the things they use to make paper airplanes. There are billions of them. Who has this much paper? Apparently *we* do, and all those sheets have now been repurposed into airplanes.

The other day, I found a paper airplane in the toilet, looking like it had nosedived straight into the bowl. No one fessed up, but I have my theories as to who it was.

I understand the lure of paper airplanes, but enough is enough.

5. No more swimsuits.

I'm not a big fan of swimsuits. This is mostly because I've had six kids, which changes a body, stretches it in places you didn't think could stretch. I don't like the way I look in swimsuits, but my sons are always asking, during the summer, "When are we going to the pool?" Our neighborhood has a pool right down the road; we can easily walk to it.

I most often want to answer, "Never." But it's summer. And summer is for swimming. The days after summer are for folding away that swimsuit and hoping next year's better (if you're me).

I also get a little tired of my sons begging to wear their swimsuits, which happens pretty much every day of the summer. They want to be ready in case we're going to the pool. But because they wear their swim trunks all the time, they never get washed; the pool counts as a wash, they think (at least until they watched the science video that showed them how much pee is in public pools. You know it's bad when your sons, who love swimming and would do it every day of their lives if given the choice, say, "Ew! I'm never swimming in our neighborhood pool again!"). Which means these swimsuits, by the end of the summer, are so stiff you could hold them up without a body, and they would stay molded to an imaginary one.

Gross.

6. Less laundry

When they're not wearing their swim trunks, my sons change their clothes a billion times during the summer. They don't like to be wet, unless it's because of a pool, and staying dry is impossible outside, because it's Texas, and a Texas summer averages triple digits. So my sons come in after thirty minutes, not to remain inside, but to change their sweaty shirt and head back out into the heat wave, only to return half an hour later to change into yet another shirt.

I guess now would be a good time to teach them how to do their own laundry.

7. Fewer words

My sons have so many words to say. And I'm thankful that they want to share those words with me, but mercy. Sometimes I just need a break from them. Sometimes I need to sit in the peaceful quiet and hear myself think. With six boys in the house who can talk—and the sixth one is doing a great job holding his own, vying for attention—I crave silence, which I'll get when they're all in school and the youngest is taking a nap.

Truth be told, I'm not really looking forward to school starting as much as I say I am, because then we'll be drowning in papers again. This year I'll have almost double the folders and agendas to sign, and that's to say nothing of homework.

But mostly because I'll miss my sons when they're gone all day. Contrary to what this entire essay says, I actually enjoy having them home with me because we get to do some really cool things together and share some special moments, and time is finite. I want to enjoy it as much as I can.

At least when they're not fighting. Which is about every other minute. We're due for an argument in three…two…one…

Right on time.

How to Know You're No Longer 'The Cool Parent'

He was starting middle school.

It was a brand new school, construction finished only days ago, and Husband wanted to take him to his sixth-grade orientation so they could walk through his schedule together. His schedule came in the mail, science and math and English and pre-Athletics and orchestra and critical thinking and social studies. He had a different teacher for every class, just as it had been for Husband and me.

When the invitation for this walk-through came, Husband and I disagreed momentarily about who would take him. I wanted to go. He wanted to go. Someone had to watch the other kids.

In the end, I ceded to him. He is Dad. My son is beginning a new chapter of his life. He leans more on his dad now, as it should be. It is the natural way of growing up for boys.

Husband was excited. He took his video camera with him, intent on filming a video of our son walking through all his classes. The transition from elementary to middle school is a

The Days Are Long, But the Years Are Short

big deal; we wanted to see it captured forever and ever and remember what he looked like, the way he talked, the emotions in his eyes as he asked questions and answered them himself.

Husband thought our son would be excited about this adventure, too. He was, instead, the opposite of excited. I would be willing to say he was not just indifferent, he was a touch mortified.

As Husband walked through the halls of the school, our son walked faster—to get away from him. My son had the schedule, along with all the room numbers of his classes, in his hand, so Husband pulled out the camera and started filming, thinking he'd just follow our son around, let the boy lead. Every scene only shows our son's back. Husband, a few times, called out to him, but to no avail. Our son just walked faster, speeding through the halls of an unknown school, his purple shirt fairly flapping behind him.

He left his father in the dust.

It's hard to tell if our son was embarrassed or annoyed or simply trying to act sophisticated and grown-up among all these new classmates, but what was clear in that video is that Dad is no longer cool.

This sad, humbling time eventually presents itself—sometimes with an announcement, sometimes with a silent race to get away—in every parent's life. One day you're proudly telling silly jokes that make your kids laugh hysterically and the next they're rolling their eyes at such a lame attempt at humor. One day they walk beside you on the way to school even though you're dressed in your workout clothes, after a particularly sweaty run, and the next they're saying, "I think I'll just walk myself today." One day they kiss you in the hallways, and the next they turn away before you can even hug them.

Parents can't stay cool forever. When kids are young, parents are the people who guide them. We are their heroes. They are proud to call us their own. My younger sons still wave to me in the hallways of their elementary school when I show up for a school visit, talking about poetry. My oldest son sits in his middle school library during my visit wishing my last name weren't Toalson.

As kids grow up and become their own people, they slowly step away from their parents, peeling themselves from our sides like pieces of removable velcro. So much of what used to be exciting—like the filming of a special day—isn't all that exciting anymore. Mostly, they just want to survive.

On the video Husband showed me when he got home, Husband asked our son a few questions, but every time a question hangs in the air, our son ignores him, like he doesn't belong to that weird guy with the camera. When our son walked down the hall, he kept a slow-jog pace, and when Husband called out to him, our son pretended he heard no one calling his name. If it weren't so humorous, it would be heartbreaking.

He's begun to peel away; he refuses our kisses, he doesn't want us to walk inside his school with him even if we have to deliver some papers to the office, and when we tell him "Remember who you are," he mumbles the rest of our goodbye ritual, which we all know by heart—but if we didn't, we wouldn't be able to decipher what he's saying. He used to look for us in the crowd at assemblies, but now he pretends like he doesn't even know us at orchestra concerts. When Husband goes up to the middle school with a guitar, to lead some worship for the Fellowship of Christian Athletes, our son doesn't even glance his direction. We are excommunicated from the public life of our son. We were kidding ourselves when we thought that our professions—musician, videographer, author—would elevate us into the "cool" category forevermore. That's impossible with kids.

Recently my son announced to Husband and me that he was going to start calling us Mom and Dad, instead of Mama and Daddy. Even though I think he forgets every time he has to tell us something, I don't imagine it will be that much longer before he actually does follow through on this declaration.

I could tell Husband was a little bit hurt by the way things had gone during that school walk-through. He has the video, as he intended, but the video doesn't show what he intended at all. I told him he could use it as a humor piece where he talks about the joys of being "uncool."

These things happen—eventually our children leave us behind. And sometimes that means literally.

Several of my sons still kiss and hug me at leaving time and wave to me when they're with their friends. Some of them still want Husband to visit their school as a "Watch Dog." But one day they won't.

For some it comes earlier than others.

The other day, my second-oldest son ran ahead of us on the way to his elementary school. I called out his name and he turned around and waited for me—at least it seemed so until one of his friends loped up behind me and I realized he wasn't waiting for me, he was waiting for his friend.

Well, it was only a matter of time, I guess.

The Destructive Kid: a True Tale

My five-year-old twins just started kindergarten this year. These are the kids we used to nickname The Destroyers—because we would leave the room for half a second and all the plants would die, the tables would turn over "all by themselves," the appliances would stop working, and the cat would tear up the wall and hang upside down from the ceiling just to get away from them.

Before their first day of school, I warned their teachers about their characteristic sneakiness, their opportunistic sense that kicks in the moment they notice someone's eyes are off them, and their maddening impulsivity. I chalk this up to being sons number five and six in a family of so many boys; Husband and I are often tied up with other crises (not the least of which is what's for dinner, because there's no more food in our refrigerator), which leaves plenty of opportunity for them to practice their cunning and truly perfect it.

In spite of my warnings, two days into the school year, one of my five-year-olds came home with a gaping hole in the middle of his shirt, right where his belly button was.

"What did you do to your shirt?" I said.

"Nothing," he said. (He also really likes to skirt the truth.)

"Did you cut it with scissors?"

He shrugged.

"Why did you cut your shirt with scissors?" I'm practiced in these confession interrogations; I knew I'd trip him up with this question.

"I don't know," he said, thereby admitting his guilt.

I sent an email to his teacher about the hole in his shirt, hoping she'd monitor him a little closer when it was time to use the scissors again. A week later, he returned home with a shirt that looked like a flag football belt—it was hanging in tatters down his torso.

It was not like that when he left for school.

"What did you do to your shirt?" I said. I felt like this was becoming an all-too-familiar conversation, already.

"Nothing," he said.

"It wasn't like that when you left this morning," I said, folding my arms across my chest and leveling at him my fiercest Mom Look. He knows the one. It says, *I know what happened, and your best move is to confess.* He squirmed a little but still shrugged.

"I fell into a bush," he said.

I sighed.

This particular five-year-old is the more destructive of the two. He once wrestled a bathtub, and the bathtub lost and surrendered its faucet and its drain so we had to replace both. It was astonishing, the destruction in that room. I still have nightmares about it.

The Days Are Long, But the Years Are Short

Three days after I handed over his brand-new shoes for the start of the school year, he cut the end of the shoelaces off, so now every time they come unlaced, we can't fix them. Plus, to tie the shoelaces, you need miniature hands. I told him he's getting shirts and shoes for Christmas, since there's no "replacement parts" in the budget. He cried a little, but even that didn't stop him from cutting the top of his shoe with some scissors he found on the floor while I was attempting to prevent one of his brothers from racing out the door with a knife. (You'll notice a theme here. Maybe we should just get rid of all the scissors. And sharp objects.)

The chairs out on our back deck have been stripped of almost all their wicker so they now resemble stick-furniture with wicker streams flapping in the wind. He and his twin brother tried, inefficiently, to weave them back together, which only served to make them dangerously deceptive; if you try to sit in one of them, you will fall all the way through the hole, which is much larger than it appears until your weight evenly distributes the barely-hanging-on threads. You will only bemoan the consequences of your foolish desire to sit out on the back deck, unless you're Husband with stallion thighs and can catch your fall in an impressive hover position before standing again as though nothing just happened. I'm not so graceful and, for weeks, have been carrying around a magnificent bruise I can't show anyone.

I wish I could say that all of this surprises me, but it doesn't. These two are, after all, the kids who only had a mattress in their room for a while. We eventually moved in a bed frame, no harm done (except it sags a little in the middle; they have no idea why.). We recently added a bookshelf with a few books, thinking that maybe since they were a little older and learning to read it would be safe to add something to their woefully bare room. Two days later, one of the bookshelves was hanging sideways.

These two see something and think: *I should probably destroy that*. Or maybe they don't think that at all; maybe it's just the curiosity that dooms them. Maybe they see something and think, "I wonder what would happen if…" and because they lack both the experience and the necessary self-regulatory process of talking themselves out of something stupid, they just act. And so they chew on their spoons, pull their backpack strings until they don't work anymore, move their jacket zippers up and down so rapidly and frequently that they peel away from the cloth. They dig holes in the yard big enough for you to fall in and get lost for hours (hypothetically speaking). They leave things out in the yard, like their shoes and their shirts and so many socks, with no regard for what the sun and rain and elements might do to them.

They both got some new scooters for their birthday this year, and we recently pulled them out of the box. They've been riding them nonstop for the last three days. One of the wheels is about to come off, for some unknown reason, likely just by virtue of being the property of a destructive child. Their LEGO sets are already missing pieces and pocked by teeth marks. And the book I got one of them is now falling apart, and no one can tell me why.

These two have the opposite of the Midas touch; everything they touch turns to ash. They destroy everything they can get their hands on—especially the food.

But they get what's coming to them. Every time they eat a whole three pounds of apples while a parent isn't looking, they spend the rest of the evening in the bathroom, wondering aloud why they're so sick when they didn't eat all the apples.

That's what you call natural consequences.

Children Spin the Most Incredible Stories

"I don't trust children. It isn't that they mean to lie, it's just that by omission or fancy mouth work they spin some of the most incredible stories since Jack London."

—Erma Bombeck, *I Lost Everything in the Post-Natal Depression*

After a long and nearly interminable summer, my kids started school this week, which means we shifted back into our regular routine of asking questions about their days while lingering around the dinner table. We don't ask as many questions during the summertime, because we're home with our kids all day; we know everything they do and say and argue about and sneak and try and accomplish.

One of my favorite questions that's not really a question is, "Tell me a story about your day."

Husband and I have been using this tactic for quite some time, to learn about our sons' days. "Did you have a good day?" is not an open-ended question that encourages elaboration and conversation; but asking kids to tell a story about their days is a perfect way to find out what happened that was important to them.

And boy can my sons tell stories.

My five-year-old twins started kindergarten this week, and they had quite a whopper to tell on the first day of school.

"My teacher said I could play on the computer for as much time as I wanted today," one of them blissfully informed me. "At home, I mean."

This particular boy is really good at putting words into anyone's mouth—especially if those words serve his own desires and purposes.

So this is how I imagine that conversation with his teacher went:

Him: My brothers get to have technology time. But I don't.

Teacher: That's too bad.

Him: They get to play on computers. I should get to play on computers.

Teacher: You think so, huh?

It doesn't take too many steps for this kid's mind to connect a teacher's sympathy with "I should get to play on the computer for as much time as I want."

Kids embellish their stories. My seven-year-old once told me there was a humongous spider in the house, and I was the only parent home to get rid of it (and by get rid of it, of course I mean relocate it because while every boy in my house is terrified of spiders, none of them want those spiders killed). When I spied the spider, it was barely as big as the scrap of fingernail I'd just trimmed off my pinkie, which, to me, is a scarier spider, because of how easily it can get lost among the fibers of the carpet. And, of course, it *did* get lost.

This exaggerating the size of a spider is not such an unusual thing; I do it myself. Spiders are always humongous, no matter what their size. If ever I should meet an actual humongous spider, you will have to peel me off the floor and restart my heart.

What my sons tell me sometimes rivals the Dr Seuss book *And to Think That I Saw It on Mulberry Street*, which is the tale of a kid who really wants to tell his dad an amazing story about his walk home from school, and he keeps making what he saw on Mulberry Street bigger and bigger and more and more unbelievable, until he gets home and just tells the boring truth. My kids forget the part about just telling the boring truth.

The five-year-olds told me the other day that they had been playing outside when a monstrous alien-like squirrel came up to them and started chattering like he was angry at them. And they almost understood what he was saying.

I knew they belonged to the animal kingdom. (Of course I didn't say that. What kind of mother do you think I am?)

Kids tell stories for many different reasons. They tell them to make something more exciting than it really is. This happens regularly when one of my sons is genuinely telling me about a dream he had, and then another kid breaks in and starts telling me about a dream that he didn't have, which sounds suspiciously like his brother's, only more fantastical. It's a competition of creativity. They'll start trying to trump each other in the Whose Dream Was Weirder Contest (which is *not*

The Days Are Long, But the Years Are Short

a real contest in our house), and I realize I'm probably not supposed to be listening anymore; I'm just a pawn in this game.

They also tell stories to get out of trouble. This happens quite regularly with my five-year-olds, who must think Husband and I are the densest parents in the known universe. The other day, I stepped into their bedroom, and the hook that secures their bookshelf to the wall so they can't move it or accidentally cause it to fall on top of them, was bent and nearly broken.

"What happened here?" I said, eyeing the metal bar that was not supposed to be curved. I tried bending it back and nearly broke my fingers off. It should have been impossible to bend that thing, but my twins somehow managed it, as they so often manage other impossible things, like escaping from dead bolted doors, scaling pantry shelves to grab an unauthorized and forbidden sweet snack, and twirling grass snakes by their tails without sustaining a bite.

"I think River might have tried to squeeze behind it and bent it," said one of the five-year-olds.

"Uhhhh," I said, drawing out the non-word and turning upon them a look that said, "Do you think I was born last night?" River is a tiny little kitten who weighs less than my left foot. "I don't think so, guys. What really happened?"

"I don't know," one twin said at the same time the other one said, "I think someone came in while we were sleeping, maybe through the window, and tried to take the bookshelf with them."

"And you didn't wake up?" I said, engaging the one with the fantastical answer.

They looked at me like this was the stupidest question ever.

"The window was locked," I said. "How'd they get in?"

"They had a key," one twin said. He looked extremely proud of himself.

"Windows don't have a keyhole," I said. "Try again."

This back-and-forth went on for some time before I sighed and said, "Seriously, guys. What happened? I know you're not telling the truth. I'm not an imbecile."

They looked at the ground for a minute before the one who'd started the yarn finally said, "I climbed on top of it and was sitting up there and I *guess* it started to fall over."

He *guesses* it started to fall over.

The kid was given a stern talking-to, but I'm sure he'll try it again, because it's just too fun to resist, sitting on top of a bookshelf when no one is looking. And who can be looking all the time?

My sons like to tell stories for dramatic effect, too. An obvious example of this is when they choose exaggerated verbs to embellish the telling. Their brother *slammed* them into the trampoline, they nearly *ripped* their toe off, the ground *sliced* their foot (it's just a tiny little poke). I'm proud that they're really good at using such action-filled verbs, which attests to their gifts in elaboration, but the drama could chill a little. It sometimes reminds me of the headlines people slap on their blogs and stories, to entice people to click. Click bait without the click. Sensational.

Maybe I'll hire them out as freelancers and enjoy a little return for all the stories I hear every day. It's never too early (or too late) to start saving for college.

September

The Back to School Season: a Short Examination

The madness has begun: It is back-to-school season. In my household, this season holds the yearly frenzied dash to collect all the school supplies, meet this year's new teachers, and hang up all the new clothes (so my sons don't look like bright pieces of tissue paper walking into their classrooms on the first day of school).

We've been doing this back-to-school routine for seven years now, and here are a few things I've learned:

1. Don't take your kids school shopping.

I've written an entire essay about this, so suffice it to say that if you are brave enough to take all your kids out on your state's tax-free weekend (if you have one) just to save a few dollars, you'll regret it less than thirty seconds in. I've never bought so many crayon packages in my life (someone slipped them in while I was digging around for wide-ruled spirals). Not only that, but one kid managed to come home with black and orange knee-high socks he says he'll wear with everything (and look like Halloween walking), another thought "Go pick out some new underwear" meant "Make sure to get the most expensive Marvel boxers on the shelf), and all that seemed to concern another was what he'd pack in his lunchbox this year as he merrily swung it around, obliviously knocking things off the shelves he passed, while he dreamed about pizza and hot dogs and macaroni and cheese (none of which he ever gets in his lunchbox. Sorry, kid.).

2. Have realistic expectations.

Every year I send a note to all my sons' teachers not just to "introduce" them to my sons, but also to apologize. There are multiple shortcomings for which to apologize: I'm sorry I'll stop signing folders by mid-September, I'm sorry I won't be able to keep up with anything, I'm sorry I'll miss teacher appreciation week, I'm sorry my kid probably won't do his homework, I'm sorry I'm *that* parent.

It's important to make sure everyone involved has proper expectations.

3. Remember that the last few weeks of summer vacation are the hardest.

During the last weeks of the summer, I can often be hard on myself for my lack of compassion and patience, my rising level of annoyance, and my increased eagerness for school to start. But the truth is, those weeks really *are* the hardest: Family togetherness has reached its saturation point, and we're all a little tired of each other and ready for the routine and stability that a new school year offers. I like to counter this by squeezing in one last family trip, to give us new horizons in which to fight.

The Days Are Long, But the Years Are Short

The good news is you've made it through another summer.
The bad news is you've made it through another summer.
Oh, time! Slow down!

When Back to School Success is Shattered By a Holiday

We've just gotten into the swing of the school schedule, and here comes Labor Day.

I love a holiday just as much as the next person, but when it comes so close to re-introducing my children to the concept of getting up when I tell them it's time, dressing in both pants *and* shirts (I'll pretend I don't notice the lack of underwear), and grabbing everything they need for school (someone always forgets something), Labor Day can become a bit of an annoyance.

On school days, my children must be dragged out of bed at 6 a.m., hurried down to breakfast, and ushered out the door. But on Labor Day, they were knocking on my door, begging for breakfast at 5 a.m.

Get your own breakfast.

That's what I wanted to say. But the last time I told them that, the kitchen was dusted with a fine film of raw oats, I almost fell into a milk puddle the size of Rhode Island, and a bowl of sludge—presumably oats and milk, though I can't be

The Days Are Long, But the Years Are Short

completely certain—waited by the sink, and my sons were all passed out from extreme hunger.

In other words, things didn't go so well. And I still had to fix breakfast.

So on Labor Day, I dragged myself out of bed at a ridiculous hour for a holiday, slid down the stairs, and fumbled around in the kitchen for a light switch. Once I found it, my oldest son jumped out from behind a door leading into a dark room, and I had to visit the bathroom.

How many times do I have to tell him it's not funny to scare me like that?

He laughed himself into the garage, which Husband and I converted into a playroom, while I delayed their breakfast by fifteen purposeful minutes spent examining my fingernails. Every time someone asked me why breakfast wasn't yet ready, I told them to go ask their brother. He'd already forgotten what he'd done to deserve the delay.

I love spending time with my kids, but it always feels like Labor Day comes too close to the first week of school to really enjoy the break. Who wants to start the back-to-school boot camp only to restart it two weeks later?

This year my twins are kindergarteners. They started school on a Tuesday. The next week was Labor Day. It's taken me weeks to convince them that they have to go to school on Mondays. Yes, every Monday. Except Labor Day. And Thanksgiving week. And—oh, forget it.

This whole summer I haven't been able to get any work done, and I was looking forward to getting started again—but a holiday delayed my productivity. And here's what happened during this holiday that is no longer summer but is also not quite the school year (at least not the regular one).

1. They interrupted me 12.5 billion times. My door, which I close when I am working, never quite shut. They tried to talk to me, but I have noise-canceling headphones, so they just thought I was ignoring them. Wonderful for their self-esteem, I'm sure.

I still feel guilty.

2. They were wildly wild. It seems like Labor Day always announces itself with either pouring-down rain or obscene temperatures here in South Texas; sending them outside is usually out of the question, to the detriment of all in this house.

3. The routine went down the drain. Tomorrow morning they won't know what it means to "wake up, it's time for school," and we'll start the fun all over again.

I guess it doesn't hurt to practice. Practice, after all, makes…

Well, it makes us, at the very least, good at trying. That's about all you can ask as a parent.

How to Have a Successful School Year: an Aside

I might be strange (I've never denied it), but I enjoy the start of a new school year. Even if it means getting up an hour earlier than we did during the summer (though my kids get up earlier on their days off than they do on school days), it also means we are back to our regular routines and schedules—although I have a kid who is now in middle school, and that's a brand new development of significant proportions, but please don't ask me to talk about it because I am guaranteed cry. And maybe break down completely.

With so many first days and weeks of school under my belt, I have some experience with how to be successful.

All you really need is this advice: Do everything for your kid.

I'm just kidding. When you're the parent of multiple kids, there's no way you can do everything for each one. It's a lost cause. They come home trailing art camp and martial arts and kids symphony fliers and thrust in your face the ones they didn't actually lose. They have a billion lunch containers. And the school papers—why are all these papers necessary?

The key to a successful school year is actually storage and systems. You'll want

1. A place for storing pens.

Your kids will likely steal them and you'll have to sign agendas with crayons or your kids' purple glue stick (the glue disappears, just in case you didn't know—but you can attach bits of lint to it before it dries; that's as good a signature as any), but what counts is the possibility of having a pen in that storage place. You will hope every morning. And one morning you might be surprised, which is good enough for hope.

2. A paper sorting technique.

A paper sorting factory would be nice, but at the very least you need a technique. Mine includes piles labeled: "To Sort," "To Keep," "To Recycle." Never mind that most of the papers get stuck in the pile "To Sort." They'll just wind up in the recycling basket at the end of the school year, when we have thoroughly drowned in paper. At least they have a place. (If you repeat it often enough, you begin to believe this.)

3. A place for backpacks.

They may make it to that place fifty percent of the time, but, again, at least you know there's a chance.

With these simple things in place and a hopeful attitude, I'm sure a successful school year is right around the corner. Or maybe they'll only guarantee a successful first month, but hey—at least you tried.

When Your Mother's Voice Becomes Your Own

When I was a kid, my mom used to say things that completely confounded me. My brother and sister and I would just be settling a massive half-hour argument, during which we'd periodically invoked my mother's help for things as trivial as "how you're supposed to wash dishes" and "what phase of the moon will show up tonight" and "how many pretzels are in the pantry package," and my mother would mumble, "I want to change my name." She didn't mean for us to hear, but I had exceptional hearing (confirmed by an actual doctor months after my second son was born and I experienced vertigo issues; the doctor actually said I could be asleep in my bedroom upstairs in my house and still hear a rabbit crossing the street).

Within our hearing, she would say things like, "If I hear this one more time..." (which she never finished, so I'm not sure if it was a threat or just a complaint—but judging by how often I've said it to my kids, I'd be willing to guess it was both); "I really need a vacation," which I assumed meant that all of us would be going on vacation; and "You kids are driving me up the wall," which I interpreted literally, as in we were actually driving her up a wall, which was theoretically impossible because we didn't know how to drive and we were still on the ground, both of which I would helpfully point out.

Now that I'm an adult and a parent, I completely understand the things my mother said. That's because I say them myself.

1. If all your friends did it, would you?

My sons often enjoy saying things like, "But my friends get to watch TV all the time during the summer," "But my friends get to play as many video games as they want to and don't have a limit on screen time" and "But my friends don't have to read for this long! Why do we?" In response, I like to break out the old classic, "If all your friends did it, would you?" I like to get creative, though, because it infuriates my sons.

Here are some of the "if all your friends did it" scenarios I've used.

"If all your friends wanted to jump off the high diving board into a pool someone forgot to fill with water, would you do it, too?"

"If all your friends wanted to dig a tunnel to the mantel of the earth and see if touching it would burn off their hands, would you do it, too?"

"If all your friends wanted to stand on the edge of a volcano while it was rumbling and about to explode, would you do it, too?"

"If all your friends ate dog poop, would you do it, too?"

Sometimes Husband will get in on the act, and he and I

will trade scenarios back and forth, each one more fantastical or gross than the last. We have a lot of fun with it (probably way too much), and my sons love it about as much as I did when I was a kid.

2. Can you go write it down first and then come talk to me?

Those who know me today may not believe it, but I used to be a chatterbox. I talked all the time. I would talk until I had no more words—which was never, because even back then I was a writer and had a great vocabulary and so many words from which to choose. I would tell my mom about elaborate dreams, the plans I had for my day, and everything I wanted to read in the next fifteen years.

Now my sons do the same to me, and I feel compelled to apologize to my mother every chance I get.

3. Go put on some deodorant.

I always thought this one was weird, because I couldn't smell myself.

Well, now I understand.

Puberty stinks.

4. Were you born in a barn?

My sons wait until the hottest part of the summer to forget how to close a door. It's such a complicated thing. I'm sure they're just trying to be polite to the people who might be coming out after them. There are still a few brothers left inside the house, so the last one out the door will leave it open a crack so it's easier for those remaining brothers to get out. Sometimes the person going out just needs to be out for a second, and he'll leave the door gaping wide open so as to expend the least amount of energy possible for getting back inside the door. You know it's too hot during a summer in Texas to do things like open and close a door.

5. Unfortunately, I am not made of money.

Kids have very little concept of money. Of course Husband and I will teach them and have already begun that teaching with our older sons. But for now, a significant population of my children think their father and I can just buy whatever we want whenever we want, because we happen to have a credit card. Two, actually—one for personal expenses, one for business expenses. But because we are a large family and Husband and I both chose creative careers, which means it's either feast or famine, we keep to a pretty tight budget. When we mention this fact to our sons, to help explain why we can't buy all the LEGO collections in Target today, why we can't take them out to eat every Friday, and why their friends get to see movies more often than they do, my sons' eyes glaze over. Why do you need a budget if you have a credit card?

After a number of really tight financial years, my sons at least no longer believe that money grows on trees or that I'm made of money or that I can just drop a load in the toilet and come back out with, you guessed it, money. But if I had a dollar for every time I enter a bathroom with a toilet that hasn't been flushed, well we'd be singing a different tune financially.

6. You're not hungry, you're bored.

I had just finished feeding everyone lunch when the eight-year-old asked me if he could have a snack. Uh…what? I gently reminded him that he'd seconds ago finished his lunch. I smiled a little. He tilted his head and said, "Oh, yeah," like he'd completely forgotten.

Boredom can clean out a fridge in a matter of hours in a house like mine.

7. Please take your stuff to your room.

When I was a kid, I didn't really understand why this was such a big deal to my mom. Why couldn't I leave my backpack on the floor beside the table? It was out of the way, in a corner, and I was about to pull out my homework, after I practiced my clarinet for an hour and then read for another hour. I didn't want to haul that thing all the way to my room and then haul it back out when I needed my homework. I lived in the Land of Least Effort.

Sorry, Mom. I get it now. I remind my sons multiple times a day to put their things where they belong, and those things still rarely get to their designated places, which means I rarely have the peace I really need—peace that comes from tidy, uncluttered living.

Sometimes it takes becoming a parent to understand all the strange and seemingly unexplainable things our parents did and said. We develop a greater sense of empathy for not only our parents—who we are now—but also our children—who we once were. It is a cyclical understanding that deepens our bonds through memory and simultaneously humors us in the present.

So today I want to say, Thanks for putting up with me, Mom.

And also: Paybacks really *are* torture.

The Lice Personalties of Children: What You Never Wanted to Know

It was the letter you never want to get. It came home with the second grader, in an unmarked envelope. It said, "A student in your child's classroom has lice. Please check your child's hair every day to ensure your child does not have lice, too."

Or something like that; I've forgotten the small details of the letter and only remember the large one: lice.

Such a large dread for such a small creature.

I didn't see anything for the first several days, and then… one day…what did I find, oh, my gosh what did I find?

That's right. You guessed it. A little bug waving at me.

Thus began our first mad rush to wash everything in the house, vacuum anything that couldn't be washed but might still have felt the touch of my kids' heads (which is pretty much every single thing in the house, because my sons walk on their heads, couch jump on their heads, take books off shelves with their heads), and comb out hair. Obsessively. Because, poor things, they have a mother who detests lice.

We did everything short of shaving off my sons' hair. And,

by the end of that year, this would be a serious consideration.

The second time the letter came home about another second-grade classmate, one of my sons had an infestation. I was horrified to find that they had also decided to infiltrate my hair. We did the drill again, and I stopped hugging my sons.

Not really. What kind of mom would I be if I stopped hugging my sons because of lice? I do hold my head away from them when we hug. Kidding again. I only do that to people outside our house—not so much because I'm afraid of getting lice from them but more because what if we have an undetected case and I unwittingly pass it along to them?

That year became a practice year, because every time a letter came home—which was no less than six times—I would find, a few days later, a bug in at least one of my sons' hair. It was an informative, exhausting, traumatic year.

But Husband and I are now lice pros. We don't even wait for a letter to come home anymore; we maintain. We have lice exterminatory shampoo (the healthy kind) and hair spritzer, multiple lice combs, and a black light that helps illuminate nits, if kids have them. Every week my sons groan as I comb out their hair before breakfast. We are proactive—because I don't ever want my kids to have an infestation again. It makes my skin (or my scalp) crawl just thinking about it.

Because we had so much practice eliminating lice from our lives, my sons emerged as having all sorts of different personalities during the combing-out stage.

I had the **Sensitive Kid**, who bristles every time you touch his scalp.

I only had to lift the lice comb to make him hunch up his shoulders, scrunch his face into a look that communicates severe pain, and cry out, "Ow, ow, ow!"

"I haven't even touched you yet," I said.

"But it hurts," he said.

"Well, we could shave your head," I said. "And then we wouldn't have to use the comb."

He shut up after that, for the most part. But he still hunched his shoulders and cried out every time I lifted the comb. I'm a little reluctant to admit that I had a tiny bit of fun with this after a while, but you deserve the truth.

If you ever see this kid out and about and you wonder why he flinches every time you raise your hands, it's not because he's hit at home; it's because of this year of intimate familiarity with lice. It changes a person (I know; I now have a permanent eye twitch.).

Next there is the **Curious Kid**.

This is the kid who wants to inspect everything. Every single time you swipe his hair, he wants to see if you've found any bugs or nits. You can tell him that you'll show him if or when you find something, but this means nothing to him. He wants to examine the comb himself; you might have missed something.

It took twice as long to finish combing out this kid's hair, because every time I wiped onto a paper towel the dirt and fuzz these combs (the good ones, at least) inevitably removed from his scalp, he wanted to examine what I'd found. I suspect he hid some treasure in his massive head of hair, and he was trying to make sure I hadn't yet discovered it.

I would have been glad that his curiosity distracted him from the discomfort of the combing out—except that after every swipe, as I was examining the lice comb to make sure I hadn't picked anything up, he would lean over, and little tendrils of his hair would touch mine. "Don't touch my head!" I'd yell.

He'd meekly turn around, only to do it again after the next swipe.

There is also the **Optimistic Kid**.

This is the kid who will make a comment on every swipe—always to the positive.

"I'm sure you won't find anything," he said after the first swipe.

"I don't think I even had it," he said after the second swipe.

"I don't ever touch the heads of my brothers or friends," he said after the third swipe.

"You probably don't even need to do this again." Four.

"My hair is thinner, too." Five.

"And it's shorter." Six.

"Right, Mama? I probably don't have it." Seven.

I'm sure the hopefulness was actually masking a bit of anxiety; there is a stigma that comes with lice, and this boy is getting older. He intuits these things. No one wants to be the kid with lice. During that comb-out I found one bug and two nits in his hair and I didn't have the heart to tell him. When I combed out all their hair two days later, I told him it was just part of the game; as long as any of his brothers had nits, he, too, must undergo a comb-out. He let his hopes fly high then, too. It was charming.

And then he stayed far away from his brothers for weeks.

Now we've normalized the comb-out. They don't even bother staying away from each other anymore.

There is also the **Energizer Kid**.

This is the kid who can't stop moving while you're trying to comb out his hair.

"Please stay still," I said.

"Okay," he said. He'd oblige for half a second before he'd turn around and look at one of his brothers.

"Still," I said. "That means don't move."

"Yeah," he said, his head jerking constantly.

"You're still moving."

"No I'm not."

"Yes. You are."

"I'm not!"

"It's just going to take longer if you keep moving."

"I'M NOT MOVING!"

I might have missed a few on this kid.

Then there is the **Blabber Kid**.

This is the kid who goes around telling people that he had bugs in his hair. He doesn't actually use the past tense, because he's too young to know about tenses. He will announce to the world that he has bugs. As in now, today. It could be months since we've actually combed out a bug, and he will still blab.

He's young, and I get that this whole process is probably a pretty traumatic thing. I remember having lice as a kid, and it was one of the worst weeks in my eleventh year. That could be because I was a girl and girls are much more complicated because of much more hair, but still. Bugs living in your hair is not the nicest image for a child's imagination, particularly if that imagination is a wild one.

Lastly, there is the **Opportunist Kid**.

This is the kid who masks his opportunist tendencies with helpfulness.

"We should probably order pizza tonight, shouldn't we, Mama," he said.

Yes. We should. I have no time to cook dinner because I've been combing out six boys' hair for the last two hours (what can I say? Obsession costs time.).

"We probably don't have time for chores, do we, Mama," he said.

Nope. We sure don't.

"We should watch a movie while you comb out our hair," he said.

Great idea.

All week we did what this kid said—because Mom against lice is a full-time job.

Which is why I hope they never, ever come again.

Honestly, I'd rather not know my kids' lice personalities, but, hey, life is life, right? You can't predict everything that will happen to your kids. Most people get lice at least once in their lives. We just happened to get it four times in one year. I'd say we've put in our time. Now leave us alone, lice.

Although, if you don't, prepare to meet your end at the

hands of the most persistent lice exterminator you've likely ever met.

What Can Happen While You're Listening to Emerging Readers Read

I currently have two emerging readers in my house.

It's always an exciting time when your kid is learning how to read; what better thing in the world is there than learning to read? Reading opens up so many magical doorways—to all sorts of things: knowledge, fantastical places, lands beyond the sea, even horrors.

The problem with emerging readers, however, is that emerging readers are not yet all that great at reading.

Now. I taught my oldest three sons how to read. I sat with them and pointed out letters, educated them about what sounds those letters make, and then painfully listened to all of them practice, every single day, their reading. It was magical at the time.

But after about the third kid, it gets a little old. Especially when your emerging readers are twins—and you have to listen to the same *Dan Pet the Wet Cat* story twice. The only thing worse than listening to an early reader try to sound out fifteen words in a book for half an hour is listening to two early

The Days Are Long, But the Years Are Short

readers trying to sound out fifteen words for two half-hours (which, for the mathematically disinclined, equals a WHOLE HOUR. Listening to a child read. One book. With fifteen words.).

My twins are in kindergarten, and they were the first of my children who did not know how to read before they went to school. I didn't have it in me to teach them. It was all I could do to (a) keep them alive and (b) keep them out of (most) things. These two are my most skilled opportunists. When I would sit down with one to work on his letters, the other would sneak away and empty all the eco-friendly toilet paper rolls into the downstairs toilet because he thought it was fun to watch the water overflow when he tried to flush it down.

Now that they're in school, they bring home books to read every day. I have to listen to them. I am teetering on the edge of madness—and my balance has never been that great in the first place.

There are a lot of things that can happen in my house while I'm listening to the excruciating-yet-wondrous sound of one of my twins sounding out the word "if."

Take, for example, our reading session three days ago. Someone ran out the door with five bananas in his hands (one for every finger! What an amazing feat of flexibility and acrobatics!). The only reason I noticed was because he tripped on his way out and left a smashed banana offering at the entrance to the back door (I know; it's a wonder he didn't leave five banana offerings. He's very protective of his food.). He claimed he didn't know racing out the door with five bananas was against the rules. Please.

This happened while one of my early readers tried to sound out "The End" for almost ten minutes; I refused to tell him the answer, because it's against my principles. Let them work hard for their victories. He was saying the word *while* he was sounding it out, and then his brain would tell him, in some mysterious and unexplainable way, that "end" was actually the word "ed." No, it's not "The Ed." Try again.

I wanted him to get it himself, teach him that he has agency in this reading-aloud practice. Ten minutes later, after a few hints ("What do you say when a story is over?" "What do you think the last words of a story are?" "It's not the beginning but…") he finally got it. And Banana Man was caught, though he'd already shoved the other four bananas in his mouth.

During another book that this same emerging reader brought home (the teacher didn't think one was enough, but our struggle over "The End" made it more than enough; still, I'm never one to give up too soon), my oldest son started listening to music and forgot he was grounded from devices. That ended in a half-hour fight, a massive headache, and a late dinner, which made a late bath time, which made a late bedtime, which compounded the massive headache.

Yesterday, during Emerging Reader Time, someone who was chomping on a humongous wad of gum launched himself onto my bed (Why was he there? What was he doing? These questions are woefully unanswerable), which knocked the gum right out of Lauchpad's mouth, and, after a good bit of looking (right—I don't know if I really believe he looked), he gave it up

The Days Are Long, But the Years Are Short

for lost. Turns out it stuck to the middle of my bed, and this morning I ripped off a piece of my fleshy backside while I was trying to get up (It was a big wad. Don't ask me how I didn't see it...I stumble around after 8:45 p.m. because I'm so tired. And I've already taken out my contacts.).

A few days ago another kid drew pictures on one of my brainstorm notecards, and another took a dry erase marker to a framed family picture, which he's seen his Uncle Kelly do (thanks, Uncle Kelly). He thought it would be funny to give the baby red eyes, Mama a mustache and the kind of beard that would make his father envious, and Daddy a pirate's patch and some black-spotted cheeks.

Someone else, who knows when, found my chocolate stash I was saving for my Friday Treat Night, when I was planning to reward myself for not yelling at my kids—well, now I lost the reward along with the chocolate.

Someone tied my shoelaces together and this morning, when I wanted nothing more than to go for a quick run, I was stuck trying to unknot them, a thing of tedium I'd like to avoid ever after.

Someone else dumped out all the thumbtacks—but so far no one's fessed up to that. It must have been that ghost who's come to live with us on the days no one wants to admit they did something.

Well, today's reading is finally done; it was a record: forty-five minutes each. My older sons are arguing about something, loudly, it appears—but my ears are so numb I can't hear a thing.

Rachel Toalson

Maybe there's a silver lining after all.

Welcome to The Funk: a Sarcastic Celebration

The other day, as I sat at the kitchen table with my roasted chicken and side of sautéed broccoli and spinach salad, my stomach grumbling about its empty chasm, forking my first bite into my mouth, my senses were assaulted by something rank. At first I thought it was the broccoli; it doesn't smell all that great the first time around—even less so the second time, if you know what I mean.

But the smell did not emanate from my plate.

I looked around, trying to locate the source of this stench. I have a very acute sense of smell, and sometimes it can interfere adversely with my daily life—how much I enjoy my food, how comfortable I feel in my home, whether or not I can remove my shoes.

I could see nothing obvious that might be responsible for the smell, so I carried on, took a bite. Everything tasted splendid. What was the smell, then?

And then I saw my oldest son, lounging in another kitchen chair, a foot tucked up under his thigh. His chair sits beside mine, so the socked foot pointed directly at me. It was the only logical culprit I could find for the pungent odor.

"Can you please put your foot down?" I said, and he obliged, with uncharacteristic acquiescence. The smell lessened, yes, but it did not go away.

"Maybe you could put on some shoes," I suggested.

He looked at me like he didn't quite understand what I'd said. I clarified in a halting, somewhat apologetic way: "It's just that…well…your feet smell a little funky."

Then he looked at me like I was the worst parent ever for noticing, for pointing it out, for asking him to be other than his smelly self. I'm sorry, kid.

But what I'm really sorry about is that I have discovered The Funk.

Being the mom of boys has introduced me to a lot of things—audacious pranks, the importance of double dog dares, how to do things without thinking twice. Some of these things have improved my life; some of them I'd rather not know.

I'd most definitely rather not know The Funk.

What is The Funk? Well, it's difficult to explain and much easier to experience. At the heart of it, though, The Funk boils down to this: A pervasive, disgusting, haunting smell capable of rendering every other lovely scent in a house (like, say, my delightful Love Beauty and Planet shea butter and sandalwood body lotion or my Peace & Calming essential oil constantly pouring from an overworked diffuser or even the peppermint and clove dishwashing liquid I stocked up on during the

The Days Are Long, But the Years Are Short

holidays) completely fictional.

My sons are malodorous. I don't know if there's any other way to say it or any way around it. Once they hit a particular age, the nice smells in your house do battle with the stronger, less nice smells of your sons. There is no amount of essential oil you can dump into a diffuser with obsessive regularity that will extract The Funk from the walls of your house.

You will find The Funk in a variety of places: feet, armpits, sometimes the top of a boy's head. Their shoes, especially. And socks (the crustier the funkier). My walls.

The Funk is the kind of smell that you will notice first upon walking into a house. I'm thinking about closing my own house to visitors for a while, because these smells leach into walls and carpet and mostly toilets. Until spring comes and I can open windows to let my house air out (so long as The Funk Cloud doesn't threaten the trees in our yard), I'm afraid my house is practically uninhabitable.

We do have visitors coming in January, and I'm already considering how many walls we might have to knock out and rebuild in order to rid ourselves of The Funk (but it will come back; I am not so ideally optimistic that I don't know this).

In my more recent interactions with The Funk, I've learned that there's not really much you can do about it—though I'm trying. I diffuse essential oils every morning, afternoon, and evening. I give my sons roller vials of oil and encourage them to rub it on their feet (do they? That's anyone's guess) before putting on their socks. I spray the inside of their shoes with citrus and mint hand sanitizer. But The Funk doesn't need much to grow and survive. My sons don't like to take showers, and their feet sweat so much in their shoes that every time they take them off, I don't have to work too hard to imagine the green fumes seeping out of them. Deodorant is a strong suggestion—about to become a mandatory demand—but try telling a ten-year-old he smells. He doesn't care.

The other day this ten-year-old approached his next-in-line brother and said, "I double dog dare you to smell my shoe." He then, before his brother could even respond, shoved it under Brother's nose. Brother passed out. I had to scrape him off the ground and wave smelling salts under his nose to lure him back to consciousness (and clean out his sinuses—because The Funk can get caught there semi-permanently). Poor kid. I don't think his nose will ever be the same.

When we were eating dinner later that night, he said, "I don't really want to eat this turkey burger. It smells gross." I didn't have the heart to tell him The Funk must still be in his nostrils, because the turkey burgers smelled delicious.

Well, at least he won't be able to smell his own Funk when the time comes—silver lining for him (not us).

I guess the next time they'll start caring about the way they smell is when they're romantically interested in someone else. And since I'm not ready for that, I'll just patiently plug my nose, hold my breath, and pretend my house is an aromatic paradise.

At least my imagination's getting consistent, challenging practice.

October

The Delight and Challenge of Creative Kids

I am the proud parent of creative kids.

I actually believe that all kids are creative and will remain creative so long as they are provided the space and permission to cultivate that creativity. But before you celebrate being the parent of a creative kid (which, as I said, is all of them) I must pass on the wonders that come standard in creative kids.

Things like

1. Mess

Creative kids can make masterful messes. My sons are allowed to read, write in journals, or draw in their drawing pads at night before they go to bed—anything to promote calm and relaxation. Husband and I let them have fifteen minutes of this free time before warning them they have five minutes to brush their teeth and get in bed. I am always astonished by how much mess greets us when we walk out of our room to make the bedtime announcement, which must also be accompanied by a cleanup order.

Which, of course, makes brushing teeth a much more

attractive task (who wants to clean up?). A purposeful ploy the on the part of intelligent parents? Or an accidental arrangement?

We'll never tell.

2. The products of creativity

Not only am I regularly surprised by the things my sons dream up (you should hear their tales!), but I am also regularly surprised by the materials they use for their creative projects. One day my eight-year-old brought into my room a cereal box, out of which he was carving a miniature bookshelf for his LEGO figures. I caught my seven-year-old painting a canvas with cherry juice the other day; at least he wasn't painting his clothes, which is more than I can say for my twins. My oldest son enjoys using the boxes that come with our Amazon deliveries for things like housing LEGO instructions, storing books (though he has a perfectly fine bookshelf in his room), and sliding down stairs to shrieks of delight—or is it fear? Well, natural consequences.

You might imagine that this makes throwing away or recycling anything incredibly complicated—and you would be right. Who regularly goes to bed with a piece of trash sitting on her pillow, along with a handwritten entreaty to "imagine what it could be"?

That would be me.

3. The rewards.

I have bins of drawings and crafts and paper airplanes (the really intricately designed and folded ones) in my closet that I will keep forever and ever. Kid paintings—quite good, I must say—hang on my walls. Music clings to the corners of my home and gets stuck in my head as I'm walking upstairs. Stories keep us entertained around the dinner table. I keep the written ones hidden away like my mother once did for me.

There are few things better than having creative kids show you how beautiful life can be.

How to Contain Creative Mess: an Aside

Creative kids—and, to reiterate, I believe that's all of them (have I said this enough?)—come standard with mess. And sometimes, as a person who feels anxious when clutter is anywhere close to me, the promise of mess makes me want to limit the times when and places where my children can exercise their creativity.

Fortunately, there's a solution (as there is to practically every problem). Here are some helpful ways I've found to contain the creative mess:

1. Designate a creativity cabinet.

Our creativity cabinet is my grandmother's old china cabinet; she would be thrilled to know it's used to house my children's creative supplies now.

Warning: you'll likely have to label shelves. My sons get zealous during cleanup (which is another way of saying they have exceptionally lazy clean-up habits), and the cabinet can quickly become a storehouse for junk, junk, and more junk, which will burst out of the cabinet every time the doors are opened.

Sometimes it'll even open the doors for my sons, which provides a convenient gateway to a very serious conversation (on my part) about how the ghost that lives with us obviously doesn't like clutter, and if they want to keep the ghost happy, they better clean up the mess. They've read too many *Goosebumps* stories to want an unhappy ghost around.

2. Make screen/technology time contingent on whether or not they've cleaned up.

Making screen/technology time contingent on anything ensures that anything will get done. My sons will never willingly forfeit their tech time—even if I tell them they have to clean out our cats' litter boxes first. Tech time is magical like that—and adding to the list of What They Will Do to Make Sure They Get Tech Time never grows old.

3. Buy supplies only once.

My twins are notoriously destructive. They once complained that their crayons were all broken three days after I bought them. I had seen them, before they filed their formal complaint, sitting at the table, snapping crayons in half, just for the fun of it. How unfortunate.

I told them they weren't getting more crayons for a couple of months and that's why they should take care of their stuff—it's not always replaceable. The next time I bought crayons to resupply the broken ones, they lasted six months.

Creativity is messy—but it doesn't have to break you.

The Difference Between Disney Brochures and Reality

We had just reached the The Twilight Zone Tower of Terror, with its artfully placed spider webs and the overturned furniture and eyes peering at you from the walls. My eight-year-old looked at me. He said, "I don't want to go!"

We tried to convince him that it was just a ride, that everything would be okay, that there was really no such thing as the twilight zone and ghosts, but when I saw him break out into a sweat, I knew the game was over.

Husband said, "I'll wait with him outside."

Which was exactly what *I* wanted—and I'm not being sarcastic. I would have enjoyed skipping a ride that made my stomach feel like it had climbed into my throat, but the seven-year-old had my hand in a death grip. So we followed the flow of people into a small square room, where the lights went out—and as soon as they did, my ten-year-old said, "I think I'm gonna throw up."

You have to understand that this entire week, which we'd planned without our sons knowing and which was supposed to

The Days Are Long, But the Years Are Short

be the surprise of their lives, all three of my older sons had been intermittently vomiting. We didn't know if it was from the rich food at Disney World, to which they are unaccustomed, or if it was a virus picked up on the plane ride to Florida. So it wasn't my ten-year-old saying he was afraid; he was actually about to hurl.

I felt the panic slide into my throat. They'd already closed the doors. This was *Disney World*. Everything is so clean. Tidy. Perfect. I didn't want to be the one to mess all that up! But I found an attendant and said, "My son wants to get out." She nodded politely and said as soon as the introduction show was over, he'd be able to slip out and return to the entrance, where Husband and the eight-year-old were already waiting (the seven-year-old still wanted to ride, so I was stuck).

My sick son managed to hold his vomit for the entire duration of the short film and, I'm pleased to report, made it all the way to the bathroom, for maybe the first time in his life. I wasn't even there to witness it and feel the pride of "Finally!" steal over me. I was, instead, screaming for my life on the Tower of Terror that plummeted straight down to the earth, the seven-year-old gripping the safety bar instead of my hand (Thank goodness. That bar was a little dented before it was all said and done.).

This was not an ideal moment in our carefully planned-out Disney trip. Not many of the moments were ideal, actually.

We've all seen them. The Disney World brochures with the smiling children and the happy parents. The videos that show you you'll have a magical time in that magical place. The images of families with loving expressions on each individual's face as they make memories that will last forever.

Those promotional images draw you in and convince you this is what you need to complete your family life (as they should; that's what good marketing does). But they don't really reflect reality.

Those brochures and videos and images don't show kids complaining about how much their feet hurt even though we've only just arrived at the entrance to the park. They don't show a parent retorting that we paid for these tickets and we paid a lot of money, and we're going to ride every single ride there is to ride and we're going to have fun while doing it. They don't show the kids finally getting in line for a ride and fighting with each other about who gets to ride with Mama and Daddy and who is going to sit all by his lonesome because there's an odd number of kids on this trip. They don't show how every other minute kids are talking about how hungry they are and then, once they eat, they puke it all up anyway.

In those promotional materials it never rains. Parents don't clothe their kids in Frog Suits so that no one has to walk around in soggy shorts and T-shirts all day (but the shoes are another matter entirely—and you can be sure those brochures will never tell you how awful the wet shoes of a ten-year-old smell). You'll never see kids complain about standing in the backpack-check line, where attendants rifle through books they've brought, chapstick they stuck in a pocket, and random LEGO pieces they thought they might have time to play with. You won't see parents smirking at the complaints, because they told their kids to leave the backpacks at the hotel and this could have gone much faster if the kids had listened (and the kids won't listen, the entire trip).

The materials that lure you to visit Disney for a magical trip don't feature a kid puking on his mom's shoes outside a shop in the Animal Kingdom because he shoved an ice cream sandwich in his pie hole right before riding Expedition Everest. They don't illuminate what happens when a dad sits down on the asphalt to wait for his one kid (out of three) and his wife to brave the Tower of Terror—but I can tell you. When his one kid and his wife are finished with that ride, and he stands up to greet them and ask how it went, he will leave a sweaty buttprint on the ground because it's a thousand degrees in Florida in the middle of October, and those promotional brochures and videos won't tell you this. The people in them don't even have a sheen of sweat marking their upper lip.

In those beautiful marketing materials you will never see a parent wagging a finger in a kid's face, insisting they're going to have fun because we paid a lot of money to have fun (yes, again). You'll never see parents dragging kids to Epcot on the first day, where the kids will complain the entire time about how they want to ride a roller coaster, won't you just let them ride a roller coaster, instead of showing them all these places where their mom and dad fell more in love on their honeymoon, gag, gross, let's just ride a ride? Who cares about honeymoons? You won't see images of kids waiting in line for a ride, saying, "Stop touching me." Or fighting with Pirates of the Caribbean swords they bought with their own money. Or sitting down to rest during the wait in line for a ride and then getting up again when the line moves forward an inch, even though this defeats the purpose of sitting down: doesn't it take more energy to get up and sit back down all the time?

Those promotional materials don't show parents hanging out for an hour outside a bathroom while one or more kids empties his stomach. They don't show a husband and wife arguing about what is the better method: schedule the fast passes or simply go with the flow (in an ironic trading of our personalities, it turns out Husband, the anal Disney World vacationer, was right. We got a lot more done scheduling). They don't show how one kid will need his magic band reattached every few minutes because he likes to play with it; nor will it show the kid who will remove his magic band and stash it in the pocket of the roller coaster he's riding because he's so good at following the instructions of "place all your belongings in the pocket in front of you" and forget to grab it once the thrill is over, and the exceedingly bored (and worried, on the part of the mother) faces of his family as they wait ten minutes for the same coaster to return so they can see if the magic band still waits in the pocket (it was still there! It's a miracle, because this is a magical place.).

No one will ever see, if those promotional materials have anything to say about it, the mother's eye twitching at the end of the day and the way they'll all snore in their hotel beds from both exhaustion and relief. Or the plane trip home, when turbulence makes them either fear they're about to die or feel like they're on a roller coaster again—one too many. Or the two-year-old who throws up all over his mother as soon as the plane lands in San Antonio, Texas, a little after midnight, and the way she must wash out her hair and her shirt as best she can in the airport bathroom sink—but they will all still ride home with the windows rolled down because none of them has the stomach to bear her Vomit Smell.

The one accurate thing about those promotional materials for Disney World is the bit where kids ask their parents when they're going back. Husband and I looked at each other with the same expression on our faces, upon hearing this question. Haha. Never.

Just kidding. Or are we?

A few months removed from that vacation, I can say that memory has done its work. I only look on that time with fondness and delight. I actually can't wait to go back.

And that's probably all that really matters at the end of a family vacation, no matter how many times you hear, "My feet hurt. When are we going home?"

How to Hide a Trip from Kids: a Semi-Successful Story

Husband and I recently pulled off a surprise trip to Disney World. We booked it four months in advance and then kept the secret from all our children (even the ones not going—blabbermouths abound in my family) until the day we left.

It was one of the hardest things we've done to date.

I say that not only because Disney World is a magically wonderful place for kids, but also because Disney World is where Husband and I honeymooned. We also returned there for our first anniversary and our ten-year anniversary. So it's a special place for us, and all we wanted to do in the days leading up to the trip was talk about how excited we were to go again—this time with some of our sons.

Many times we caught ourselves in the middle of a sentence, about to blow the whole secret, and our sons would look at us like we were out of our minds—which, to be fair, we generally are, so they didn't ask any questions. (Good cover, huh? Just pretend you're always out of your mind and you won't have to explain accidental almost-ruined-the-surprise slip-ups.)

Fortunately, the majority of our sons are not all that observant, nor are they usually listening to Husband or me for pleasure. Unless they hear their names mentioned, they're more typically completely oblivious to what's going on around them.

Because we pulled this off so successfully, I have some tips for how to keep surprise vacations from children:

1. Have unobservant kids.

As mentioned before, there were many times throughout the duration of this secret-keeping when Husband and I almost spilled the news—and then we'd quickly shut our mouths, even if we were in the middle of a sentence. Other times we'd accidentally leave something out on our bed—the Disney World luggage tags the folks at Disney sent us for our suitcases, the complimentary pin on a lanyard that came in another mailing, the plane tickets we printed and almost forgot to hide away in a folder.

Once, my father-in-law came over and asked when our plane was going to arrive in Florida, and Husband and I shushed him very loudly. Our sons all turned around with confused looks on their faces, likely because of the very loud shushing; not one of them asked about the plane he mentioned.

Their inability to pick up on such clues was both amazing and a bit alarming. I didn't realize my sons fail to listen to me as much as they do.

But it sure makes secret keeping that much easier.

2. Talk about the trip all you want behind the closed door of your bedroom.

After Husband and I put our sons to bed for the night, we would talk at length about the trip and the things we wanted to do while at the parks. When they were away at school and we were sitting down to our quiet breakfast, we would pull up the Disney app and plan out routes and itineraries. When they were concentrating on doing their homework or watching a movie we'd share secret smiles and winks.

3. Keep a messy room.

Husband and I try really hard to keep our room clean, but the majority of the time there's a little more mess than we want (particularly on Husband's side of the bed). Turns out this is an unexpected advantage when trying to conceal something as big as a family trip to Disney World. When our sons walked into our room without an invitation two days before the trip, while we were packing all their clothes into suitcases, they didn't think twice about the extra baggage in the room. They thought it was part of the usual mess. This allowed us to freely pack and, when we heard their footsteps heading toward our room for who knew what now, quickly close the suitcases and act as though nothing at all was out of the ordinary.

The only time they noticed anything amiss was when they went searching for socks and found their sock bin empty. But this isn't all that unusual, either; on any given day they leave their socks outside by the trampoline so they can shrivel up and crustify (I know that's not a word, but I've made it a word) in the sun. They assumed that's where all their socks were and took it upon themselves to clean up the backyard.

4. Have a cover story.

Husband and I told our older sons that we were going to take them on a Family Fun Day the Saturday after their twin brothers went to their grandparents' house, to leave for their own trip to Disney (we knew we couldn't handle six kids at Disney World, so we recruited grandparents to take the two most notorious for wandering). We told them we wanted it to be just them and the littlest one. They were all excited, asking where we were planning to go. We told them we were just going to play it by ear, and, for once, that was enough.

Did they guess it was Disney World? No way. They were completely surprised. When we woke them up early the next morning, waiting at their breakfast plates were tickets to Disney World. I think Mickey Mouse heard them shrieking all the way from San Antonio, Texas.

And, honestly, he probably heard Husband and me, too.

Co-Parenting: a Tale of Inconsistency and Chaos

One of the most frequent arguments Husband and I have is about the way we do things as parents.

Co-parenting is a wondrous thing, and I'm exceedingly grateful that I have a husband who believes that raising our sons is his responsibility, too, and I am not the only one saddled with childcare. Things too often lean in that direction in our larger society, but we both work and we both contribute to the economic well being of our family, which means we share duties in every way we can. If he needs a weekend off to go see his brother in North Carolina, I can handle the kids on my own. If I need a weekend to attend a conference in a nearby city, he can handle the kids on his own.

Sharing the load requires communication.

Husband and I talk frequently about parenting strategies and goals. We agree on all the important, underlying principles: that children are treasures; that every emotion is acceptable, though not every expression of those emotions is (namely, when they harm others); that we are teachers more than dictators; that children are people, just like us, and deserve to be treated as such.

Within those principles, however, we have our own way of doing things.

This took me a long while to admit and accept. I used to get frustrated when I would watch my sons getting away with something on Husband's shift that they would never get away with on mine (they would never even try!). My sons have said, in my hearing, "Mama's stricter than Daddy." And it's true. It's our personalities. We are different people, which means we parent differently.

One of my kids is very much an opportunist. I realize that most kids are, but this one takes the cake. I remember when he was only eighteen months old and he learned how to climb out of a playpen at his grandfather's house. My father and Husband and I sat around talking one night, and out he struts from the room where all the children were sleeping (except for him, apparently), like he owned the place. We had to put him back in that playpen six times, and then one of us had to sit in the room until he fell asleep, because he refused to stay put when someone wasn't in there watching him.

Because of this kid's tendency to try something he's forbidden to do when eyes are not on him, I watch him diligently on my shifts. But Husband? Not so much. When Husband is on duty, this kid (who shall remain nameless—but those who know my family will know exactly which twin it is) will color himself purple, eat twelve cookies that he shoved in his mouth while Husband was glancing away for a minute too long, and sneak out into the garage to unleash his tornado on the LEGOs. Husband won't even notice.

As soon as I come down the stairs, off my shift of work, he will sit docilely, along with his twin brother, both choosing to do what they're supposed to do, because they know by now that Mama sees everything and puts up with practically nothing.

Who took a bite out of this cookie and put it back on the plate? Why are there permanent markers on the table? How did your shirt get such a massive hole in it? There are so many questions that don't have answers (but which I can totally answer on my own) when I take over as Parent in Charge.

Here are some of the most obvious differences between Husband's and my parenting styles.

Me: I'm watching you. Always watching.
Him: I think I'll sit down at the piano and write a song.

As mentioned before, my sons know that they will not get away with anything while I'm on duty. They will be able to play outside or with the Hot Wheels or color and draw or do a puzzle or play Uno, as long as they ask permission. They will not be able to wander, without permission, over to the dress-up clothes and put on four costumes without a parent noticing and then go jump on the trampoline, get overheated, and strip those costumes off, where they'll be left on the ground and forgotten. They will not be able to walk by the television and "accidentally" turn it on so it's blaring a Netflix show in the background (How'd it get on "Octonauts"? They have no idea.). They will not be able to take the scissors to one another's hair.

Sometimes, when Husband hasn't noticed something that would be glaringly obvious to me—and is to him, now that he's paying attention—he will ask our sons if they thought they were going to get away with what they did. They always say yes. Yes, they did. Daddy wasn't paying attention. Husband will remind them that Mama always comes home from work—and she notices pretty much everything.

Me: Homework and reading time first.
Him: Meh. They'll get around to it.

I'm not a big fan of homework, so I can't say I require that my children do it with any regularity, but I *am* militant about reading time. I know how important reading time is for kids, so when mine come home asking, "Can we go out and play?" the most frequent answer, when I'm on duty, is, "First we have to do our reading time."

My twins, who are currently emerging readers and take three days to read one fifty-word book, will excitedly snuggle into the couch, waiting for me to sit between them so I can listen to them sound out every word on the page. By the time they're done, or the timer goes off, whichever comes first (usually it's the timer), my teeth have fallen asleep. That's to say nothing about my ears, my legs, my arms, my rump, and everything else. Someone's going to have to pull me out of this couch, because I can't do it myself. I have been turned to stone by letter sounds.

I'm looking forward to the days when I will be able to read my own book and not be required to listen to the whispered guesses of my twins as they navigate *What Peggy Did* and other equally riveting books.

The reason I have to suffer through this agonizing ritual is because Husband never requires my emerging readers to sit down and read. In fact, he doesn't require that they do their reading time at all. He sends them all outside to play, and, you know, they'll get around to homework and reading eventually. When a twin bursts through the door to announce to him that he *must* listen to them read their book, Husband waves a hand and says, "I'm sure Mama would love to hear it. She's the one who taught you to read anyway."

Guess I didn't think that one through entirely.

Me: Go outside and play while I'm cooking.

Him: You can stick around as long as you stay out of the way.

What do they do when they "stay out of the way?" Husband doesn't know. But I do. Oh, yes I do. There is evidence of it everywhere, evidence Husband does not see quite as easily as I do. Twelve fresh apple cores in the compost bin; sixteen LEGO sets transported from the play room into the living room; the cards for Go Fish, all the squares that belong to the Dr. Seuss matching game, and the pieces to Go Nuts for Donuts, spread around the table like someone thought they made an adequate dinner (but they'll complain come dinnertime, of course).

"Notice anything different about this room?" I sometimes say when I've emerged from my bedroom-cave where I do my writing in the afternoons.

Husband will look around the wrecked living room and

shrug. "Not really," he says.

I guess, in his defense, it doesn't look all that different. I can't seem to keep a tidy house anymore. In fact, I wrote a whole book about the impossibility of it. Yes. There was enough material for an entire book.

"Stay out of the way" should come with a disclaimer, like: "As long as you and everything else you get out stays out of the way, which is to say you clean up every tiny piece you touch." Not that it would help. My sons believe that getting something out uses every bit of energy they have; when they're done playing with it, they can't be bothered to put it back where it belongs. They're too tired. Have you seen how long and hard they played?!!

Me: No one opens the fridge without my knowing.
Husband: Did someone open the fridge?

If you haven't already gathered from some of these other examples, Husband does not have the most sophisticated skills of observation when it comes to our children. He often disappears into his own world—which I totally understand, as a creative person; don't get me wrong—and will be completely blindsided when someone shoves through the door to say, "My brother has an entire bag of apples outside, and he's eating all of them." How did the bag of apples get past Husband while he was cooking dinner? No one knows. Least of all Husband.

I know. It was probably during the moments when he watched a Netflix show while stirring the spaghetti. You can't really hear a refrigerator door opening when you're watching the latest episode of *The Good Doctor*, can you?

By the time dinner rolls around, my sons have, collectively, crammed sixteen bananas, three pounds of carrots, and an entire container of strawberries into their pie holes. Good luck finding something to pack in your lunches tomorrow. Grocery day's still five days away.

Me: No, you may not cannonball from the top of your father's shed to the trampoline, wearing a superhero cape.

Him: What's the worst that can happen?

I am convinced that for some (perhaps even many) males, the brain develops in such a way that it does not fully consider the consequences of particular actions. For example, when my twins received roller blades for their birthday and, despite never having roller bladed before, they strapped them on their feet and tried to walk up our stairs, their brain was clearly not scanning the multiple consequences that could smack them in the face—literally—were they to continue on their oblivious path. When two of my sons decided that one would roller blade while pulling the other down the hill on a skateboard, their brains did not consider (a) what would happen if their weights were significantly disproportionate, (b) how they would stop once they reached the bottom of the hill, and (c) how much asphalt hurts when you're headed toward disaster. When Husband once told me, as I biked through the nature trails of Huntsville State Park, rife with above-ground tree roots that sometimes made popping a wheelie feel like child's play, that I was going too slow, after which he pedaled around me, promptly hit a massive tree root, and flew over the handlebars of his bike in a graceful, slow-motion wipeout, his brain had not fully considered the consequences of what he was about to do.

So "What's the worst that can happen?" I'm almost certain I don't want to know.

These examples only scratch the surface of how different our parenting is. I realize I might sound like a militant, by-the-books, routine-obsessed mother, but I really am. Someone needs to bring order and predictability to the unruly lives of rowdy boys, and it may as well be me.

It's good for my sons to see these differences between their daddy and me. They adjust. We're consistent on what really matters—respect, honor, the way we treat other people, how many times a kid needs to brush his teeth (at least twice a day) and bathe (at least four times a week).

Coparenting is way more important than maintaining all the control. And I realized that early on—soon enough to see how much Husband adds to the life of my sons with his presence, his relaxed rules, and his play.

Thank goodness he's here.

The Sick-Day Personalities of Children

For the past several weeks, the Toalson home has been a sick house. My sons have brought home the flu (twice), a stomach bug (once), and all the residual things with which kids come standard when they're not that great at washing hands and wiping their own noses: buckets and buckets of snot, everywhere.

The good thing about all this sickness is that I've had volumes of time to sit and observe them and their sickness personalities. You gotta find humor where you can, don't you?

I am pleased to report that one of my sons is **The Sprinkler**. This is the kid who doesn't quite know how to tuck his mouth into the crook of his elbow when he needs to sneeze, so he ejects little droplets of spit and germs and who knows what else—whatever's in his mouth (sometimes it's bread, which is fun when he's standing in front of your computer trying to explain something)—all over you and whatever you're holding. Sometimes he remembers to bring the crook of his elbow to his mouth, just in delayed fashion, and splashes it with a load of snot from his sneeze. Then he'll hold the now repulsive (I know it's a value statement and an opinion at that, but I've never liked snot) elbow toward you like he expects you to utter the kind of magical spell that will make the slime disappear.

How I wish I could.

The Sprinkler also doesn't like having his nose wiped, so he'll typically walk around with way too much snot dangling from his nose, which he'll periodically suck back up into his nostrils.

Next we have **The Wailer**. No, this is not a kid who goes around searching for whales, though sometimes I wish that's what he was doing (at least that would be productive). This kid is, instead, the one who, when he has the least little hurt, like, say, his throat is a teensy bit sore (but it's not Strep, and it's not even red), he will wail for a very long time. He apparently cannot take a single dose of pain (he wails when a brother flicks his arm), and he would like everyone in our house (and our neighborhood and our city) to know that he is not feeling his best and he would like to be excused from any and all responsibilities that his mean parents might make him do on this very very sick day when his throat is so, so sore and he might even be dying (but he can still swallow his spaghetti dinner—at least two servings of it).

We get the most notes home about this son and his frequent visits to the school nurse—for a scratch sustained at recess, for a cough he developed during lunch (which was miraculously "cured" by a tasty cough drop), for the little ant bite on his pinky. I'm glad the school nurse is patient.

Then we have **Puke and Run**. This kid has so much talent. He will execute a drive-by vomit comet into the toilet, on his way out to jump on the trampoline, because when he's sick, he's still going a mile a minute. There are moments when he's perfectly healthy and perfectly boisterous that I half-jokingly think, *I would like him to be sick*, and then when he is sick and he's only slowed down marginally from his vigorous and overeager attempts to be everywhere all at once, I think it's really a miracle that sickness seems to have no dampening effect on his energy.

Puke and Run is also the kid who used to spend his nap time playing with his own poop and come inside from the backyard with his face full of dirt because he'd been snacking on it all afternoon (he still sometimes takes a little taste or four), so maybe he actually never gets sick. It's quite astonishing, because, given the same stomach virus, Husband and I can only curl up in bed and try not to die.

Puke and Run is quite the delight.

Next we have **School Skipper**. This is the kid who will wake up and ask me to check his forehead, does he have a fever, should he stay home from school because he's really not feeling well. He will tell me about the tummy ache he thinks he has (thinks? I always know when I have a tummy ache) and proceed straight to trying to convince me that he deserves to stay home from school, he's been working really hard, can't he just have a break? Does he think moms don't put together context clues? He's not sick. Get up and go to school, School

Skipper.

One of my sons is his opposite, **Mr. Tough Guy**. Mr. Tough Guy is quite the marvel. He could have two broken legs and he would still be running. He could be walking around with a ruptured appendix (something I'm actually, genuinely afraid will happen, and we'll never know it), and he would still race his brothers to school. He takes no sick days whatsoever but will bravely bear whatever ails him with hardly a mention. He never goes to the school nurse. When he's running a fever, he's extremely upset that he can't do all the things he wants to do. We have to pay the closest attention to this kid or else he'll walk out into the world with diphtheria and take out a city. Just kidding. He's vaccinated.

And lastly, we have **The Worrier**. This kid worries about every little thing—his arm was hurting a little bit today, do you think it's maybe going to fall off? His throat is a little sore—will he die? His stomach really doesn't feel well, could it be that maybe he has a parasite and it's eating him from the inside out?

I'm really sorry The Worrier got this from me. He's going to have a fun future ahead of him.

Nursing sick sons doesn't always make me sick, fortunately, but when it does, they all come to nurse me, too. Puke and Run will ask me why I'm not running around, and Mr. Tough Guy will second that question. School Skipper will tell me I should probably take the next four days off (as if a mom could do that). The Wailer will wail for me, and I'll have to point him out of the room, because my head is already aching, thank you. And The Sprinkler will likely gift me with what he does best: a sneeze shower.

And then there's The Worrier. The Worrier will ask me if I'm dying, because my lips are kind of blue and my eyes are so glassy and my voice sounds like it's made of gravel and a frog's croak, and his worries will seep into me and become my worries because, yes, maybe I am dying, maybe…

Should have locked the door behind me.

Keeping Boys Alive is a Full-Time Job

Living with sons for so long has made many things clearer —but one thing in particular: There are a thousand ways to die when you're a boy.

Husband and I used to occasionally watch a show called "1,000 Ways to Die," back before my awareness of how utterly fragile life is was fully developed—that is to say, before I had children of my own. We all feel invincible until we have children. And when those children are males, well...

Keeping boys alive is pretty much a full-time job. Here are just a few ways boys can die from their own sometimes-unfortunate curiosity, liberal experimentation, and exceedingly horrible ideas.

1. The Step Stool

A few days ago I snuck out of my bedroom, which is my home office, hoping no one would see me and bombard me with questions like, "Where's the iPad?" or "Do you have any idea what this math question is asking?" and, the most frequent one of late, "Can you please get me some toilet paper?" (Why are they always out of toilet paper? And why don't they confirm the bathroom has a roll before they sit?) I was so intent on not being seen that I almost died tripping over a step stool sitting at the top of my stairs. It wasn't just sitting at the top, either. It was pushed up against the edge of the first stair drop, as though someone wanted to see just how close that leg could be to empty space without the entire thing toppling down twenty-six stairs.

Had someone been climbing on it? I can't say. I snapped a picture and posted it on my social media page with the words, "I don't think I want to know what they were trying to do with this." And I didn't. But, of course, my mind has a will of its own and filed through all the gruesome outcomes that could have arisen from such a bad idea. Husband and I had a stern talk with our sons: Step stools must not be used near stairs.

Apparently we needed to be more inclusive.

Two days later we had to add to this limitations of the step stool, when I took a break from cooking an elaborate dinner of beans and rice, only to find my ten-year-old climbing atop the step stool, which was balanced precariously on two padded dining room chairs, so he could get the story cubes I'd put on top of the art cabinet when three of them couldn't stop fighting about whose story was more creative.

2. Races

If you're the parent of a son, you'll quickly notice that with boys, everything becomes a fierce competition. My sons race down stairs, race scooters down hills, race in bear crawl position only to stub their nose skin on cement. If they don't die they will almost assuredly break something at least once (although we've been thankfully lucky).

3. Double Dog Dares

My seven-year-old came home from second grade one day and said, "I double dog dared my friend to stand in an ant pile for a whole minute, and he dared me and we both did it." Husband and I looked at him and said, "Why would you do that?" at the same exact time. He was unable to answer the question. There is no logical reason for double dog dares. My sons dare each other to jump off high places, do dangerous bike stunts, and eat disgusting things. Every day it's a wonder they are still alive.

4. The Desire to Fly

While doing chores the other night, my seven-year-old asked me if the trash bag he was putting in our can would grant him the ability to fly if he jumped off the roof. Um...no.

You will never be able to fly without proper equipment, boys. Please don't try.

5. Homemade Obstacle Courses

My sons love making obstacle courses. They will turn things inside out, rearrange furniture, cut boxes into tunnels, and build enormous LEGO structures to create an impossible obstacle course. But the best ones are those they create outside (and I'm speaking with every ounce of sarcasm I possess), with old boards they've pulled from the fence; and crown molding stashed in their father's shed, intended for a project we planned five years ago; and a woefully unsupervised circular hand saw (we bought a lock for Husband's shed. No more unsupervised hand saws in the near future...well, not until they learn to pick the lock, that is). Not least of these perils is the grass we like to let become proper wilderness, so all manner of natural dangers hide out: insects, gigantic black squirrels, and, most recently, a rat snake.

6. The Stairs

Husband and I taught our sons to take care on stairs, especially back when they were still unsteady on their feet. They mastered stairs early and efficiently, and after that, it was much easier to just look the other way and pretend we couldn't see what they could do—or couldn't do?—on the stairs. Sometimes I look, and I see them making the stairs into a game: Roll down on your stomach, slide face first, ride boxes to the bottom (I might have been responsible for showing them this one, and I regret it every day; my back has never been the same. Turns out you don't slide down stairs so much as you bump down stairs when you're as old as I am), and jumping pogo style with whatever they can find.

Walking down stairs like a normal human being is simply not challenging enough. Even my two-year-old now jumps down the stairs. I cringe and close my eyes.

7. Beds

Because we are eight people living in a three-bedroom house, we have several bunk beds. You would be amazed at the ridiculous things boys do on bunk beds. They roll off the top, they jump on the bottom (sometimes forgetting to duck—hey, natural consequences), they tie their comforters around boards and swing like Tarzan on a Spider-Man-decorated vine. I've had to make so many rules about what is acceptable and unacceptable behavior on bunk beds that no one would even believe me if I shared them all. Don't shove your brother off, don't hang from your feet, don't pile up pillows like they'll save you from your cannonball jump off the side—and if you do, don't come crying to me when your bum breaks in half. I told you so.

8. Spiders, centipedes, and snakes—oh my!

My sons are not afraid to pick up and collect all sorts of creepy crawlies, including but not limited to spiders, centipedes, snakes, hammerhead worms, asps, earwigs, grasshoppers, and flies. I know that not all of these are dangerous, but have you seen how often boys wash their hands?

9. Anything small

This could be a piece of chalk, a button, even edamame. All of which have ended up in my kids' ears, noses, and other unmentionable places. Why do they expend energy on putting things where they shouldn't go and neglect putting things where they should go? Some things we'll never understand.

This is, by no means, an exhaustive list; my point is simply to show a small fraction of the millions of dumb ways boys can find to die. Moms of sons have their work cut out for them.

The other day my eight-year-old burst through the back door. He was laughing so hard he'd turned breathless. He told me a story about a rock catapult he and his brothers had constructed in the back yard. He said, "One of the rocks almost hit me, and I was like AHHHHHH!" He wasn't concerned at all for his well being—not for the head that could have been cracked or the legs that could have gotten crushed or the arms that might have bent in unnatural ways under the weight of a giant rock. He thought the near-death incident was the funniest thing he'd experienced that day.

Holy mother of—

As brilliant as it was, the rock catapult was confiscated. They don't need any more help in the Whoops I Almost Died Department.

November

Fostering Gratitude in the Most Annoying Places

We're coming up on the Thanksgiving season. I've had a busy stretch of book signings, panel participations, school visits and all sorts of activities that have taken me (and my family, usually) away from home. When my schedule starts filling up—no matter how productive those activities may be—I start feeling grumpy and irritated.

I recognized this week (after biting off my sons' heads continuously for the last few days) that I really needed an attitude adjustment. So I decided to write a gratitude list.

These are just a few of the items that made the list. There are, of course, many more reasons I'm grateful to be the mom of my sons.

1. The single-minded focus

More than once in the last few days my oldest son has decided he's tired of living in a disaster area, and he will make a plan to reorganize his room. By reorganize, he means tediously take every book off his two bookshelves and put them back in alphabetical order—except he consistently gets stuck on the letter D. He likes to listen to an audiobook while he attempts this daunting task, which means he can be found, at any time during the process, sitting on the floor, staring into space, imagining the story unfolding in his mind, every now and then jolting awake and remembering for a few seconds what he was doing before the story carries him away again. When it's not annoying, it's endearing.

My other sons showcase this single-minded focus when I'm trying to tell them something cool—like did they know that some beautiful butterflies eat poop?—but they're so captivated by their brother's game of Breath of the Wild that they hear absolutely nothing else.

2. Rowdiness

Anyone who lives with boys (multiple ones, at least) knows how active and noisy they are. I feel exhausted after watching their continuous activity for less than five minutes. When Husband takes them out of the house for a "quick" trip to the store (which is never quick) because one of our sons has two dollars that's burning a hole in his pocket, it's incredibly quiet at home. And then they burst through the door fighting, arguing (which is not the same thing as fighting), tattling, yelling, and/or singing (sometimes all of them at the same time), and the word "peace" becomes a memory.

Silence is overrated. Their sounds are life-giving.

3. Use It, Leave It

My sons take off their socks and shoes in the kitchen, I trip over them and sprain my ankle (because aging is a blast). They take out the Hot Wheels and build elaborate garages for them out of wooden blocks, and the garages are still there (along with every Hot Wheels car we own, stuffed inside), five days later. Lately they've been into origami, and there are so many pieces of paper in my living room we could probably build a tree (solid, not hollow). And still have some decorative swans and butterflies and flowers to spare for the papery leaves.

But hey, at least with this Use It, Leave It method everyone always has something to play with.

My sons give me plenty for which to be thankful; I'm glad they can turn my attitude around so efficiently.

Most days.

Rules You'll Need for a Daily Thankful Practice with Kids: an Aside

My sons and Husband and I try to name thankfuls every night around the dinner table, because good practice makes for marginally more grateful children. We focus even more intentionally on this practice during the month of November.

If you'd like to do thankfuls around your own dinner table, here are some standards we've had to establish with our children that you might likely need as well:

1. Share the floor.

I have some talkers who have to be reminded that there are others waiting to share their thankful, too. I'm glad my sons are so thankful for such small things (the color purple, the broccoli we're eating tonight, the roly poly he still has in his pocket), but....

Sometimes I wonder if they just like hearing themselves talk.

**2. Try not to have food in your mouth when

communicating your thankful (because see-food is definitely not my thankful).

My sons look for any excuse to talk with their mouths full, so we try to mitigate this at the very beginning.

3. No sarcasm.

There are, of course, times when a kid is not at all in the mood for thankfuls (generally this happens when one or all of them have lost tech time because they didn't bother to tidy up their messes). But we practice them anyway, and in these cases I have to remind my sons not to use sarcasm like "I'm so thankful for my parents who didn't let me have tech time today because I didn't clean up the mess my brothers made."

Gratitude is a worthwhile practice as a family. We (the parents, that is) might even find our own attitudes turned around when exposed to the innocent thankfuls of children.

Rainy Days With Children: a Humorous Timeline

Every single day my kids have a holiday off from school, it rains. I know this can't possibly be the case, but it certainly seems to be the case, because it happens so frequently and the results of a day like this are so traumatic that my brain remembers it as though it happens all the time.

Rain is good, but not for kids—at least not for mine. While I encourage them to go outside and play in the rain—so long as they stay on the concrete and out of the mud (right)—that's a pain, too. They come in dripping like a rag that hasn't been wrung out.

After many, many opportunities to test whether they understand the words, "If you play in the rain, you're responsible for cleaning up the mess you bring inside," and discovering that no, no they don't, not at all, I make them stay inside instead. Which is not a solution, because here is what they do:

1. Whine

They whine about how there's nothing to do inside the

house, like we don't have a full art cabinet that I just stocked yesterday. They don't have crayons they could take out or coloring books (even the fancy kind) or any of the other supplies they might need to have wonderful art fun. They whine about how they wish they could have tech time or watch a movie. Can they have tech time or watch a movie? When the answer is no, guess what they do in response? That's right: they whine.

They whine that there isn't anything good to eat (as though they didn't just have a snack five minutes ago). They whine that their daddy and I won't ever let them do anything fun because we're the meanest parents on the face of the planet. They whine that they don't have rain boots and if they did they could actually go play outside (it's more fun barefoot, but they don't believe me).

The last time it rained my sons raced out to jump on the trampoline in the rain, which I encouraged them wholeheartedly to do (a trampoline is pretty far from mud) because they'd spent the last 14.47 minutes whining. They came back in whining about how they kept slipping and hitting each other unintentionally.

There's just so much to whine about.

2. Beg

Next my sons move on to begging. They will beg to have something to eat, please, they're starving. I will tell them that unless they want to head to school tomorrow with empty lunch boxes, they'd better lay off the food. They will beg me to please, please, please let them get out the permanent markers because they really want to draw something, can't they draw something, why won't I let them draw something? What they fail to understand is that there are certain children in our house I simply cannot trust with permanent markers, because they will draw a lion's mane on their face and then they will have to go to their kindergarten class like that for the next five days—because permanent marker is semi-permanent on skin.

They will beg to have early tech time. They will beg to play a video game or watch a show or just surf on the computer with no clear purpose at all. They will beg to do anything but sleep.

I wish they'd beg to sleep.

3. Question

After my sons spend a good bit of time begging and they find that my answer is still no (I'm a rock of resilience—with an eye twitch), they will move on to the questioning phase of their routine. They will ask "Why" about a billion different things. Why can't they watch a movie, why can't they play a little with the computer, why can't they listen to music on the extra phone, they're just listening to music, they're not even looking at the screen, watch, they'll show me. Why can't they just have a nice mother and father who let them do whatever they want like the mothers and fathers of all their friends—of all the kids in their school. Probably even all the kids in the world!

I don't deign to answer that last question; they'll figure out soon enough that the grass is almost always greener on the other side.

4. Pontificate

This is my favorite part of the routine. My sons will pontificate about how they should have another family and what would life possibly be like with another family, why couldn't they have been born into another family. They would probably be able to have tech time all the time and eat cereal for every meal and have pizza and dessert and, yes, probably even as many snacks as they desired, and the food would never run out. They could stay up as late as they wanted, they could draw with permanent markers—on the walls, no less—they could watch as many movies as they wanted.

My sons will do this pontificating out loud, which is probably for the purpose of offending me. Instead, I just feel amused. Utopia doesn't exist, I'm sorry to say.

5. Settle

Finally, at last, just when I'm at my wits' end and I'm about to cave and actually let them do what I don't want to let them do (watch a movie, usually), my sons will settle in to read a book. But there is irony here, too. My sons will settle in with a book as soon as the sun starts shining.

And when they're done with books, you can bet it will be raining again.

The Facts of Life: Adolescent Version

As parents, we only have a certain number of years with our children, at least in such close capacity as when they're young. My newly-turned eleven-year-old has taken to reminding me of this every chance he gets. "I'll be old enough to move out in seven years," he says.

I hope he's ready.

This is the kid who would forget his shoes if I didn't warn him about how cold it is outside this winter (It's really not. But I can always convince him it is). He's the kid who will find his school agenda—three months after he lost it—in the dress-up clothes that he doesn't even play with anymore. He's the kid who will set something down in a place he deems logical and unforgettable, only to come crying when he can't remember where he set it.

So "I hope he's ready," is a legitimate, terrifyingly desperate hope.

Every parent worries, to some extent, whether their kid will be ready to strike out on their own. There are certain facts of life that must be passed along to them—because kids don't come standard knowing what seems to be the most obvious things. We have only a limited number of years to teach them everything in the world. It's daunting.

But parenting happens in stages, which means we don't have to teach them all at once. We teach them what they need to know at every stage.

Here are some of the important facts of life my sons, in this current stage of life, need to know:

Deodorant is a necessity.

Even though my oldest son is eleven, he still considers deodorant an option. He can either choose to wear it not. Most of the time he chooses the latter—either because he forgets or because he doesn't even think about the importance of applying some odor-neutralizing cream to his underarms. When he comes in from outside smelling like he's made of armpits, I have to point him in the direction of the basket upstairs, where his deodorant, which smells of tweed and spice and everything nice, patiently waits for him to apply it. It's been waiting since we bought it for him two months ago. I might have to hang up a checklist in the bathroom like I did when he was two, just to help him remember. Shower, brush teeth, floss, apply deodorant.

Flush the toilet. Your nose will thank you.

Sometimes I will wake in the middle of the night sweating, with thoughts of my sons living on their own swirling in my head. What will they do when there is no mom around to flush the toilet for them? They will one day be bachelors, living in homes or apartments without their mother. I will want to come visit them—but will there be a working toilet? I'm the kind of woman who won't use public toilets unless they're spotless; what happens when I visit my sons and find the public toilets not only *not* spotless but also filled with feces because they can't be bothered to flush?

Maybe I'm thinking too far ahead. Maybe it all evens out. I certainly hope so.

One son in particular is notoriously bad at flushing the toilet. He will download all his insides into the porcelain throne and soon thereafter skip happily out, three pounds lighter. "Did you flush the toilet?" I'll say.

His face will register that familiar stricken look. He's either thinking or reconsidering the wisdom of cutting off his download a few seconds too early. "Oh," he'll say and skip back in to complete the ritual.

Any time I pass my sons' bathroom, which I have to do every time I walk upstairs, my nose wrinkles involuntarily. Someone hasn't flushed in days. How do they ignore that stench? I know my sense of smell is highly sophisticated, but theirs must be close to nonexistent.

It's not lost on me, the irony that when they were younger, the only thing they wanted to do was flush the toilet.

Socks should be worn with shoes.

We have a shoe basket that sits right beside our front door, because I like my kids to take their shoes off when they come inside the house. The problem is, when you step into that little entryway, it smells like a combination of old, stale corn chips and sour milk. When one of my sons couldn't find his shoes one day before school and I looked in the basket where they're supposed to be and they were, miraculously, there, I picked them up and noticed that the smell—that same old, stale corn chips mixed with soured milk—grew stronger. I didn't mean to press those shoes closer to my face, but something about the mystery moved my hands for me. I think I might have ruined my nose.

After that horrifying encounter, I started to wonder why my sons' shoes smell so badly. They only wear them to school. Most of the time, when they're home, they're barefoot or they have roller blades strapped to their feet. I pondered this for some minutes before I saw one son slip on his shoes without any socks to form a necessary barrier between boy foot and sole.

We had a talk. I'm not sure it helped.

Homework is crap.

I mean—I didn't mean to say that.

(But truly. I don't make my sons do homework because I think it's ridiculous—especially in elementary school.)

Everything in moderation.

Boys have a really hard time with the concept of moderation. I'm talking about this in regard to food, video games, and fun. All of life is a balance between work and play (although, truly, to reach our fullest potential, work should be a lot like play), but my sons sometimes believe that their life should not include any work at all. That's why they complain about having to sweep the floor when it's their turn for the dreaded chore. They also complain about the dishes, the trash, wiping the table, cleaning out the cat litter, and picking up after themselves. To hear them tell it, they live in the worst house ever, and they're the only kids in the world whose parents expect them to do chores.

My sons would, instead, play video games all hours every day if Husband and I weren't notoriously thick-headed about monitoring their time on screens. And as far as food is concerned—my house's air conditioner doesn't cool it as much as my refrigerator does. It's always gaping open, a boy standing in front of it, bemoaning the opinion (not the fact) that there's nothing to eat while he's pulling out three apples, a jar of pickles, and last night's chicken.

It is, I presume, every parent's hope that their children will learn about the way life works and their place inside the world before they leave the comfort and safety of their first home, but some things we, as parents, will have to repeat over and over and over again. Like the fact that the back door should be closed as soon as someone walks through it. Like the knowledge that hair *does* need to be brushed occasionally, even when it's short. Like the revolutionary idea that if you get your clothes in the laundry hamper they will actually get washed, rather than remaining dirty on the floor for two weeks and counting.

One thing I've learned in this parenting adventure is that eventually everything works out. Kids learn what they need to learn. We teach them, we reteach them, we reteach them again and again and again, and we hope that one of those billions of lessons will stick.

And if not, well, life has a pretty good way of teaching us what we most need to learn, too.

The Day I Stopped Eating Food Where Kids Could See It

Every Friday night, Husband and I have a standing date. We order in, because it's tough to find a babysitter who's willing to watch six rowdy kids on a Friday night (not to mention expensive) and watch one of our shows (right now it's "Stranger Things") and pretend like we're at the movies but one where we can recline and snuggle and glance toward the door every so often.

The problem's not the show or whatever we happen to be watching; it holds our attention well enough. The problem is that we live with a bunch of vultures.

As soon as Husband returns from picking up whatever it is we've decided to order (if it's Husband's turn to pick, it's always the same thing: a fried chicken sandwich with gobs of avocado and Swiss cheese, some fries, fried pickles, and chips and queso. For all my rigidity, I prefer to vary it up, but we share the meal, which means we trade off on who gets to pick every week.), it begins.

My sons will press their faces to the carpet to try to see

underneath the door. They will shove their eyes through any cracks. They will knock on the door to tell us one more goodnight, and once they're inside the room, they will embark on their elaborate, creative asking routine.

First, they will ask for another kiss and hug.

Next, they will say, "Wow. That looks really good." (It doesn't matter if what they're seeing is something we've made from home, which we do twice a month or so, in order to cut down on restaurant costs. Anything not made for them looks good.)

Then they will say, "I wish I had some of that."

Then they will look at us like they're the most pitifully underfed kids on the planet.

I swear, it's just like having dogs.

Husband and I usually send them on their way with a lecture about how it's important that Mama and Daddy get this alone time together, because parents need time away from their children. Lecturing generally works wonders to clear a room of its kids. One or two might hang around for one last longing look at the food spread out on our bed.

I used to hear parents joking about how they ate food in secret, and I didn't know how true it was until I became a parent myself. Now there are things I've bought for myself that I don't even want Husband to find. I used to have a secret hiding place for my stash. There aren't many places to hide in a house that's less than two thousand square feet when it's occupied by seven other people, so invariably someone would stumble upon my stash and ask why there was a package of chocolate chips in the closet that he didn't know about. This someone was usually Husband, who is an expert at sniffing out treats. I skip the hiding places now (mostly because there aren't any undiscovered ones left) and just label my food. If the food has an "R" on it, everyone knows better than to touch it.

Maybe that sounds selfish. But living in a house of males makes you do things you never thought you'd do. If I shared my food, I'd never have any left. I can make a package of chocolate chips last two months; if I shared with Husband, it would be gone in two days. Any time I bake cookies or brownies, which isn't often anymore because of Lifestyle Change, I will set some aside for myself, because Husband likes the method known as Eat As Many As You Can As Fast As You Can, and I prefer the Savor and Have Some Self Control. We are diametrically opposed, and if I didn't set some aside, I would only get one. I want at least three.

The problem with setting something aside for myself is that when they're the only treats in the house, everyone can sense when I'm eating them.

I will be hiding out in the pantry with a gallon of milk so I can take a sip of it every time I take a bite of my saved-for-later cookie, and someone will say, "I smell cookie," and then their wonderful noses—which work on everything except boy stench—will track me into said pantry, where they will stand watching me while I eat, begging without words for a bite.

I suppose I should thank them for chipping away at the calorie count of whatever I'm eating, because by the time I give six boys a "taste—just a small one" I have the crumb of a brownie left.

The worst beggar of them all is my youngest, who is now three and is, arguably, the cutest three-year-old I remember raising. (Not really. The only three-year-olds I really remember are my twins, and that's only because their third year could be called the Worst Year in the History of Parenting). When Husband makes me a peanut butter chocolate smoothie, which is actually a healthy alternative to treats on the six days a week when we restrict our sugar intake, he will follow me around saying, "Mama, may I please have a taste of your smoothie?"

Who could ever say no to a sweet, polite three-year-old?

He works the system now.

My sons have, to date, caught me shoveling brownies in my mouth the morning after a birthday party, after I've just told them that brownies are not an appropriate breakfast. They have caught me stuffing cookie cake in my piehole before I've even had my morning green tea, and they will call me out for saying they can't have anything with sugar before noon. I have an answer for this. It's called Being an Adult. When you're an adult, I tell them, you can do anything you want. Unfortunately, I also tell them, I don't have someone like me to tell me I can't have a cookie for breakfast.

Sometimes I wish I did.

This phenomenon of eating foods in secret is not limited to just yummy treats; it happens for healthy foods, too. When my sons had spaghetti one night, Husband and I, because we try not to eat too many carbs, cooked some spaghetti squash for ourselves. My sons complained that they didn't get what we were having. We gaped at them. The last time we tried to have spaghetti squash as a family, no one ate it. We reminded them of this. They insisted that they had, actually, liked it. So we caved and gave each of them a small bite of our spaghetti squash. One wrinkled his nose while eating, another swallowed it without chewing and proclaimed it disgusting, and a third one gagged.

It's the same with our beet juice, our green smoothie, and the eggplant we roasted for dinner last night.

The other day my third son caught me in the pantry. I was stuffing salad in my trap.

"What are you doing?" he said.

"Eating some salad," I said. I had to work hard to maneuver those words around all the leaves without them falling out of my mouth.

"No fair," he said. "I want some."

He changed his tune when I decided that's what we were having for dinner.

When You Feel Like a Walking Disaster: a Personal Reflection

It's been a helluva month.

We started it with an unintentional baptism: a leak in our kitchen. One fine Saturday morning our eleven-year-old burst into our bedroom before it was time to get up, with the words every homeowner wants to hear while still in the middle of a fine dream about Disney asking her if they could option her book into a movie: "Our kitchen is flooded."

We thought he was joking, so it took Husband and me some minutes to respond. This kid likes to play practical jokes on us, and we were right in the middle of telling him that it wasn't funny to play practical jokes on parents on a Saturday morning when we were trying to sleep in and we stayed up too late the night before (and I, for one, was thinking of all the ways I would enact paybacks when he's a teenager and sleeps his Saturdays away), when the seven-year-old launched into our bed and brought with him a soggy shirt.

"Why are you all wet?" Husband said, bolting out of bed. I followed soon thereafter, when the wet boy rolled over to my side.

"There's a swimming pool in our kitchen," he said.

Husband ran faster than he's ever run, taking the stairs three at a time. I was, for the moment, a tad bit calmer and took the stairs one at a time, knowing I did not want to repeat what happened two summers ago, when I fell down the stairs and broke my foot. Husband passed me on the way down, heading back up for "all the towels we have," he said.

Husband's a pretty handy guy, but it took him an entire hour to figure out what had happened: Rats had chewed the lines between our upper and lower floors. This caused our ceiling to flood and bend and finally crack under the water load, which then caused the water to cascade onto the floor. It was a royal mess.

We used every towel and every kid in our house to mop it all up (well, every kid but one; read on), while the eleven-year-old complained on the couch that he was starving and we complained back that the least he could do was be helpful, and then he fell asleep while we and his brothers tried to fix the disaster and reclaim our Saturday.

We set out some traps for the rats and thought that was that; we'd repair the ceiling and all would be well.

Later that day the eleven-year-old came back into the kitchen from the garage, where we keep the extra refrigerator, and said, his face impassive, "There's another leak."

Again, not a good joke.

It wasn't a joke. We could hear the water splattering into the garage.

The Days Are Long, But the Years Are Short

We thought there was a rat infestation, maybe, so we called an exterminator and paid way too much money for a service that, to date, has only caught one rat (and it's been a month with no new water leaks). I feel like we probably could have done that on our own, but you know what they say about hindsight.

The following Saturday, Husband and his dad worked on repairing the ceiling. We still haven't fixed one of the water leaks, because Husband likes leaving things unfinished in our house. But nature didn't care about the unfinished disaster repair, because on Sunday, as we were driving home from church, a deer ran into the side of our Honda Odyssey.

There is something that you must understand about the deer that live in the wilderness around San Antonio, Texas. They are always on a suicide mission, seemingly. They will run into cars like they don't even see them. One morning several years ago, I drove to work in the pitch darkness, my headlights scanning the roadways. Halfway into my commute a deer dropped out of the sky and landed on my windshield. I could see its eyes as it slid all the way across the glass in slow motion and ran off like it hadn't been hurt at all. Me, well. I'd had a near heart-attack and I was eight months pregnant with twins. I thought I was about to die. Or give birth. The windshield was shattered and the whole hood of my car dented. I turned around and drove very slowly back home, thinking this deer falling from the sky was probably a sign that I shouldn't go to work that day.

So it wasn't entirely off our radar that a deer could possibly run into the side of our van as we traversed the wild roads of San Antonio. Husband had been in the middle of saying something to me, and we heard a crash like a car had hit us. We didn't know what it was until we looked behind us and saw a deer loping off. At least it wasn't a person. He left a pretty good dent in the van and took our sideview mirror, too.

On Monday a letter came home to say that one of my second grader's classmates had been sent home with lice. I hate lice. No, I loathe lice. So I checked my sons' heads obsessively.

They were clear on Monday. On Tuesday…well, not so much.

We'll just say I'm not a big fan of Mother Nature right now.

I feel like a walking disaster, like if I get too close to someone else, this Walking Disaster condition might be contagious. (That's true for the lice, but, hey, at least it's a good reason to hole up in our house and not emerge into the light of day for anyone. And to not have extra kids around.)

Last night my kids ate sugary cereal and tortilla chips for dinner. I had three brownies for breakfast.

Me: I would like to have an easy time of things for a while.

Husband: Well, at least we'll be really good at overcoming adversity.

Me: Hahahahaha hahahahaha (sob)

Sometimes getting into this disastrous place narrows our focus, makes us feel alone, makes us feel contagious, makes us feel like there will never be anything else but this, a disaster walking. I didn't go to my book club meeting the week the sky fell (or seemed to), not just because they canceled it but because I probably wouldn't have gone anyway. There's nothing I need more after a week with seven males than hanging out with four females, eating chocolate and discussing life, but during disasters, I can hardly keep my head above water, let alone breathe.

But here is one thing I've learned about these seasons: They pass. Soon we'll be back on our feet again, and then we'll be waiting for the next shoe to drop, but that's the way it is when you're the parent of young kids. I'm starting to think that life will always feel like a three-ring circus, as long as they're little. Maybe even when they're big. And I want to enjoy the circus as much as I can for as long as I can.

Rats, deer, lice, and all.

Fall and Winter Fashion Report: Kids' Edition

My sons have the worst fashion sense.

I don't say that to be mean; a couple of them actually do have a bit of a sense for what goes with what. The problem is that what they choose to wear doesn't always match the season.

Now that we're heading into the cooler months of the year here in Texas (which is to say, temperatures that hit seventy degrees instead of two hundred), my sons have taken their fall style up a notch. They like to look good and feel good during the course of their day, the majority of which they spend in school, at desks. Here are some things you'll see in my sons' (and probably many boys') wardrobes for the fall and winter season:

A pair of shorts paired with a thick winter jacket.

Even though the entire walk to school they'll complain about how cold their legs are and you'll remind them that you tried to warn them how chilly it was before they walked out the door and they argued and stubbornly refused to change out of shorts and, instead, simply grabbed their winter coat, they will fail to see reason and logic before reaching the school grounds. They wanted to look cool. Now they are, literally, cool—bordering on freezing cold.

At the door to their classrooms, they will tell me, in their typical overly optimistic way, that it will probably warm up by the end of the day, so it was good that they wore shorts, isn't it? I never have the heart to tell them that the highest it'll get today is forty-five degrees.

Maybe next time they'll actually listen when I tell them the projected temperature. But probably not.

One tennis shoe and one flip flop.

Don't ask me why my five-year-old twins like to dress their feet this way, but their little fun exercise in self-expression generally happens on the coldest days of the year. They don't do this at school, of course, because they lose points in P.E. if they're not wearing tennis shoes, and they're all about the points (I wish I'd known that the first four years of their lives)! But any time we have a Family Fun Day or an errand day or a church day, they will share a pair of flip flops and a pair of tennis shoes and be perfectly satisfied that they are ready to go. Well, okay then. Don't complain about your freezing foot; maybe if it hits frost-bite-cold, you can just swap shoes and let the frozen one warm up and the other one air out.

When I've asked them why they like to wear this strange combination, they usually tell me they can't find their shoes and decided to share what they *could* find. I'll reply, "We have plenty of places for shoes, and you probably didn't even look," to which they'll reply, "I did, too!" And we'll go round and round on the argument carousel while I stare at the other pair of tennis shoes sticking out of someone's shoe basket, eliminating the necessity of sharing. They never follow my pointed gaze; they're too busy insisting there are no other shoes in the house that fit them. And if they did follow my pointed gaze, they'd probably argue about whether or not those shoes are real because such is life with twins.

Some fleece mittens if it's lower than eighty-five degrees.

Of course every outfit needs a pair of fleece mittens, so my sons will drag out every pair we have (and usually they're not really pairs, so (a) they're mismatched and (b) you can bet there will be a fight about who owns which). What this looks like, in practice, is one boy donning a bright orange mitten on one hand and a camouflaged mitten on the other. He'll call it a pair, at least until a brother tries to rip it off his hand and claim it for his own.

I don't have time for this.

A scarf from the scarf collection, or, you know, preferably five.

It's not winter or fall outside in Texas if my sons are not able to wrap their entire upper half like a mummy. I've tried to explain to them the purpose of a scarf. Scarves are not to be used as hats. Scarves are not to be wrapped around eyes so you have to look through the crocheted spaces to walk. Scarves are not means to tie a brother's wrist to his forehead.

Do they listen? I'm sure you can guess the answer to that rhetorical question. And, if you can't guess, I'll just say that when my sons load up on scarves, someone is going to trip through the doorway and bust his nose on the side of the wall because he can't see. But with luck, his face was padded enough by five scarves to escape a bloody encounter.

Workout clothes that are warm and comfy—paired with a tie.

It's a little casual and a little formal. The one who likes to claim this style will typically choose a fluorescent green shirt paired with a bright blue tie and some red shorts. He wanted to be all the colors today and couldn't be bothered with a thing called Matching.

One of my sons will routinely take a shower and dry himself off and then put back on the same clothes he was wearing before the—it must be said—much-needed shower. "Why are you doing that?" I'll say.

"Because they're comfortable," he'll say.

"You have other sweatpants and T-shirts," I'll say. A whole closet full of them, actually. He wears nothing else. I stopped buying him jeans when he was eight—not because I wouldn't love to see him wear jeans every now and then but because when it came time to pack away his too-small clothes, every pair of jeans still had its price tag attached. No sense in buying what isn't used.

"But not like these," he'll say.

I consider it gross, but that's the thing: Boys don't understand gross. They can't smell sweaty pits, stinky feet, rancid farts—at least not like I can. My nose is assaulted on a daily basis in my home.

Part of being a mom to boys is learning to be okay with

their clothing choices and remembering that what they wear does not reflect in any way on me. If it did, I'd probably be seen as eclectic, weird, and possibly even neglectful (see shorts with winter coat and forty-degree weather).

The other day my sons streaked out the door to jump on the trampoline, even though it was fifty-four degrees outside. They only had their underwear on.

"What are you doing?" I yelled at their backs.

"Playing 'Freeze' on the trampoline," they yelled back.

"Umm…." I said. "You can't go out in just underwear."

They shrugged, looked at each other, and filed back inside, disappearing to their rooms. When they returned downstairs they were clad in the shortest shorts imaginable. I don't even know where they got these cheek-a-boos.

"That'll do," the oldest said.

I was rendered speechless.

December

How Kids Exacerbate the Holiday Drama

Every year the holidays creep and then speed and then effectively catch us off guard—how is it possible that we're already here again? It seems like just yesterday we were gearing up for all the traveling our holidays require, and now here we are, again, trying not to stress because we didn't record all the family get-togethers on the master calendar and, because of our lack of initiative, we'll probably forget about one and offend someone we don't want to offend.

Our holidays with our sons look a lot like the holiday featured in the picture book by Anna Dewdney, *Llama Llama Holiday Drama*: full of questions, destructive opportunities (when parents are distracted), and intolerable waiting.

Here's what the breakdown typically looks like in my house:

Step 1: Incessant questions

For us, this question is most frequently, "When will it be Christmas?" (By the end of their two-week holiday from school, the question will shift to, "When do we get to go to school again?" But more on that in a minute.)

The question is asked marginally less frequently now because our older sons have reached an age where they can retain dates, but our younger ones—particularly the six-year-old twins—ask the question like it's the only one worth asking (unless we're on a trip, and then the only question worth asking, in their estimation, is "How much longer until we're there?"). After the four thousandth time they ask (or maybe just the third), we stop answering and pretend like they're not talking.

Step 2: Examination of the presents

I don't usually get my sons' wrapped presents under the tree until right before Christmas, but they will eagerly await my move. And then they will shake it, examine the shape—which they should know by now doesn't indicate the size or the shape of the gifts—and make ridiculous guesses as to its contents (with the exception of LEGO boxes; they always know what those are).

No, I did not get you the latest iPhone for Christmas; *I* don't even have one of those!

Step 3: Everyone grows weary of each other

There's the drama leading up to the big day and then there's the added drama of being around each other all day every day. By the time Christmas Eve rolls around, my sons are all trying to figure out whether or not they love each other (of course they do; they've just momentarily forgotten how).

Step 4: Major meltdowns, here we come.

Husband and I have come to expect major meltdowns

from our sons as we near Christmas. It has to do with kids not sleeping as well (excitement is hard to take to bed), countdowns, and trips that disrupt our normal schedule and routines. For some reason, even though Husband and I have the most kids out of anyone in our family, we have never been able to convince our extended family to come visit us for the holidays. So we get to cram into our car (which holds exactly eight people) for five hours and listen to our kids argue about what Pikachu would eat if he were real.

I'm not bitter.

Step 5: New things to play with (finally!).

Peace is restored for a couple of hours on Christmas Day because my sons all have new toys to play with—until they look around and see that their brothers' toys are so much better. They wish they'd asked for that!

With all the drama, I still love the holiday season because it means family togetherness, a chance to take each day slowly (sometimes we have to work really hard at it), and an opportunity to press more deeply into love.

Which is worth all the drama in the world.

How to Get Kids Involved in Gift-Making: an Aside

My family and I like to make homemade gifts for the holidays, not only because we don't have a large budget for our gift-giving, but also because most of our friends and family already have everything they need or could possibly want (at least everything that's not hundreds or thousands of dollars).

And making gifts is a good way for little hands to stay busy over the holidays, even if those gifts don't end up getting wrapped and given away.

Kids are pretty generous by nature, and when it comes to making gifts for the people they love, I've found that they hardly ever disagree. But if your kids don't feel particularly inclined to practice their generosity today and would rather spend their time watching a holiday movie, here are three ways to get them involved:

1. Tell them Santa needs them.

We don't make a big deal about Santa in our home, but my kids will still do whatever they can to make sure they're on Santa's good side. Any time I mention Santa or elves, they are more than happy to participate. They will smile and put on their elf hats and work (some harder than others) at making the holidays magical for someone else.

2. Don't worry about the mess.

Yes, this suggestion is for the parents, but it's also for the kids. Kids feel much more inclined to make things when they don't have a parent hovering over them reminding them to "be careful not to let the hot glue drip onto the table," "don't wipe the paint on your shirt," "watch out—all the color pastels are rolling onto the floor!" Plan accordingly (protect the table with a tablecloth, use paint shirts or smocks, keep pastels in a pencil box), and just have fun.

3. Use some of the creations as gifts.

When kids see their creations used as actual gifts, they are so excited about the opportunity to use their talents and bring joy to others. And that means the next time you're in a pinch (like when your six-year-old comes home and tells you his teacher's birthday is tomorrow), you'll have a solution: make something—and he'll be confident enough in his work to do it.

Have fun crafting!

Travel Games that Will Keep Your Kids Occupied

We had just gotten in the car, and already Husband was wrinkling his nose. "What's that smell?" he said.

"I just took off my shoes," said the eleven-year-old.

Well, that explains it.

If you've ever had the pleasure of traveling with kids anywhere, you know that it's always a treat: You'll hear "Are we almost there?" on repeat, you'll witness things you never wanted to see or hear, and you'll be trapped in a vehicle with SBDs (Silent But Deadlies: an advanced flatulation technique).

Holiday trips can be a long and torturous adventure when you're traveling with kids, so here are some fool-proof ways to distract children from the endlessness of their journey.

1. I Spy

You know the game. It works for about ten minutes before you realize your kids keep saying they spy something that will pass in three seconds and they're the spy forever and ever.

2. What Do You See in the Clouds?

This works for about the same amount of time, until

someone gets mad or upset about the fact that they can't see the dragon someone else pointed out, because seeing shapes in clouds is nothing more than subjective, dependent on an individual's imagination. Should have thought about that before I suggested it and became responsible for the beginning of World War III.

3. Kick the Back of Mama's Seat

My twins made up this game without even trying. It was fun for them, but not for me. At the same time they were playing this game, I played the one-player Repeat Yourself game; every time they started kicking and I had to remind them that a seat is not for kicking, I won.

Mama: 1, 784, 342, 921; Twins: 0

4. How Much Longer?

Kids have no concept of time. My sons would ask Husband and me this question and all its derivatives (Are we almost there, are we close, how much farther, etc.) every other minute. So we turned it into math and then listened to them complain about how much they hate math, which was the best thing ever.

5. Count the ABC Signs

This game was the winner for our trip. My kids were occupied for hours trying to find signs that started with each consecutive letter of the alphabet, especially during the long stretches of lone wilderness between San Antonio and Edna, where my parents live. I think they played it three times.

6. Where Did I Put My Shoes?

I'm sure it's just my sons who are masters at this game, but every time we reach our destination, they bemoan the tragic circumstances in which they find themselves: they can't find their shoes. They're not so great at looking, but that's neither here nor there. We've attended two family Christmases where at least one boy didn't have any shoes, because our van has a mysterious black hole that swallows them up (they're probably lodged under a seat, along with the eleven-year-old's entire last month of homework and the lunch box that went missing a week ago, so pardon me if I don't want to go excavating). Either that or my sons misremember grabbing shoes in the first place. Hard to say which is more likely.

Fortunately, we live in Texas, which means they can walk around barefoot in December and it won't really matter. At least until climate change catches up with us—which seems to be happening. Today it reached thirty-three degrees here—an anomaly in early December.

Ideally, one or several of these games will keep your kids occupied for the duration of your travels. If not, well, let the record show: I did the best I could.

When You Give a Parent the Flu

One lovely Friday night, Husband insisted that we all pack up in the minivan and drive to the local grocery store to get our flu shots. I argued that I didn't really need the flu shot; I'm a hermit, so I probably would be safe without it. Husband looked at me like I was dashing a dream.

I've only had the flu shot once in my life—when I was pregnant with twins, which apparently reduces your body's resistance to illness so efficiently that your obstetrician practically requires you to get a flu shot. I still ended up with the flu.

So it was with great anxiety and not a little doomsday apprehension that I trudged into the store behind my children and Husband. I let them all go first, watched a couple of them brave the shot without tears and a couple of them cry. I turned my face away when it was my turn. Only a small prick and it was over.

What came after was much, much worse.

Husband (and medical experts) say there is no connection to the flu shot and coming down with the flu. In fact, they say the symptoms of the flu are much worse for those who don't get shots. All I know is the day after I got my flu shot, I felt like I was dying.

Parents don't get sick days. That's especially true in my home, where Husband and I break our days in half so that both of us can work while the kids are still (mostly) supervised (except for a few busy days when the backyard becomes our babysitter or we bribe the eleven-year-old to keep an eye on his brothers for a while. He never does a good job. We should know better by now). From 6 a.m. until 12:30 p.m., one parent takes care of the kids, and from 12:30 p.m. until 5:30 p.m., it's the other parent's turn.

You'll notice that this arrangement means one parent is always on duty with six kids. One against six is hard enough when you don't feel like you're about to die. It's practically impossible when you do.

My coming down with the flu was fortuitously aligned with my sons' holiday break from school, which meant that, rather than send them to school so I could burrow beneath a blanket and try to live while one child played docilely with his Hot Wheels, I was forced to burrow beneath a blanket and try to live with six children arguing over LEGOs, raiding the board game closet, and attempting to bounce up the stairs on a pogo stick (seriously? AGAIN?).

I didn't even have the energy to care.

Here's what a parent's sick day tends to look like:

1. Someone is going to get away with something they don't normally get away with.

My sons have very strict rules about technology time in

our house. They get to play on screens for only a small window of time during their day, and that window is limited to how much is healthy for them at their individual ages, but it is also contingent on how much they read for the day.

The day I tried to live, I didn't monitor anything. I was too busy trying to keep breathing. I'm pretty sure my sons started playing with their screens at the normal time—3 p.m.—and didn't finish until Husband came down the stairs at 5:30 p.m. I just couldn't grasp enough molecules of energy to say, "I'm pretty sure I heard your timer go off. Turn the screens off." I know it's not many words, but the flu wiped me out. It's much harder to recover, the older you get.

My sons had a ball on my watch. They generally call me the stricter parent, and it's true; I monitor everything, I enforce the rules, I uphold the consequences. I'm rigid, almost to a fault. But by the time Husband pried the devices from their hands, my sons were all slobbering out the sides of their mouths; they'd been playing long enough to become zombies. I was horrified at myself for a second or two, but that required too much energy, so instead I crawled upstairs and went to bed.

2. The house will be a wreck.

When I don't feel up to tidying the high-traffic rooms in my house, it simply won't get done. I shouldn't have to tidy the high-traffic rooms of my house; what's strewn all over the floor belongs to my sons, and on the days I'm fed up with the mess, I'll stick that stuff in a box and put it on top of the refrigerator out in our playroom and see if they notice it's missing. It takes them days to notice, which tells me all those items aren't as important as they claim. If any of my stuff was put in a box and I couldn't find it, I would notice immediately.

All that aside, on the day I courted the flu, the dishes were piled high (apparently no one knows how to do dishes unless I'm right beside them—that needs to change), the floor was littered with books and clothes and toilet paper, and someone had scattered a puzzle, a Dr. Seuss matching game, and all the paper money from Monopoly all over the table. There were apple cores and orange and banana peels on the kitchen floor, the living room floor, and the library floor. The only place they should have been was nowhere—but the only place my sons should have been eating was in the kitchen.

I thought I was living in a trash heap for a minute. Wading through all that made getting to my bed harder but also much more necessary. Mess makes me tired on a normal day. On a flu day it makes me dead. Or nearly so.

3. There will be no real dinner.

Husband and I take great care to feed our sons healthy meals. Yes, we are those parents who serve hummus and vegetables along with pita bread for a filling and satisfactory dinner. We have salad at nearly every meal. We save pizza or hot dogs or highly processed foods for one night a week, which our sons call Cheat Night.

But on the first day of the flu, I could not even manage a single care about the food my children would eat. I didn't feel like eating myself, which means my passion for food preparation (which is already pretty low) was completely nonexistent. At least when you feel like eating you'll get to partake in the fruit of your labors. When you don't feel like eating, someone else should provide dinner.

Someone else *did* provide dinner; Husband ordered some pizza the first night I was down. The next night I summoned what little energy I had and tossed a salad with a little leftover chicken—one tiny slice for each person. Day Three of the flu I broke up some celery and spooned out a little peanut butter on their plate, gave them a piece of bread and told them if they were still hungry they could eat a frozen banana from the container in the freezer (it was also a problem that I hadn't been to the grocery store and we were running out of food). Day Four I fed them dry cereal; we'd run out of milk.

The good news is my sons thought they were having a special Cheat Week instead of a Cheat Night. "What are we celebrating?" they said.

I wasn't sure how to answer that one.

4. The sick parent will likely fall asleep on the job.

This is, of course, a dangerous thing in my house. In the amount of time it will take to rouse a sick parent, my sons can do any number of things: Climb in the washing machine and commission another brother to turn it on so they can see if they'll spin inside it; kneeboard down the stairs; decide the wall needs a layer of the blue paint Husband forgot to secure a few days ago.

They will get into their leftover Halloween treats (arguably, they're hungry), leave any and all doors to the outside wide open (they need my yell to remind them to close doors, I guess), and dirty every cup in the house. It's too bad there's a Day After Sickness.

5. Someone will not get dressed.

Only one of my sons needs any amount of help getting dressed: the three-year-old. He could do it himself, really, but we're letting him be the baby for as long as we possibly can. He wore his pajamas for three days straight which also means, yes, my kids didn't take a bath for three nights straight. My kids taking a bath requires two parents on duty, and, to reiterate, I was otherwise occupied with trying not to die. As soon as Husband came downstairs for our normal family dinner, I crawled up the stairs and back into bed.

By the time I got back on my feet, the counters were so sticky there were papers plastered all over them, and we had to use a quart of alcohol to scrub them off; the kids hadn't brushed their teeth in five days; and they were eating organic whole grain graham crackers for dinner—the only food left in the pantry. Well. At least they were organic whole grain.

I'd say we made it out pretty well.

The Fart Cloud: a Smelly Tale

The other day I walked my sons up to their school in the early evening, because the second grader had a special musical program that his two older brothers had also participated in when they were his age. I always look forward to special events like this, because I love music, and seeing my children engage in playing an instrument or singing is a deep and meaningful experience for me.

As soon as we walked through the front doors of their school we saw one of my sons' kindergarten teacher. He rushed to hug her, and when I caught up with him and the brothers who had followed him in the race, I caught up with something else, too: a whiff of Fart.

You might think it's a typo that I've capitalized the word "Fart." No. That's purposeful. This Fart deserved a capital letter. You had to smell it to believe it. It was so bad I thought I was going to pass out, but I caught myself at the last minute, and only because I wasn't sure if I'd wake back up again.

It didn't take me long to realize that the whiff of Fart was us.

In fact, it's not even atypical.

When I am out and about with my sons, we move in a perpetual Fart Cloud. We take this Fart Cloud with us wherever we go. I don't know how to escape from it. I smile apologetically to every person we pass and just keep going like nothing happened. Maybe they can smell it, maybe they can't—well, I don't think anyone can *not* smell it. But I try to stay positive: Maybe they won't think it was us. Maybe they'll assume someone stepped in dog poop. Maybe they'll think it's just the way the air smells in here—what is that, Rotten Egg Mixed with (sniff) Dead Possum?

Having so much experience with this Fart Cloud—you probably don't believe me, but I'll say it again: It's everywhere we go—you'd think I'd get used to it. But I have never, in my eleven years of braving this Fart Cloud, gotten used to it. Maybe that's a good thing. It means, at least, that I still retain my sense of smell.

Or maybe that's not such a good thing.

Sometimes, when we're walking together, I imagine you can actually see this cloud if you squint really hard and look really close. It resembles a sickly brown aura that wraps around all of us, and no matter how much I wrinkle my nose and pretend I'm not a part of it, it clings to me, miles away from my sons. There is no escaping the ever-present Fart Cloud.

If you're ever standing downwind of this Fart Cloud, you better have someone strong standing beside you, because your knees are going to buckle, and your body is going to want you to fold up and go to sleep to escape from the atrocious stench of it. My problem is I wake up still in it.

My sons' gastrointestinal systems are working overtime to produce such a noxious aroma.

When I stop to consider it, I can't really say how the cloud forms so quickly and efficiently around us. It's like everyone in the assembly—two sons beside me, two flanked on the stroller, where their baby brother sits, another walking behind me, stepping on my heels every few minutes—innocently takes a turn with a fart, and they time it in such a way that it has a ripple effect. Even if we're moving, the smell is constantly there, contributing to the cloud.

I also can't say why it happens; we eat mostly fruits and vegetables and other whole foods, and every now and then my sons have something out of the ordinary (now that I think about it, it's probably more like every day when school is in session, because every time a classmate has a birthday, parents bring Krispy Kreme donuts). But they still have exceedingly smelly gas. Or maybe that's just something that comes standard with boys and I'm still living in denial. I don't know.

When we pack up in the car and I'm the last one in, I have to roll down the window and ride miles like a dog, my tongue hanging out, because the cloud trapped inside has almost suffocated me. No one else seems to notice. Maybe all their noses are broken now.

The Fart Cloud is especially embarrassing when you're walking past important people—like the school principal or your pastor or your husband's boss. But there's not really anything I can do about it. Sometimes I just want to clear the air (not literally, obviously) and say, "Hey, sorry about the smell; I've tried getting them to eat essential oils, but I don't think it'd come out the same way."

I really thought this was something special and unique about my sons—at least until we embarked on our first sleepover and had six eleven-year-old boys hanging out in our living room. By 7 p.m. I couldn't even venture downstairs for fear I'd never make it back up.

I think the Fart Cloud has now seeped into our walls.

And I have to admit: A small part of me was a little disappointed that others can produce such an efficient Fart Cloud, too.

The Hidden Time Costs of Children

When I first became a parent, I was fully prepared for the extra time it would take to care for my children, feed them, put them to sleep (even multiple times; I read a lot of parenting books), dress them, bathe them, keep them out of trouble. I knew I would take the time to teach them certain things, like stranger danger and all their ABCs and letter sounds and even, for most of them (all but the twins, actually), how to read. My time-cost analysis included the moments I would need to explain the ways of the world, to assure them of my undying love, to impress on them the need to always, always be kind.

Though I felt fully prepared for all of these time-consuming things, there was a whole world of time suck that I was nevertheless missing.

Here are some of the most frequent hijackers of my time.

1. The talking

Parents spend so much time listening to talking. I don't think anyone can actually prepare you for this. We spend so many hours of that first year with our children trying to convince them to talk—and then once they do we never have a moment of peace.

I have a son who wakes up talking and goes to bed talking. He talks so much that his brothers get mad and tell him he's hogging all the words—and all the time we spend at dinner discussing everyone's days. By the time he's finished talking, everyone's done with their after-dinner chores. And he's been interrupted a billion times, to get kids back on task, but he doesn't mind. If Husband or I tell him now's not a great time to talk, he will either walk away from us talking to the air (that's if we're lucky) or bulldoze right through our protests. Sometimes I will sneak by his room and hear him talking, expecting to see one of his brothers inside. No one's with him; he's just talking.

How many words is a parent expected to hear in the course of a day? Sorry. I cannot even make an educated estimate. All I know is that by the end of the day, I would like to ban words from the face of the earth, though I know I would miss them—at least the writing and reading kind.

2. The constant questions

Kids ask so many questions. I knew this about them already; I babysat for a while as a teenager (not for long, though; I found I didn't really like keeping other people's kids) and was a substitute teacher during college (this also didn't last long), but I never knew the massive volume of space and time those questions required.

When you have multiple children, those questions are compounded. While one child may ask three hundred questions in a day, two children will ask six hundred, three children nine hundred, and on and on it goes. How many questions do six children ask? At least a million.

Kids ask things like, "Why is my leg attached to my hip?" "What shade of blue is the sky?" "How are tiger sharks different from regular sharks?" I don't mind these questions so much, because the answers are interesting; they make me think. Sometimes they're quite delightful, if they aren't asked too liberally. Every now and then I've gotten a book idea out of their questions, so I would never begrudge them these.

The questions that take my sanity and shove it are the ones where kids ask what time their uncle will be here three days before he's supposed to come; why their poop is so green today (I've already answered this one four times; they just think it's funny); and whether it's okay for their baby brother to be coloring himself with a red Sharpie.

3. Food preparation

Who would have ever thought that I would get tired of feeding my children? I mean, I'm no chef, and I don't really like to cook at all, but this is giving them life and nourishment, right? Still, every day I have to fix some kind of wholesome breakfast, lunch, or dinner, I shuffle my feet like I'm heading for the execution block. Part of this is likely due to the fact that I'm a little burned out on food preparation; the other part of it is that I know, no matter what I fix, they'll complain about it. It's not enough or it's too much or they wanted pancakes or if we're having pancakes they thought we were having spaghetti or this cheese is stringy or the mushrooms I tried to hide in the chicken's cream sauce taste like feet (according to one who bites off his toenails instead of clipping them like a normal person).

The only meal that will please with any regularity is pizza.

4. The re-teaching process

Of course, as a parent, I knew I would be required to teach my kids certain things. How to brush their teeth, how to return a mean word with a kind word, how to be human. It's the re-teaching that gets to me. I'm not a big fan of repeating myself, but for some reason my sons require multiple teaching lessons on the following:

How to cross a street safely

How to whisper

How to clean up

How to sit correctly in the car

How to sit correctly at the table

How to follow simple instructions

How to do their after-dinner chores

How to take a proper bath

How (and why) to apply deodorant

This list goes on and on and on. I can't possibly include the entire thing here; it would be irresponsible.

5. The protection measures

My children are all boys. Sons do incredibly stupid things. Not all of them; sometimes sons can be level-headed and cautious. I have two of that kind. The other four act without thinking.

Not long ago, Husband and I had to board up the window in my twins' room, because one day we found them leaning out the window, which they had figured out how to unlock and pry open, like fools, wondering what it would be like to slide down the roof. We kept the board up for a day or two, until one night I woke with a panic attack and realized it was a fire hazard. Now they have prison locks on their windows, but at least we'll be able to get out in case of fire.

Some of my sons have also tried to "power jump" their brothers off the trampoline onto the roof of their daddy's shed. They have tried to pick up snakes with their bare hands, though they are city boys and have no formal education in which species are poisonous and which are not. They have tried to capture yellow jackets in their little insect containers, heedless of the pain that might cause (miraculously, no one was stung).

Protecting my sons is almost a full-time job. At the end of a day, it's a miracle any one of them is still alive.

6. The Finding Game

This game has one and only one object: Find the socks and shoes.

My sons leave their things everywhere. Because we live in Texas, where the temperature regularly courts a triple-digit count, they enjoy stripping off all their clothes except their shorts and jumping on the trampoline. This wouldn't be a problem; boys are lucky to be given leave to expose their skin. The problem is that they leave these stripped clothes right where they took them off—outside.

Especially their socks and shoes. Husband and I spend way too much time trying to locate socks and shoes. My sons have multiple pairs of socks, so often we won't even notice how the socks have piled up in the backyard until one of my sons says, "I don't have any socks" the day after I washed laundry. But the shoes. I am the mean mom who only buys my sons one pair of shoes. This is mostly because they'll only choose to wear one pair of shoes once school starts, and by Halloween they'll already need another pair. One pair of shoes, however, means it is imperative to find those shoes before we can go anywhere.

I could do without the Finding Game.

7. The relentless reminders

Most days I feel like such a nag. I have to remind my sons to put their bowls away, hang up their backpacks where they're supposed to go, wash their lunch containers, do their homework, close the door, turn off the lights. And it's not just the one time that this reminder is needed; it's multiple times. My sons will hear the reminder, acknowledge it, and promptly forget. They will, instead, see the cardboard boxes collected at the front door, waiting to be transported to recycling, and decide they would rather make a LEGO mini figure mansion, completely forgetting their mother is not the maid.

8. Observation time

My sons are rather remarkable. I never, ever expected to spend so much time blissfully watching them with my heart squeezing and bursting at the same time.

Yesterday my youngest son, who is three, asked me if he could sit on my lap. He's my last child, so I do everything I can to accommodate his requests, because I know that he will not be asking for long. He stayed in my lap for a while, talking about all the animals on the little matching cards he had in his hands. He would giggle, look up at me with those big blue eyes, lean his head back into the space between my chest and my neck. I would press my mouth to the top of his head and just breathe.

I didn't get any work done that morning.

But it didn't matter. The weight of his form in my lap, the tickle of his hair against my nose, the sweet smell of him that lingered long after he'd slipped away—*that* was the work that needed to be done.

A breathtaking moment in time.

What Working Out Looks Like with Kids

The other day I made the lazy decision to sleep in when I should have gotten up so I could work out in peace and quiet like I did every other, normal morning. But the youngest hasn't been sleeping well, and I just needed a few extra minutes in bed. I know what they say about the early worm, but the few extra minutes in bed only kept me in bed until 4:45 a.m. instead of the regular 4:15. I'm still an early bird. I just missed my workout time slot, which means I don't get to have a worm (the gummy kind, that is).

Because I really wanted that gummy worm, I thought I would simply shift this workout to the afternoon and cut out some of my work time, because I was feeling tired anyway, which generally happens when I don't get to start my day with a workout. I would solve two problems at one time.

However, in the afternoon, there are six additional problems that need solving: kids and what to do with them.

My typical workout is a high intensity interval training session, except for two days a week when I go on runs with my toddler in the running stroller and just about die jogging up and down the hills because he and the stroller, collectively, weigh about a thousand pounds and my legs can only carry so much. Rather than try to work out the logistics of a run with six kids running behind me (or more likely in front of me, taunting me all the way), I opted to do the interval training workout, which I could set up on my laptop. Besides, it was too cold outside for a run.

I guess the toddler heard me bouncing around, because he came bursting into the room when I was in the middle of some back exercises, and, thinking my lying on my belly was an invitation, he promptly climbed on my back. Fortunately, at exactly that moment, the back exercises finished, and it was now time to do a plank. I managed to hold a perfect plank position for thirty-nine seconds before my arms collapsed with the added weight of a three-year-old's thirty-five pounds rolling around on my back.

As if a plank isn't hard enough. But I never back down from a challenge.

Sometimes I don't want to get up as early as necessary to work out, but, being a hyper-disciplined person, I do it anyway (my kids refer to me as The General. Not really. But if they had the vocabulary, they probably would). But sometimes my discipline disintegrates during a night of someone's sick or someone burst into our room after a nightmare or someone just never went to bed. On those mornings, I cut myself some slack and sleep for an extra half hour—never more than that, or the whole day falls off the rails.

Still, I always regret it.

I start the day thinking it won't be that big a deal for me to squeeze in a workout between when I'm done with work, which coincides with when my kids get home from school, and dinner preparation. Somewhere along the way, I remember what it's like.

It can go one of many ways.

They do the workout with me, and I trip all over them.

If you've ever engaged in high intensity interval training, you know that it requires a bit of movement. I'm usually jumping over imaginary side-hurdles, which are not so imaginary when you have four kids who want to join your workout. Their reaction times are woefully bad. This means I burn extra calories keeping myself on my feet. I guess that's not really a bad thing, if you're in it for the calorie burn.

My sons are all over the place—beside me, behind me, in front of me. Inevitably, I must do a burpee at some point, which means one—or, if I'm really skilled at taking them down, all four of the workout joiners—will be in the way. Oops. Sorry. They'll then complain that I've cut off their leg with my foot. And I'll have to pause the video and make sure they're really okay (they are; they all have a penchant for drama. They get it from Husband.).

They tell me I'm doing it wrong.

Once they realize they can't quite keep up, my sons will move to the sidelines. Have you ever been so completely out of breath you're two inches from collapsing but still trying to perfectly execute your fortieth burpee, only to have a kid study the screen and then watch your form and tell you you're doing it wrong? And then, as you're about to die from the lack of oxygen that's in this house (he's using valuable oxygen to tell you how wrong you're doing it), he will proceed to show you how to do it, except he looks exactly like a seal. It's about as annoying as it sounds. These are the same kids who will tell me that people on the screen are not doing push-ups from their knees. Yeah, well, I don't care. I'm not as strong as they are.

They leave weights everywhere.

Most of my workouts require weights. I only use one pair of weights, but when my sons see them, they gleefully race out to the playroom, where there are four additional sets, and bring all of them back in, spreading them out in my workout space. This means that not only must I dodge children during my sashay, but I must also dodge weights. Those things hurt if you don't pick up your feet while racing with high knees. They also hurt when dropping to the ground for more planks, when unfolding into yet another burpee, and when stepping into a reverse squat. Next time I visit the skin doctor, I'll have to explain all the bruises.

They comment that the workout must be hard because I'm breathing really hard.

This seems harmless and innocent, but when you're in the middle of a workout, sweat now streaming down your face, while your kids are watching, you're not exactly in the best frame of mind. I get offended when they say I'm breathing hard, because I equate that with the insinuation that I'm out of shape. I'm not out of shape, I just have a few extra pounds I've carried around for the last eleven years. You stick with the workout and see if *you're* not breathing hard by the end of it. Or the beginning. Whatever.

Someone ends up getting hurt.

If it doesn't happen at the beginning of the workout, it will most definitely happen at the end of it. This is the time when I'm running out of steam, when I'm not as carefully placing my hands or my feet, when anyone in my way is going to get barreled down. I want to get finished as fast as I can. Sorry, kids. Stay out of the way.

I used to run six miles a day; I don't have that kind of time anymore. Every now and then Husband and I experiment with family runs, when our sons will strap on roller blades or dust off their bikes, but after the first half-mile they're already complaining about how they want to go home. So interval training, at home, with my computer, is about the best I can do right now. For now, working out looks like pockets of time here and there. It won't always be that way.

One day I might even miss their comments.

Well, that's probably stretching it.

The Sleep Personalities of Children

Husband and I feel exceptionally fortunate that our children are good sleepers. They've been good sleepers since the very beginning. Our oldest son started sleeping through the night at six weeks old, our second son at seven weeks, the third around that time, the last at eight weeks, and only because I stretched it out longer, purposefully. The two worst sleepers were our twins, who started sleeping through the night at about twelve weeks (they finally stopped waking each other up), and I thought *that* was bad.

Hearing the stories of other parents, I know how truly fortunate we are. Some friends have three-year-olds still waking during the night. They would've had to put me in a strait jacket if that were the case in my life.

My sons are older now, and they're still good sleepers—but some very distinct sleeping personalities have emerged in recent years.

First we have the **Stay Up All Night Guy**. This is the kid who would willingly stay up for as long as we would let him, and he often claims that he *does* stay up all night, even though I check on him and his brothers before going to bed myself, and I have never seen him with open eyes; instead he is, usually, mouth-breathing with his eyes closed, just like the others. When I tell him this, he'll usually say something along the lines of, "I was just resting my eyes. I knew you were there." Yeah, right, kid.

In reality, he has so much on his mind, so much creativity pulsing through his bones, that he has a hard time shutting his eyes. I get that. Sometimes my stories wake me up at night, and I can't help but write them in my head—only to forget them in the morning (I really should sleep with a notebook nearby). The world will pass on by while he sleeps, and he doesn't want to miss a thing.

This is also the kid who, at four years old, spent a few weeks fearing that an asteroid would hit our house while we were sleeping, and he wanted to know if we had an evacuation plan. So he's got anxiety like me, which I'm sure plays a part in this temporary insomnia that ends, usually, in sleep.

There is also the **Can Sleep Anywhere Guy**.

My second son has been able to tell when he's tired from the time he was very young. This is a wonderful capability in children, because it means Husband and I don't have to tell him to go to bed; he just does. He's like a magical child. Sometimes he'll go so far as to take a nap, even though he's eight. He has an almost eerie ability to feel when his body is in need of refreshment, and he will take it upon himself to refresh it. He will sometimes stay up too late, but you can bet that the next day he'll put himself to bed early.

Favorite child, come bedtime.

He could sleep anywhere, too. He could sleep rolled up in a blanket or in the car or even on his daddy's back. If he is much too tired to hold up his head, he doesn't care where he is. He'll sleep standing up if necessary.

Then there's the **Spread Out Everywhere Guy**.

A few times this summer, I tried to nap with this one, because when he was a little boy, I used to lie down on our couch, position him in the crook of my arm, and take a nap while he sweat into my elbow (he's always been a sweater). That was before he moved much. Now he moves all the time. He is a relentless mover (and yet still sleeps like the dead), and just when I feel myself falling into a light doze, he'll twitch or smack his hand into my face, accidentally. He doesn't leave space in a bed for anyone else, and he's always kicking someone. He loves sleeping with his brothers, but they certainly don't like sleeping with him.

Don't try to tell him he moves too much, though. He'll argue with you until you're ready to go to bed now, this minute.

Next we have the **Go Until Gone Guy**.

You likely know this kid. He will go, go, go and never stop. He will fall asleep where he was standing up, likely in a running position. Most of my sons have been this guy for a short time, but one particular son may never grow out of it. He has the remarkable ability to bounce off a wall, land in a crime-scene position, and suddenly be asleep.

To be quite honest, sometimes I wish I had this ability, but, unfortunately, it takes me a while to wind down when I've been riled up. He has no problem with going Elevated Heart Rate to Hibernation in mere seconds. Most mornings, when I venture into his room to wake him up, it looks as though he'd been attempting circus moves before he passed out. Sometimes he has carpet burn on his cheek.

Empathy is hard with a kid like this.

There is also the **Needs Everything Perfect Guy**.

This is the kid who will protest and fight and complain until we have everything perfect—pillow fluffed just so, blanket pulled over him exactly like it was yesterday, bed not sagging the slightest bit in the middle (can't help him there; all the beds sag now because everything in my house gives up around boys). The darkness has to be balanced just right, the temperature has to be cool but not cold, the water in his cup must be filled to a certain level. Did we put the nightlight where it's supposed to go? Is his shirt twisted underneath him? Does he still have socks on?

We must do Monkey Kiss, Pig Kiss, Fish Kiss, Tiger Kiss, Chicken Kiss, in that order, every night. Not too much to ask for a good sleeper, is it? At least when he's out he's out.

Lastly we have the **Sleep Anytime You Want Him to Guy**.

This kid is my youngest, and he's the most delightfully easy kid I've ever met. If I wake him up from his night time sleep, he'll go to sleep three minutes later if I tell him it's time. He'll just say, "Okay," and lie back down and close his eyes. He fights occasionally, of course (no kid is perfect, though this one is close), like when he's having a good time playing with his brothers and he doesn't understand why he has to stop that and take a nap—but after the fight (which isn't really a fight; I have several strong-willed kids, and I know what fights look like) he will be asleep within two minutes.

He's accommodating and wonderful, and it's a miracle that we ended with this one.

Of course Husband and I have sleep personalities of our own—his is **Lie Down and Fall Asleep Within Minutes Guy**. I always try to be in bed before he is, because I don't like being the last one up. But what inevitably happens is that my mind will sort through all the worries of the day—did we turn off all the lights, did he lock the door, will someone break in to murder me, which spawns a whole series of imaginative scenarios that I tell myself I'll eventually use in books but probably never will—and it'll take me much too long to shake off thoughts and fall asleep, rendering me the **Plagued by Worries Girl.**

Well, at least I'm up to witness the eventual surrender of Stay Up All Night Guy. Tonight I'll get it on camera. Resting your eyes, huh? How do you explain that string of drool connecting your mouth to your pillow?

Tomorrow's breakfast will come with a heaping dish of I Told You So.

The Days Are Long, But the Years Are Short

The other day, upon returning from picking up all our kids from the grandparents, after a weekend spent in bliss away from them, one of my six-year-olds raced into the house before the rest of us. We were a little slow-going, to be perfectly honest, because the travel wearied us (or maybe it was all the whining and complaining we'd heard on the way home) and he had at least a whole minute to devise his masterful plan. He snuck a pen out to the trampoline, mistakenly believing he would get away with this deviousness, and there proceeded to mark up his arms and legs with black-gel-pen tattoos (he must have thought they were invisible) and, when that bored him, he decided to take his artistic skills to a toy truck someone had left outside.

I happened to look out the window and see him bent intently over this truck for much too long, my mother sense screaming that something was amiss—he was doing something wrong. And, sure enough, my mother sense was right (it's actually never been wrong yet).

The Days Are Long, But the Years Are Short

First of all, pens are mine. They're not allowed to migrate anywhere; they must stay in the pen holder that sits on our counter, because when it's time to sign school folders, I would like to have something besides a broken crayon, an unsharpened pencil, and a water color paint palette at my disposal. Rule number one, broken.

Secondly, we don't allow sharp objects (like pens) out on the trampoline, because of the potential for injury and also damage to the trampoline. Rule number two, broken.

Thirdly, we don't allow hieroglyphs on anything besides paper and art supplies (I know. It's so mean.). Rule number three, broken.

Because of this recent weekend spent without kids, I wasn't quite ready to get them back and do what always must be done upon picking up kids from the grandparents: detox. And now, right out of the gate, there was this.

I thought, *Man, I can't wait until they're older.* I thought, *It will be so nice when stealing a pen to mark on skin and a toy truck doesn't seem like a fun activity.* I thought, *When are you ever going to grow up?*

Parenting elicits so many emotions.

There is frustration that rises up when they destroy a terra cotta pot that used to house a perfectly beautiful plant growing healthily—until the moment kids got hold of it and the pot shattered into tiny mosaic pieces and the plant lost most of its vital soil. There is frustration that happens when they get down from the table a thousand times while you're eating lunch or dinner even though it's been drilled into them that everyone—

even parents—stay at the table until they've been excused. There is frustration when bedtime already passed and they're still horsing around in their beds and you think, *When are you going to grow up? When will I be able to stop nagging?*

There is horror when you walk into their bathroom, which smells like a rotten swamp, and when you see what they can do outside of your presence—like chew apart some wooden blinds (!)—and when they look like they're about to jump off the top of the deck and over the fence and out into the great unknown of a twenty-foot drop and you think, *When are you going to grow up? When will you decide, for yourself, that danger is not an enjoyable dance partner?*

There is overwhelm when everyone talks at once and they all ask for things simultaneously and everybody has something to say about everybody else; and when you're about to leave and you try to make it out the door without any major catastrophes and you almost make it and someone slips on water someone else spilled without saying anything and now there's blood all over the kitchen floor from a busted-up chin; and when it's past their bedtime and they're still horsing around and you're so tired you just want to go to sleep and you think, *When are you going to grow up? When will you get in your bed by yourself, without supervision from me?*

There is annoyance when the oldest son is late to school even though you told him it was time to leave and you walked out the door with his brothers where he could clearly see you leaving; and when they can't find their shoes, even though you have several designated places for the shoes to be stored; and

The Days Are Long, But the Years Are Short

when they leave their possessions everywhere—their backpacks on the floor and not on the backpack hooks, their plates and forks and spoons and bowls on the table instead of in the sink, their clothes two inches from the laundry hamper, and you want to ask, *When are you going to grow up? Will I ever be done with the reminders of where things go?*

There is embarrassment when the twins tell people your age, without anyone asking for it; and when the eleven-year-old melts down in public—because he makes you look like a terrible parent and sometimes you care too much about what other people think, unfortunately; and when they go to school without brushing their hair so it sticks up everywhere, and you think, *When are you going to grow up? Will you ever be done with offering random information and melting down in public and looking like you never take baths?*

There is panic when they disappear for half an hour at the local museum because they decided they wanted to see a different display than the one the family was observing; and when they try to cross a street by themselves and you see a driver who's looking down at his phone in the early morning hours; and when the house gets too quiet, and you think, *When are you going to grow up? I don't want to always have to worry about you wandering off and whether or not you can safely cross a street by yourself and what the silence means.*

There is also, of course, an abundance of positive emotions —love, joy, wonder, pride. When they learn to read and when they fall in love with books and when they use the manners— without intervention—you've drilled into them. When they tell you they think they know the meaning of life: to create beautiful things and to love others. When they do really well on a test or bring home an amazing piece of art or finally decide what they want to do for the rest of their lives.

But so much of early childhood, for parents, is spent molding and shaping and redirecting, and sometimes it grows a bit stale and we find ourselves thinking, at almost every turn —

> *When will you do this for yourself?*
> *When will you manage your own life?*
> *When are you going to grow up?*
> And they say:
> *Now. You see?*
> *I'm all grown up now.*

THE END

About the Author

Rachel is the Chief Remembrance Officer (CRO) of the Toalson household, not only planning new memories to make but diligently recording old memories in volumes of notebooks—some hilarious, some sappy, all necessary to preserve important moments in time. Though her sons are older, she still secretly records their lives in essays, poems, and stories.

When she isn't carried away by a string of words that need writing, she can often be found baking delicious treats with her sons, running miles and miles through the streets of her city, and kicking her feet up with a good book she finally gets to read for more than a minute at a time (but, oh, how she'd love to return to those constant-interruption days when her sons were tiny, if only to savor them a fraction more…).

She is the author of the humor essay books *Parenthood: Has Anyone Seen My Sanity?*, *This Life With Boys*, *The Life-Changing Madness of Tidying Up After Children*, *Hills I'll Probably Lie Down On* and *If These Walls Could Talk*; multiple poetry books; and several stories for kids under the pen names R.L. Toalson and L.R. Patton. Rachel lives with her husband and six sons in San Antonio, Texas.

Author's Note

My dear reader,

It really is astounding how fast they grow.

I published my first humor essay ten years ago, when my oldest son was three. That essay kicked off a decade of capturing the hard and sour parts of parenting and wrestling them into something humorous, something that would etch into my memory a positive note, rather than a constantly-overwhelmed, constantly-tired, constantly-frustrated one. What a journey it has been.

I am not sure I have enjoyed anything in my life as much as I have enjoyed strengthening my humor muscle, opening my eyes and heart to the laughter that hides in every moment, sharing that with others. What a fantastic privilege.

Though it feels sort of like an era is dying with the publication of this book, I also know—without a doubt—that I will still exercise my humor in day-to-day life, because I know how essential it is to carrying on, to lifting ourselves out of dark pits, to living a life of the fullest joy. I know how necessary it is to embrace the ironic, humorous places in our memories so they become more weightless than weighty. I know I need it.

So I will write humor, yes. It may not look quite the same as these Crash Test Parents books look. My sons may not agree that it's funny to write about them, and I will respect that. But I will find ways to weave humor into our lives. I will search, endlessly, if need be. And perhaps one day you will read another book by me, and maybe, hopefully, you will say, "Wow. That was really good. Funny, too."

Laughter is the best medicine for many maladies. I hope you've found that to be true in your own life.

And so, reader, this is not goodbye. This is merely see you later (and probably not even much later). I sincerely hope you have enjoyed these Crash Test Parents books, as I have certainly enjoyed writing them.

To laughter, love, and a life filled with both.

In love,

Rachel

Acknowledgments

During the editing phase of this book, one of my sons confessed that he googled me and found my web site and read some of my humor essays. At first I was mortified; I made fun of so much of our lives—including him! But then he said, "Can I read more?" I did a double take.

"Yeah, sure," I stammered.

Thus began the reading of these humor essays to my sons, who found them hilarious.

So I must first thank the ones so open to laughing at themselves: Jadon, Asa, Hosea, Zadok, Boaz, and Asher. Thank you for not taking yourselves too seriously, for sharing these laughter-filled memories with the world, and for proving, yet again, that kids are some of the most surprising people in the world.

Thank you, Ben, for your constant support during this Crash Test Parents journey and the unfolding of my writing career. I couldn't do any of what I do without you.

Thank you, Mom, for always believing in me and for laughing at my stories.

Thank you, Toalson boy teachers, for helping grow my

sons into the sweet, brilliant young men they are today.

Thank you Scott and Alana Ammons and Jared and Courtney Rawson, for providing Ben and me with friendship, camaraderie, and necessary supplies (toilet paper? Anyone have any toilet paper?). Your presence in our lives and the lives of our sons means the world.

Thank you to all the parents who have written me or pulled me aside over the years, to tell me my words make you feel less alone. You reaffirm my purpose without even knowing it.

Thank you to all the humorists out there who have shared their work and laughter and made the world a brighter, better place.

And last, but not least, thank you to all my readers who encourage me not only to share but also to be brave in what I share. Your support has carried me through many the valley.

Crash Test Parents

Enjoy more from the Crash Test Parents series:

www.crashtestparents.com

Are you a parent who needs a little dose of humor and hope?

For a limited time, pick up your FREE copies of *Guide to Surviving a Year* and *Guide to Self Esteem* and laugh your way back into hope. Or maybe just survival.

Get your FREE copies at:
racheltoalson.com/SurvivingAYear

www.ingramcontent.com/pod-product-compliance
Lightning Source LLC
Chambersburg PA
CBHW030315100526
44592CB00010B/437